# The Theory and Practice of Teaching

Teaching, like learning, is one of the most basic human activities. As a skill and a vocation, teaching is absolutely central to those who educate as well as to those who are taught. To this end, teaching as an art, as a skill and as a subject in itself has long been the focus of debate, analysis and classification. At this time of great interest in the relationship between, and the processes of, teaching and learning, the practice of teaching itself is also changing.

This second edition of Peter Jarvis' well-received book is designed to help readers understand the techniques, theories and methods of teaching. With a new emphasis on the person within the teaching and learning relationship, and by concentrating on interpersonal methods, *The Theory and Practice of Teaching* concerns itself with the issues that underpin teaching. Topics discussed in the second edition include:

- the nature of teaching
- the ethics of the teaching and learning relationship
- the relationship between learning theory and the theory of teaching
- teaching methods, including didactic, Socratic and experiential, and monitoring
- the issues of assessment of learning.

Combining theory and practice, this book offers a broad and multi-disciplinary perspective on teaching methods. It will help teachers and lecturers in schools, higher, further and adult education, plus teacher educators and mentors understand the techniques that they can call upon at different times and in different situations. This book is essential reading for anyone interested in the art of good teaching.

**Peter Jarvis** is Professor of Continuing Education, University of Surrey, UK and Adjunct Professor, Department of Adult Education, University of Georgia, USA. His latest books include *Human Learning* and *Adult Education and Lifelong Learning*.

# The Theory and Practice of Teaching

Second edition

Edited by Peter Jarvis

Routledge
Taylor & Francis Group

LONDON AND NEW YORK

First edition published 2002
by Kogan Page
This edition first published 2006
by Routledge
2 Park Square, Milton Park, Abingdon, Oxon OX14 4RN

Simultaneously published in the USA and Canada
by Routledge
270 Madison Ave, New York, NY 10016

*Routledge is an imprint of the Taylor & Francis Group, an informa business*

© 2002, 2006 selection and editorial matter, Peter Jarvis;
individual chapters, the contributors.

Typeset in Times New Roman by
Newgen Imaging Systems (P) Ltd, Chennai, India
Printed and bound in Great Britain by
TJ International Ltd, Padstow, Cornwall

*British Library Cataloguing in Publishing Data*
A catalogue record for this book is available
from the British Library

*Library of Congress Cataloging in Publication Data*
The theory and practice of teaching / edited by
Peter Jarvis. – 2nd ed.
        p. cm.
    Rev. ed. of: The theory & practice of teaching / edited by
Peter Jarvis. 2002.
    Includes bibliographical references and index.
    1. Teaching. I. Jarvis, Peter, 1937– II. Jarvis, Peter, 1937 –
Theory & practice of teaching. III. Title.

LB1025.3.T53 2006
371.102–dc22                                    2005030925

ISBN10: 0–415–36524–4 (hbk)
ISBN10: 0–415–36525–2 (pbk)
ISBN10: 0–203–01644–0 (ebk)

ISBN13: 978–0–415–36524–6 (hbk)
ISBN13: 978–0–415–36525–3 (pbk)
ISBN13: 978–0–203–01644–2 (ebk)

# Contents

# Illustrations

## Figures

## Tables

# Contributors

**Dr Josie Gregory** is a senior lecturer in the School of Management at the University of Surrey. Her particular interests are: spirituality in work and learning environments, with particular emphasis on Western mysticism. She is a dedicated humanistic adult educator exploring and teaching transformative learning and change at individual, group and organisational levels, and management learning. Josie has developed an international profile as creator and Director of the International Conference on Organisational Spirituality; she is also a trustee of a spiritual education charity.

**Dr Colin Griffin** is Visiting Senior Fellow in the Department of Political, International and Policy Studies at the University of Surrey. He was for many years in the Department of Educational Studies as a member of the Centre for Research in Lifelong Learning. His research and publication interests have been in curriculum theory in adult education and policy analysis of lifelong learning.

**Professor Peter Jarvis** is Professor of Continuing Education. He is a former Head of Department of Education Studies. He is the founding editor of *The International Journal in Lifelong Education* and Chair of the Board of Editors of *Comparative Education*. He is widely published; his most recent books include *Human Learning: A Holistic Perspective* (edited P. Jarvis and S. Parker) and *Adult and Continuing Education: Major Themes* (5 vols) (ed. P. Jarvis with C. Griffin) – published by Routledge. In addition, he has also published *The Practitioner-Researcher* (published by Jossey-Bass) and Kogan Page have published *Learning in Later Life* and *Universities and Corporate Universities: The Higher Learning Industry in Global Society* – both published in 2001.

**Dr Linda Merricks** has been Head of Adult and Continuing Education at the University of Surrey for five years. Her research has been centred on lifelong learning in Britain. She is currently heading the English team contributing to an EU funded project 'Towards a Learning Society in Europe'.

**Professor Gill Nicholls** is Professor of Education and Director of King's Institute of Learning and Teaching at King's College, University of London. She has extensive research experience and has published widely in the fields of learning, teaching and professional development. She is also involved in consultancy work evaluating university learning and teaching strategies and advising in relation to strategic development in institutional learning and teaching.

**Professor Julia Preece** is Professor of Adult Education at the University of Glasgow. Before that she was a Reader at the University of Surrey during which time she spent three years at the University of Botswana. Her current research interests include citizenship, lifelong learning, adult education and social exclusion.

**Dr Paul Tosey** is a senior lecturer in the School of Management Studies at the University of Surrey where he is programme leader for the MSc change Agent Skills and Strategies, an advanced programme for consultants. In 2004/2005 he received the University's Learning and Teaching Award. His research interests include transformative learning; he is leading an HEFCE funded project on Enquiry-Based Learning and a University-funded one on Neuro-Linguistic Programming.

# Preface to second edition

It is always pleasing when a book goes into a second edition because it is an indication that it is being used and we are grateful for that. But this is a time when teaching is beginning to be recognised, even in higher education:

> In the past, rewards in higher education – particularly promotion – have been linked much more closely to research than to teaching. Indeed, teaching has been seen by some as an extra source of income to support the main business of research, rather than recognised as a valuable and high status career in its own right. This is a situation that cannot continue. Institutions must properly reward their best teaching staff, and all those who teach must take their task seriously.
>
> (DfES 2003, para 4.17)

How things have changed – I remember writing to a Vice Chancellor in the 1980s and telling him how an American University had introduced an annual University prize for good teaching and suggesting that we should think about something similar and, unfortunately, I did not even get an acknowledgement!

Now there are many books on teaching, including this one. However, this is a considerably revised second edition, with every chapter except one being revised and updated and some being completely rewritten. There are a variety of reasons why the team is much smaller now: two of the original team have retired and are no longer actively engaged in academic work, one other has assumed senior administrative position and is, therefore, undertaking less academic work and two others have moved away from Surrey. The University of Surrey itself is also, in part, responsible for this change since it closed the Department of Educational

Studies in 2004 and so the original team has completely disbanded. Nevertheless, we hope that this second edition will be as useful as the first.

Amongst the changes made from the first edition are: the new first chapter is a revised version of the original second chapter and there is a new second chapter; the third chapter has been updated and the fourth completely re-written; the fifth and sixth chapters have been updated and the seventh re-written; Chapters 8–11 have been updated and Chapter 12 remains in its original form; Chapters 13–15 and 17 have been revised and updated and Chapter 16 is a new one. Consequently, this is a substantially different book. Nevertheless, we hope that it will also be useful to those who use it.

We have retained the same format of trying to combine theoretical ideas with practical outcomes. This is not to say that we favour the idea of theory being applied to practice since we recognise that much of our theorising comes as a result of reflection upon practice. Nevertheless, we are of the opinion that it is important that practitioners should be knowledgeable ones, whatever the age group of students whom they teach. This book, while it carries an undertone of adult and higher education, is also one that students and those training to teach in school will, we hope, find useful.

I must thank everybody who has encouraged us to prepare this second edition, especially colleagues at Routledge, such as Steve Jones (before he left), Helen Pritt (his successor) and Philip Mudd – who have been a constant source of encouragement to me. Finally, we all want to thank you, the readers, for studying our work and we do, sincerely, hope that you find it useful.

Peter Jarvis
Thatcham,
August, 2005

## Reference

Department for Education and Skills (2003) *The Future of Higher Education* Norwich: HMSO CM 5735

# Preface to first edition

While much government emphasis has been placed on the learning society in recent years, it has not omitted consideration of teaching as well. A number of reports have included it in their considerations, especially the Dearing Report (1997) which is discussed in considerable detail in the opening chapter of the book. But the traditional notion of teaching is also changing – no longer can it be conceived of just standing in front of a class and talking, with the occasional use of the chalkboard. While it is acknowledged that the practice has not changed for some teachers, teaching itself is undergoing change. For instance, this book has deliberately focused on the inter-personal, more traditional side of teaching, with only one chapter on distance education. Had time and space permitted we would have included more chapters on teaching aids and on distance education.

Many books have been written about inter-personal teaching and so it might be asked whether we need another, but many of those are entirely practical. While this book is certainly not divorced from the considerations of practice, it is also concerned with many of the theoretical issues that underlie teaching. Consequently it is designed to help practitioners think about their practice as well as extend the techniques that they employ. This book provides a multi-discipline analysis of teaching, and contains three sections:

- the first five chapters examine theoretical issues underlying teaching itself;
- the following section examines teaching methods;
- the final brief one looks at issues surrounding assessment of learning, since teachers often find this a problematic area.

This book is written primarily for teachers and lecturers in post-compulsory education, that is:

- higher education
- further education
- education for managers and professionals
- adult education.

Since the book focuses on theoretical and practical issues of teaching, those who teach school children will also find it of interest. Others will also find this book particularly useful, including:

- those who teach and assess teachers, like many of the authors of this book, will hopefully find many of the concerns in this book relevant to their work;
- school teachers;
- planners and policy makers might also wish to consider the human concerns underlying this book, since we seek to show that teaching is a moral activity concerned with the nature and identity of the learners.

The authors of the following chapters were all members of the School of Educational Studies, although one has subsequently left the School for another University. Ever since its formation soon after the University of Surrey was established, its focus has been on post-compulsory education and it still remains one of the only Schools of Educational Studies where there is no school-teacher preparation. Its main concerns now are both in the preparation of educators for all forms of post-compulsory education and also for the study of these sectors of education and learning. Members of the School are interested in all of these sectors, from policy to practice, and undertake teaching, research and consultancy in all of them. The School has a large doctoral programme, and runs Masters degrees both on a face-to-face basis and it also has the first international distance education Masters degree in post-compulsory education – one it started in the 1980s.

The authors of this book come from two Centres in the School – those of Research into Lifelong Learning and the Human Potential Research Group. This latter group has existed almost since the formation of the School which was then a Centre for Adult Education, while the former group has emerged as a result in the changes in the educational scene over the past decade or so. The Human Potential Group runs a world-renown Masters degree in Change Agent Skills while the Centre for Research in Lifelong Learning has been responsible for the distance learning Masters degree which has three strands: lifelong learning; applied professional studies; information technology.

Among the publications that have come from this group of authors in recent times has been *The Theory and Practice of Learning* (Jarvis *et al.*, 1998); *International Perspectives on Lifelong Learning* (ed. Holford *et al.*, 1998); *The Age of Learning* (ed. Jarvis, 2001); *Twentieth Century Thinkers in Adult and Continuing Education* (Second Edition – ed. Jarvis, 2001) and *Learning in Later Life* and *Universities and Corporate Universities* (both 2001 and by Jarvis). All of these books have been published by Kogan Page.

## Reference

Dearing, R. (Chair) (1997) *Higher Education in the Learning Society* London: Department for Education and Employment

# Part I

# Chapter 1

# Teaching in a changing world

*Peter Jarvis*

This book is about teaching in a learning society, in a completely different world to that in which the art and science of teaching emerged. Teaching itself has traditionally had a number of different meanings, as the *Concise Oxford English Dictionary* shows:

- To give systematic information to a person, (about a subject or skill).
- To practise this professionally.
- To enable a person to do something by instruction and training (to swim; to dance).
- To be an advocate for a moral principle (my parents taught me forgiveness).
- To communicate, instruct in a moral principle.
- To induce a person by example or punishment to do or not to do a thing (that will teach you to sit still; that will teach you not to laugh).
- To make a person disinclined to do a thing (I will teach you to interfere).

It may also be seen from these definitions that teaching has also had negative as well as positive connotations – indicating that sometimes people do not want to learn and have to be taught or that they will be punished if they do not learn. This is something that will occur again in the next chapter when we look at teaching style. Yet, it also contains moral overtones and indications that it is generally regarded as a good thing. However, this diversity of function has been increased dramatically over the past few years because the globalising forces in society and the rapid changes in knowledge, resulting in both the knowledge society and the learning society. It is interesting that the concepts of teaching mentioned about do not explicitly specify learning but, perhaps, the most significant aspect of teaching is in helping others learn.

This book seeks to analyse the nature of teaching in relation to the learning society. Its thesis is that the type of teaching will vary in relation to the status of the content (knowledge) being taught. We will examine first theories of the learning society from which we shall draw out a few points about the way that knowledge is changing. Finally, we will locate the changing nature of teaching in this context and by way of conclusion ask whether educational institutions are responding to the challenge.

## Part I: the learning society

The learning society is both a confused and a confusing idea. Indeed, one of the phenomena that makes society a society is a sense of permanence and patterns of behaviour. In other words, members of society repeat certain fundamental processes, like language and behaviour patterns and so non-learning is a feature of society (Jarvis, 1987). If learning either produces change or reflects it, then the nature of society is itself changing. This, we know to be the case, since change is endemic. But not everything is changing; there is still a degree of stability and permanence. There is both learning and non-learning.

Coffield (2000, p. 28) actually suggests that all talk of '*the* learning society will have to be abandoned rather than refined' (*italics* in original); he says that there are simply too many modern and post-modern readings of the term for any general agreement on one approach or model to be possible. He highlights ten different approaches from the various research projects on which he (p. 8) reports:

- skills growth
- personal development
- social learning
- a learning market
- local learning societies
- social control
- self-evaluation
- centrality of learning
- a reformed system of education
- structural change.

A number of things emerge from these ten approaches: first, that they are not different models of a learning society but merely different aspects of the society being studied; second, therefore, that they may be describing something of the fragmentation of contemporary post-modern society; third, they have neither a sophisticated nor an agreed model of learning on which to base the analysis which prevents genuine comparison of the fourteen projects that he reports. Since all the projects were conducted in the United Kingdom, I want to argue that it is still possible to talk about a learning society, provided that we can agree on a definition of learning, with each of these projects concentrating on but one aspect of the whole. Indeed, these models are actually Western cultural models and societies such as Hong Kong, which is very committed to the creation of a learning society and in which a tremendously high proportion of the adult population attend post-secondary education, provide other perspectives on this form of society.

On further examination into Coffield's ten types of learning society we can see that even within a single society, the forces of change do not produce standardised responses, and nor should we expect this to happen since we have not postulated a deterministic model of society. Nevertheless, we can see that it is possible to classify his types into a smaller number of categories:

- *personal development* – personal development, self-evaluation, centrality of learning;
- *utopian* – social learning, structural change;
- *planned development* – social control, skills growth, reformed system of education, local learning societies;
- *market* – learning market.

From the above that it is possible to argue that those aspects of the learning society that fall under personal development are the natural outcomes of learning. They are about the individual rather than the social, so that we do not need a learning society concept to understand them, although they will have some social outcomes. Nevertheless, when personal development issues involve planning and the control of that development, then they fall into the category of planned development – or strategy. The other three are about vision, strategy and market, and they are distinctly different from each other.

However, one aspect of a learning society not really touched upon in Coffield's report is that of learning in the risk society (Beck, 1992) – what Beck calls reflexive modernity. Coffield (2000, p. 22) makes an implicit reference to this when he claims that the phrase 'We're all learning all the time' is anodyne. The fact that we are being forced to learn all the time is actually the very basis of the learning society rather than an educative society which underlie the other three approaches. Only those who have disengaged from society are not really being forced to learn a great deal, and even they are still exposed to some of the forces of change. Much of this is either unplanned or uncontrolled, or both, but it is an aspect which is central to contemporary society – for the learning society is also reflexive modernity (Jarvis, 2000). We see this form of learning as a crucial dimension of the learning society, but one that cannot be controlled and this is important when we consider the complex nature of teaching in a society where all forms of learning are occurring in an uncontrolled and uncontrollable manner.

We suggest, therefore, that there are four dimensions to a learning society, which we will examine: vision, planning, reflexivity and market, starting with the vision.

### Vision

Early writers about the learning society, Hutchins (1968, p. 133) for instance, started with an educational vision that everybody would have access to part-time adult education throughout the whole of their lives, but it would also be a society which had 'succeeded in transforming its values in such a way that learning, fulfilment, becoming human, had become its aims and that all its institutions would be directed to this end'. For him, the learning society would be the fulfilment of Athens, made possible not by slavery but by modern machinery.

It was the realisation of the computer revolution that led Husen (1974) to very similar conclusions. Husen (1974, p. 238) argued that '*educated ability* will be democracy's replacement for passed-on social prerogatives'. He recognised that the knowledge explosion would be fostered by a combination of computers and reprographics and he (p. 240) foresaw the possibility of '*equal opportunities* for all to receive as much education as they are thought capable of absorbing'. Despite Sweden's long history of adult education, Husen still regarded the learning society as being educational and based on an extension of the school system.

There are reflections here of Dewey's (1916, p. 51) claim that:

> It is commonplace to say that education should not cease when one leaves school. The point of this commonplace is that the purpose of school education is to insure the continuance of education by organizing the powers that insure growth. The inclination to learn from life itself and to make the conditions of life such that all will learn in the process of living is the finest product of schooling.

In a more recent book on the learning society, Ranson (1994, p. 106) suggested a similar picture:

> There is the need for the creation of the learning society as a constitutive condition of a new moral and political order. It is only when the values and processes of learning are placed at the centre of polity that the conditions can be established for all individuals to develop their capacities, and that institutions can respond openly and imaginatively to a period of change.

The vision of these authors, and others who have written on this topic, is of a 'good society' that is both democratic and egalitarian; one in which individuals can fulfil their own potential through education and learning throughout the whole of their lives – something for which they have been prepared for in school.

### Planning

There have been many policy documents published by European governments in recent years, all illustrating the strategies that they regard as important in the development of the learning society. It is unnecessary to refer to many of these here, but they also recognise the significance of the knowledge economy.

In the introduction to the OECD report (1996, p. 13), the following occurred:

> Success in realising lifelong learning – from early childhood education to active learning retirement – will be an important factor in promoting employment, economic development, democracy and social cohesion in the years ahead.

In the European Union White Paper (1995, p. 18), a similar claim was made:

> The crucial problem of employment in a permanently changing economy compels the education and training system to change. The design of appropriate education and training strategies to address work and employment issues is, therefore, a crucial preoccupation.

In the British government report *The Learning Age* (DfEE, 1998, p. 13) it was clearly stated that the learning society is something to be created and that it will be educative in nature:

> In the Learning Age we will need a workforce with imagination and confidence, and the skills required will be diverse: teachers and trainers to help us acquire these skills All of these occupations...demand different types of knowledge and understanding and the skills to apply them. That is what we mean by skills, and it is through learning – with the help of those who teach us – that we acquire them.

Despite the inclusion of some rhetoric about learning enriching our humanity and even our spirituality and the democratic society, the main emphasis of planning in all of these documents is that its end-result will be the learner's employability.

### Reflexivity

The risk society (Beck, 1992) is one in which the complexities of the contemporary world make decisions based on certainty impossible, and uncertainty is introduced into an instrumentally rational world. There are now hardly any points of decision in individual or social life that do not offer alternative viable solutions, but there are rarely any such incidents that have only one certain unequivocal answer. Every decision is a risk, which Beck (1994, p. 6) sees as underlying reflexivity:

> Let us call the autonomous, undesired and unseen, transition from industrial to risk society *reflexivity* (to differentiate it from and contrast it with reflection). Then 'reflexive modernization' means self-confrontation with the effects of risk society that cannot be dealt with and assimilated in the system of industrial society – as measured by the latter's institutionalised standards. The fact that this very constellation may later, in a second stage, in turn become the object of (public, political and scientific) reflection must not obscure the unreflected, quasi-autonomous mechanism of the transition: it is precisely abstraction which produces and gives reality to risk society.
> (*italics* in the original)

That society has emerged in this way means that its leaders take risks when implementing 'solutions' to its problems because there is no necessarily proven answer. Consequently, there is always a need for it to confront itself about the outcomes of the decisions it makes, or fails to make. This is a reflexive society, one of the outcomes of which has been that people are forced to make decisions for themselves, often without having more than the everyday technical knowledge that we discussed in the third chapter to guide them. Individuals are forced to take risks, to learn and reflect upon their decisions, and so forth. They are also forced to adjust to the changes that occur in society as a result of whatever changes occur. As Beck (1994, p. 13) suggests, individuals 'must produce, stage and cobble together their biographies themselves'. People must decide for themselves, adjust to social changes and keep on learning, either by doing and reflecting upon the outcomes or thinking and planning before the action takes place. In another sense, creative discoveries and new decisions made in the work place are also individual learning. As Beck (1994, p. 16) claims, participation in work in reflexive societies 'in-turn presupposes participation in education' – or at least in learning. One of the outcomes of reflexive modernisation is that individuals are learning more often throughout the whole of their lives – both reflectively and non-reflectively. This is 'learning all the time' but it is not an anodyne statement but a necessary feature of reflexive modernity. In this sense a reflexive modern society must be a learning society, but the learning is individual and much of it is autonomous and occurs outside of the institutionalised provision of learning opportunities.

Another aspect of this form of society is that upon reflection learners can be critical about what they have learned. Traditionally, teachers taught truth propositions but now there is recognition that many decisions are made without there ever being evidence to prove that they are the correct decisions, and consequently learners should be encouraged to be critical.

### Market

Contemporary society is also a consumer society and the history of consumerism can be traced back to the eighteenth century (Campbell, 1987). Campbell traces it back to the romantic period in the eighteenth century, when pleasure became the crucial means of realising that ideal truth and beauty which imagination had revealed and, significantly, this Romantic Movement 'assisted crucially at the birth of modern consumerism' (Campbell, 1987, p. 206), so that a longing to enjoy those creations of the mind becomes the basis for consuming new phenomena. In other words, there can be no market economy unless there are consumers who want to purchase the products that are being produced. Advertising plays on imaginary pleasure – and learning becomes fun! Whilst learning was equated with education in people's minds, they remembered their unpleasant experiences at school when its was no fun to learn, a barrier to further education was erected and it was one which every adult educator sought to overcome.

As we pointed out earlier, one of the advantages of the concept of learning is that it is a consumer term, whereas 'education' is a producer concept and 'teaching' is the marketing of the product (information). Once learning became separated from education, then learning could become fun – and there is a sense in which this has become a more popular thing to do in the United Kingdom since the creation of the British Open University. Now people can learn all the things that they have wanted to learn, and they do not have to go to school to do it. They can read books, watch the television, listen to the radio, access the web and go and talk with other people – if they want to. The Open University marketed a commodity, and other organisations have followed suit. Now it is possible to learn all the things people have wanted to know – by purchasing their own multi-media personal computers and surfing the web, watching the television learning zone programmes, buying their own 'teach yourself' books and magazines and, even, purchasing their own self-directed learning courses.

There are tremendous implications of the learning society for our understanding of teaching since the social milieu in which we teach has changed, people of all ages are exposed to much more information and can, and do, learn a wide variety of things, so that, for instance, no longer can teachers be sure that they know more about their topics than do their students, and so on. There is a real sense in which the internet has assumed an all-embracing role of information provider (teacher) for many.

One of the features of the learning society upon which we have not placed a great deal of emphasis yet is that it is one in which knowledge is no longer static. Since it appears to change with great rapidity, it is difficult to construe it any longer in terms of truth propositions to be learned and memorised, but rather to be considered and utilised if it is appropriate.

## Part 2: the changing nature of knowledge

The nature of teaching might, therefore, change both with the nature of the knowledge being examined and its means of dissemination. At the same time, since it is learning that is now being encouraged rather than teaching, it might first be necessary to redefine teaching away from the definitions provided in the *Concise Oxford Dictionary* – for instance, teaching might be regarded as an activity designed to foster human learning. But then it might be asked is any activity designed to foster human learning the process of teaching? Are managers, for instance, who create a situation where any of their staff learn in the work place teachers? Clearly, however, as the nature and status of knowledge has changed, so teaching has changed – from demonstrating scientific truth through word or action. It is difficult to consider the idea that the nature of knowledge has changed and in order to illustrate this a little more we need to look at some different ways of understanding knowledge.

In the *Dictionary of Philosophy* (Flew, 1979) three types of knowledge are discussed: *knowledge that* (factual knowledge); *knowledge how* (practical); *knowledge of* (people and places). *Knowledge that* is knowledge based on argument or research; so that it is possible to claim that 'x' is a fact. *Knowledge how* is practical knowledge; I know how to do it. There is a sense in which this latter type of knowledge is also often confused with *knowledge that* since it becomes shorthand for *knowledge that this is how* it is done. *Knowledge that*, in both of the forms described here, can be taught in a traditional school, college or university setting since the knowledge is usually being mediated to the students through the lecture. By contrast, neither *knowledge how* nor *knowledge of* can be taught in this way. Neither can be mediated in the same manner.

Additionally, Scheffler (1965) has suggested that knowledge can be legitimated in at least three different ways: rationalistically, empirically and pragmatically.

### Rationalist

This form of knowledge is legitimated by reason – it is *knowledge that*. Pure mathematics is often the example provided for knowledge of this type; mathematicians need no objectives beyond the problem and no form of proof that it not to be found within its own logic. Philosophical knowledge is another form of knowledge which is legitimated in the same way. We can help students master the art of rational argument through their writing and in the way that we help them construct an argument, or a case.

### Empirical

Empirical knowledge is also *knowledge that* but relies on the sense experiences; knowledge is true if it can be shown to relate to an empirical phenomenon. Thus, I know that there is something upon which I am sitting – I can feel it and I do not sink to the ground when I sit down. There is a chair here and I know that there is an object here by my sense experience, even though the *idea* of 'chair' is a construction of my experience – but the chair is part of the situation! We can have knowledge of a reality beyond ourselves through our senses. However, facts have no meaning in themselves, so that we always have to interpret facts and give them meaning. This was a relatively easy task when the meaning of facts was undisputed, but now it is much more complex because different schools of thought provide different interpretations of phenomena and so we become interpreters rather than legislators of different theories (Bauman, 1987). Competing interpretations hardly have the status of knowledge, rather they are theories and should always be treated in this way and Foucault (1972) has shown that dominant theoretical interpretations are often those of the dominant elite, so that teachers should expect students to be critical especially when they are examining such theories.

### Pragmatic

Pragmatic knowledge is *knowledge how*; it also scientific knowledge since its validity rests on experimentation. If the experiment can be replicated, if the findings of the experiments fit the situation or achieve the desired results, then it is valid knowledge. The pragmatist also emphasises the experimental nature of certain forms of experience; individuals try something out and find that it works, or it fails. For instance, young university lecturers can be told how to lecture but until they have actually done it they do not know that they can do it, and it is only after having done it many times that expertise in lecturing might begin to develop. They find out by doing it and achieving their desired aims. As Heller (1984) points out, this is also the nature of everyday experience and everyday knowledge – we learn by experiment. Lyotard (1984) has stressed that in post-modern society knowledge will be legitimated by its performativity; that it by whether it works. But another significant thing about pragmatic knowledge is that it is practical and tends not to be based on a single discipline, so that our teaching has to take a practical turn and, as we shall see later in the book, innovations in teaching practical and pragmatic knowledge lead us into problem-based learning, among other new teaching methods.

Teachers have to recognise the type of knowledge included in their lessons and adapt their teaching to the legitimate claims of the content – we should never claim too much for the knowledge we teach because we can be assured that our learners might soon question the claims that we make especially since they have many other channels of information by which they can check what we claim. False claims for the validity of our content will expose us in an unfavourable light and lower our credibility with our learners.

## Part 3: the changing nature of teaching

The traditional image of the teacher is someone who tells students what to learn and encourages them to learn and rehearse what they have been taught. It has been they who have mediated knowledge to children and adult learners alike. Teachers were 'the fount of all wisdom' but now that has all changed. Teachers, for instance, now no longer:

- have a monopoly on transmitting knowledge;
- determine or legislate on matters of knowledge but they may be interpreters of different systems of knowledge;
- deal with truth but they certainly teach truths;
- teach with unchanging knowledge but now they deal with scientific knowledge which is transient;
- are confined to the classroom, but like the ancient teachers they may have to function where their learners are;
- teach only theoretical knowledge but now they also help learners acquire practical knowledge;
- can assume that their learners know nothing about the subjects that they teach but must learn to build on knowledge acquired by their learners from a wide variety of sources.

In addition, with the mode of delivery changing as the learning market develops, so it is no longer only an inter-personal activity – now it might be mediating knowledge through the written script and through the spoken word on audio tape and even on interactive electronic systems. As education seeks to respond to the demands of the market, so teaching is forced to change to produce in the most efficient means the learning packages that will be useful to the work situation, or the socio-cultural one, and so on.

## Conclusion

Teaching is changing; it is being forced to change by the dominant globalising forces of social change. Teachers are faced with playing new roles requiring many more and sometimes different skills. Indeed, many of the new techniques that have to be learned are ones that adult educators have learned in teaching adults over the years, but others are new for all educators.

The aim of this book is not to produce a 'how to' book (see Jarvis, 1995, *inter alia*) but to examine some of the approaches to teaching that are arising from an informed and critical perspective.

## References

Bauman, Z. (1987) *Legislators and Interpreters* Cambridge: Polity

Beck, U. (1992) *Risk Society* London: Sage

Beck, U. (1994) The Reinvention of Politics in Beck, U., Giddens, A. and Lash, S. (eds) *Reflexive Modernization* Cambridge: Polity

Beck, U. (2000) *What is Globalization?* Cambridge: Polity

Beck, U., Giddens, A. and Lash, S. (eds) (1994) *Reflexive Modernization* Cambridge: Polity

Campbell, C. (1987) *The Romantic Ethic and the Spirit of Modern Consumerism* Oxford: Blackwell

Coffield, F. (ed.) (2000) *Differing Visions of the Learning Society* Vol. 1, Bristol: Policy Press and ESRC

*Concise Oxford Dictionary* Department for Education and Employment (1998) *The Learning Age* London: Department for Education and Employment

Dewey, J. (1916) *Democracy and Education* New York: Free Press

European Union (1995) *Teaching and Learning: Towards the Learning Society* Brussels: European Union

Flew, A. (1979) *A Dictionary of Philosophy* London: Pan Books

Foucault, M. (1972) *The Archaeology of Knowledge* London: Routledge

Heller, A. (1984) *Everyday Knowledge* London: Routledge and Kegan Paul

Husen, T. (1974) *The Learning Society* London: Methuen

Hutchins, R. M. (1968) *The Learning Society* Harmondsworth: Penguin

Jarvis, P. (1987) *Adult Learning in the Social Context* London: Croom Helm

Jarvis, P. (1995) *Adult and Continuing Education: Theory and Practice* London: Routledge (2nd edition)

Jarvis, P. (2000) Globalisation, the Learning Society and Comparative Education, *Comparative Education* Vol. 36, No. 3, pp. 343–355

Lyotard, J.-F. (1984) *The Post-Modern Condition: A Report on Knowledge* Manchester: Manchester University Press

Organisation for Economic Cooperation and Development (1996) *Lifelong Learning for All* Paris: OECD

Otala, L. (1998) *European Approaches to Lifelong Learning* Geneva: European University-Industry Forum

Ranson, S. (1994) *Towards the Learning Society* London: Cassell

Scheffler, I. (1965) *Conditions of Knowledge* Chicago, IL: University of Chicago Press

# Chapter 2

# Teaching

## An art or a science (technology)?

*Peter Jarvis*

> The ideal lecture theatre is vast, truly vast.
> It is a very sombre, very old amphitheatre, and very uncomfortable.
> The professor is lodged in his chair, which is raised high enough for everyone to see him;
> there is no question that he might get down and pester you.
> You can hear him quite well, because he doesn't move.
> Only his mouth moves.
> Preferably he has white hair, a stiff neck and a Protestant air about him.
> There are a great many students, and each is perfectly anonymous.
> To reach the amphitheatre, you have to climb some stairs, and then, with the leather-lined doors closed behind, the silence is absolute, every sound stifled;
> the walls rise very high, daubed with rough paintings in half tones in which silhouettes of various monsters can be detected.
> Everything adds to the impression of being in another world.
> So one works religiously.
>
> (History student, female, aged 25 – cited by Bourdieu and Passeron, 1994, p. 1)

Academic discourse, as Bourdieu and Passeron make clear, uses a vocabulary far removed from the students' everyday experience and not well understood by them. When they try to use it, usually incorrectly, it merely reinforces the professors' perception of them as unintelligent, since they try to repeat the ideas of the professors in a language that they have not mastered. But even if they do master it, it contains only limited forms of knowledge that might, or might not, be useful to the students in their own everyday life, or even their own professional life. It is about certain forms of cognitive knowledge, omitting the other dimensions of human living and human practice. But the questions that we might want to ask is – is what we have described here actually teaching? It has certainly passed for teaching in universities for a long while. But how do we evaluate it – is it because 'correct' knowledge is being transmitted or is it because the process facilitates the learning. Universities have traditionally been concerned about the former and only recently have they become concerned about the latter. Therefore, before we can we can seek to answer the question posed by this chapter's title we need to explore what we mean by teaching. This chapter, therefore, falls into three parts: the concept of teaching; teaching as a technology; teaching as an art.

## Part I: the concept of teaching

A great deal of emphasis in contemporary education has been on learning and the learner, although concerns about teaching have continued to surface – as the Quality Assurance exercise and the emphasis in the Dearing Committee's (1997) report make clear. In the latter, we read:

> We recommend that, with immediate effect, all institutions of higher education give high priority to developing and implementing learning and teaching strategies which focus on the promotion of students' learning.
>
> (Recommendation 8)

> We recommend that institutions of higher education begin immediately to develop or seek access to programmes for teacher training of their staff, if they do not have them, and that all institutions seek national accreditation of such programmes from the Institute for Learning and Teaching in Higher Education.
>
> (Recommendation 13)

While the Dearing Committee was concerned that the image of the professor sitting high above his students had to be eradicated, the committee did not really consider the concept of teaching itself, although it did include distance education within its deliberations.

In the previous chapter we outlined the meanings to the concept given by the *Concise Oxford English Dictionary* but in order to demonstrate how even the dictionaries differ, in this chapter we record the meanings given by *Collins Dictionary*. It offers us a number of different ways of viewing teaching: to help to learn, to show; to give instruction or information; to cause to learn or understand; to teach someone a lesson. Perhaps this final one shows us something of the paradox of teaching, but the many definitions from both dictionaries illustrate that it is hard to define teaching. Indeed, Pratt (1998) offers five different approaches to it: transmission (effective delivery), apprenticeship (modelling ways of doing), developmental (cultivating ways of thinking), nurturing (facilitating self-sufficiency), and social reform (seeking a better society). Pratt is actually suggesting five different aims of teaching rather than five different conceptions of it. Nowhere does he actually offer a definition, since he recognises that people, like the dictionaries, have a variety of perspectives on the subject. Neither does he try to distil out common elements from these perspectives in order to provide a conceptual framework for understanding the concept.

Many years before this, Hirst and Peters (1970, p. 80) tried to delimit teaching by suggesting that 'teaching had to indicate or express some content, that pupils are intended to learn', and this for them was the thing that distinguished teaching from other similar activities. It certainly fits the pattern of the professor, as described by Bourdieu and Passeron, and it is also in accord with curriculum theory where content is one of its central elements, but if this is the essential nature of teaching it is hard to locate facilitation within it. In these contexts, it is perhaps no wonder that writers such as Carl Rogers (1983, p. 119) can claim that teaching is an over-rated function. But Rogers was a teacher! But not one who sought to control the content of what is taught and so Hirst's and Peters' approach is not applicable to all forms of teaching. Perhaps, an even more inclusive definition is required.

Brown and Atkins (1998, p. 2) actually offer a simple and almost self-evident definition of teaching: it is 'providing opportunities for students to learn'. Kidd (1973, p. 292) would agree with this and he suggested that we need a noun that captures the idea of 'he (sic) – who-assists-learning-to-happen' – which is rather like the idea of animation. Yet this approach is not as self-evident as it might seem. For instance:

- What happens if the students do not take the opportunities – is providing them with opportunities still teaching? One could claim that it is, but Freire (1998) would claim that there can be no teaching without learning. Nevertheless, if teachers cannot attract their learners they might be considered poor teachers rather than non-teachers. Yet poor teaching might not be the only reason why the students do not learn – it might simply be that they do not want to learn, or that they consider the subject irrelevant to their lives. It is possible to take a horse to the water but it cannot be made to drink.

- Does there have to be a relationship between the teacher and the learners for teaching to occur, as there is in the traditional classroom – or has the realignment of time and space in late modern society meant that the teacher's role has changed in dramatic ways? Clearly as teachers now prepare material on-line there can be no face-to-face relationship in these instances, but neither did the professor seated high above his students have much of a relationship with his then? In on-line teaching a relationship might emerge, although its nature will have changed, and an opportunity to learn has still been provided.

- Writing a book or a journal article might be viewed as providing an opportunity to learn, but is authorship *per se* teaching? It certainly provides opportunities for learning but authors are not necessarily teachers in the formal sense of the word, they might not regard themselves as teachers, nor might they regard their writing as teaching. Yet in writing material for print-based distance education, there is an intention to provide opportunities for learning, so that certain forms of authorship are teaching. Consequently, teaching might be seen as an intended activity.

It may be seen that it is extremely difficult to get a definition that delimits teaching from other similar activities. Nevertheless, for the purposes of this chapter, teaching is regarded as an intentional activity in which opportunities to learn are provided, and this is broad enough to include all the types of teaching mentioned above. Now the question posed by the title of this chapter might be addressed.

## Part 2: teaching as a technology

Since education has been an Enlightenment product, it is no surprise to find that the traditional concept of teaching has embraced many of its philosophies, such as the emphasis on an end-product, rationality, efficiency, scientific ideals of measurement and evidence, and both an empirical and pragmatic approach to knowledge. Significantly, learners were treated almost as if they were passive recipients of the information that they were receiving; they could be treated almost as inanimate objects so that the process could be likened in some way to natural science. Teaching could, therefore, be examined in the same way as material objects, so that the techniques by which knowledge was transmitted were regarded as crucial to the process. Therefore, teaching as we have traditionally known it might be regarded as the product of the era of Modernity. It is an activity that had to fit this paradigm, so that this calls for a discussion of at least three aspects of teaching: the end-product of teaching, the means to the end and an assessment of the process.

## The end-product

The outcome of any teaching process had to be measurable so that the emphasis on behaviourism reflected the instrumental rationality of the period. If teachers could understand how the learning process occurred they could endeavour to ensure that their activity was efficient and achieved the predetermined outcomes. Hence scientific experiments were needed to demonstrate how individuals learned and Skinner, amongst others, was able to demonstrate this case in laboratory experiments with animals. This satisfied the scientific emphases of Modernity. Consequently, the more teachers understand processes of reinforcement in learning, the more effective their teaching might become so that they achieve their specified objectives – usually behavioural in nature. Skinner (1968, p. 59) actually believed that teaching is a technology in which we can 'deduce programs and schemes and methods of instruction'. Therefore, lessons and teaching materials could be designed that provided the type of reinforcement necessary to achieve the predetermined outcomes, that could then be measured either by behavioural change or by examination and assessment of the knowledge taught. In precisely the same way he (1968, p. 65) believed that teaching machines are devices that 'arrange the contingencies of reinforcement' and, therefore, effective distance education could use the same psychological processes as face-to-face teaching and their effectiveness could be assessed in precisely the same manner.

While there is considerable evidence that conditioning is effective, fundamental questions have to be asked about the extent to which the laboratory experiments with rats and mice can be transferred to human beings. Nevertheless, behaviourism was a product of this period, and this approach to teaching seemed self-evident and was widely accepted and is still accepted.

## Means to an end

Teaching techniques are means to an end – they might be regarded as a form of instrumental rationality, and therefore fit into this paradigm of scientific Modernity. In basic curriculum theory we see the logical pattern of aims of the lesson, content to be taught and, therefore, the methods to be used. Finally, in this model, evaluation occurs – of the content and of the methods selected. The choice of method bears little or no relationship to moral or philosophical principles but only to a realistic understanding of human behaviour and its effectiveness in producing the desired outcomes. This 'scientific approach' is even more pronounced in the various approaches to instructional design, which are more common in the United States than in the United Kingdom (West *et al.*, 1991; Gagné *et al.*, 1992). Here the models for designing instruction are extremely sophisticated; they provide rational processes and pro-grammes that instructors should implement in order to make their instruction more effective. Once more, it is the technique and not the teacher what is important, so that individual instructors or the teachers are almost dispensable to the process.

Perhaps we see this even more with the use of PowerPoint presentations – I have attended conferences where there has almost been a competition for the most sophisticated power point expertise, almost irrespective of the conceptual level of its content. It is almost as if the technology has assumed a greater importance than the content or the teachers and learners.

This argument has been pursued even further when it comes to distance education, since it is possible to design the types of materials that Skinner (1968, p. 65) advocated when he suggested that 'the teaching machine is simply a device to arrange for the contingencies of reinforcement'. In another way we see teaching as no more than a trans-mission of knowledge to more students than a single lecture theatre would hold. Peters (1984) equated the production of distance education materials to a process of manufacture. In this, teaching was becoming efficient since it enabled one set of teaching materials to be mass-produced and used with a far greater number of learners. However, in a later work, Peters (1998) has also noted that other distance education mate-rial does take philosophical and humanistic concerns into consideration.

Nevertheless it is quite significant that in teacher training there has been a considerable emphasis placed on teaching methods – see the discussion in the next chapter. It is the method that is important rather than the personality of the teachers or of their behavioural and ideolog-ical dispositions. Teaching techniques are important, and few people would deny this, but the emphasis placed upon them reflects the era of Modernity. Skinner (1968, p. 91), however, actually recognised that if these techniques are used unwisely they might inhibit learners' creativity, so that he indicated that teaching might be more than tech-nique, as do other theorists of education. Not all objectives, for instance, are behavioural – some are expressive (Eisner, 1969), and more recently the focus has been on other elements of teaching, such as teaching style – a point to which we will return in the next section and even more so in the next chapter.

In my own work (Jarvis, 1995) I originally suggested that there are three different categories of method: didactic, Socratic and facilitative, but in this book we have added a fourth – experiential. Within this discussion, however, the ethics of teaching acquires a more significant place, a point to which we shall return below.

### Evaluating the teaching process

Since the emphasis of teaching has been placed on instrumental rationality, it is little wonder that one of the ways of measuring teaching success has been on the outcomes of the process. Teachers must be effective if they produce students who gain good grades – a measurable outcome. But there is no direct evidence to indicate that the teaching process has actually been the cause of the measurable outcome! It might have been, but we do not necessarily know whether it is the teaching process, or the teachers' personality or the learners and their efforts, which help achieve the success. But there is at least one other problem: students can learn from many other sources and it might even be that poor teachers drive good students to the libraries. But so does the fear of failure! Our professor sitting on high might actually be communicating relevant knowledge but fear of failing his course might mean that his students spend hours in the libraries and then it is their study skills that are as, or more, important than the lectures that they attended.

The other way of assessing the teaching process is to observe it and in some way record it. In this numerical world, we have seen teachers graded, and in some places the grade is used in helping to determine whether, or not, teachers should be promoted. But as we know from all the research on marking essays that there is a tremendous difference between different markers and how much more is this likely to be when each teaching event is unique and when it is not really possible to re-visit the event and re-consider it? We are all aware that students' evaluations of the same lesson do not all agree, and a similar disagreement might well be found if experienced lecturers all assessed a teaching process. Indeed, many years ago we tried an experiment in a workshop when we asked thirty teachers to assess a video of someone cleaning a pair of shoes – there was considerable variation in their assessments! This is not to claim that bad teaching cannot be identified, only that it is more difficult to do than many of the over-simplistic methods that are often employed in many situations.

With distance education materials, we can only evaluate the content and the way that it is produced and presented, but the writer of the material may not actually be the person who designs the format or produces the final structure. In this sense, the writer as academic can be evaluated but the presentation of that material is a skill that might other professionals might possess, so that teaching itself becomes a team activity with at least one partner not necessarily being an academic. However, it is also clear from this discussion that distance education has changed the nature of teaching; it is about content, process and design which captures the spirit of the technological age. It is an ultimate form of manufacture; it comes much closer to being a technology and a science of production than does classroom teaching. Like other occupations, the uniqueness of the person is removed. The human relationship of the classroom is displaced by impersonal transmission of knowledge and individual learning and achieving. However, in certain forms of on-line learning we are beginning to see the possibilities of relationship and individuality emerge in distance education – it is a more human and a neo-Fordist approach to education.

What we have begun to question in each of these points is the idea that teaching is just about technique. It is a technology but is this all it needs to be to provide learning opportunities intentionally? Is the teacher merely the instrument choosing the right methods, communicating the 'correct' knowledge and getting the desired results? In this process the students are treated as passive and are moulded like materials in other production processes – but this does not exhaust the process of teaching since students need individual help, need to be motivated, and so on. Learning and teaching needs a personal relationship in order to achieve the best outcomes and this is also recognised by the fact that many distance education institutions also provide opportunities for face-to-face contact.

## Part 3: the art of teaching

The concentration on content and method has led many of us to say that 'I teach sociology' or 'I teach mathematics' – but this is incorrect. Actually, 'I teach people sociology' or 'mathematics', and so on. Sentences of this nature betray the values of a technological age, but they are incorrect and they also hide something of the moral basis of teaching, a point to which we shall return in a later chapter.

Brookfield (1990, p. 2) has denied the importance of the technology of teaching by suggesting that it is rather like 'white-water rafting'. In a sense the conditions in which it occurs are not controllable. In a similar manner Eble (1988, pp. 11–12) seeks to dispel at least twelve myths of teaching, although he concentrates rather more on the teaching process than on the conditions; three of his twelve myths are that:

- teaching is not a performing art
- teaching should exclude personality
- popular teachers are bad teachers.

Basically he is saying precisely the same thing as Freire (1998) when he calls teaching a human act, but he goes a little further than Freire by implying that there is something of a performance in teaching. I do not think that Freire would disagree with this. However, this aspect of teaching – teaching style – is notably absent from many teacher-training courses.

Kidd (1973, p. 295) suggests that teaching styles are often presented as dichotomies:

- permissiveness versus control
- aggressiveness versus protectiveness
- emphasis on content versus emphasis on participation.

In my own work, I (Jarvis, 1995, p. 105) have suggested that research into leadership management styles are also useful when thinking about teaching style, such as Lippett and White (1958) who suggested that there are three leadership styles: authoritarian, democratic and laissez-faire, and McGregor's (1960) Theory X and Theory Y, with the former treating learners as if they do not want to learn and the latter assuming that they are highly motivated. The recognition of teaching style is the recognition that teachers' performances as an intrinsic part of the teaching process. More works are now focusing on teaching style as well as teaching method than in previous generations – style is the about the art of teaching rather than the science. It is also about the teachers' own humanity and personality. Style clearly overlaps with method, but is still different from it. For instance it is possible to have an authoritarian facilitator and a democratic lecturer, and so on.

However, there is more to humanistic teaching than just style. This form of teaching involves a relationship, one that is necessarily moral, for all human interaction has a moral component. I have argued elsewhere (Jarvis, 1997) that there is one universal moral value – that is being concerned for the Other – and it is never wrong to care for the Other – whoever the Other is. Consequently, teachers should be concerned for their students, but students should also be concerned for their teachers. There are many books and papers that have sought to demonstrate the significance of the moral relationship in teaching (Daloz, 1988; Freire, 1998; Palmer, 1998, *inter alia*) and they recount the lengths to which teachers should go to help students achieve their own fulfilment through the processes of teaching and learning. This is the vocation of teaching. We shall return to the moral element in teaching in a later chapter.

Palmer (1998, p. 74) highlights some of the paradoxes of classroom teaching and suggests six – the classroom space should:

- be bounded and open;
- be hospitable and 'charged';
- invite the voice of the individual and the voice of the group;
- honour the 'little' stories of the students and the 'big' stories of the disciplines and the traditions;
- support solitude and surround it with the resources of the community;
- welcome both silence and speech.

Once these paradoxical and moral elements enter into the teaching and learning process, the focus is on the humanity of the learners and much of the instrumentality of teaching fades into insignificance. Teaching is about respecting the personhood of learners and teachers and enabling human beings to achieve their own potential, without imposing of them predetermined outcomes of the teaching, although we recognise the importance of what is learned in the process. Fundamentally, teaching is a human process, in which the teachers themselves may well be the best instruments that they have in helping learners to both learn their subject and achieve their potential. We are now beginning to see recognition of this when, as in the UK recently, there have been campaigns to attract people into the teaching profession using celebrities who have proclaimed how specific teachers have most influenced them in their earlier life, and so forth. This is an implicit recognition that the emphasis on the instrumentality of the Enlightenment era, which modern teaching acquired, have always underplayed the human elements of the process – teaching is an art.

## Conclusion

Like the dictionaries that offered a number of definitions of teaching, we cannot reach a definitive conclusion as to whether teaching is a technology or an art. Clearly some forms of teaching, especially those that tend to depersonalise the teaching and learning process, like the professor with whom we opened this chapter who can lecture to hundreds of students, and those other forms the lend themselves to mass production, suggest that teaching is a technology. But when teaching is face-to-face and interactive, when it is a human process then it is much more than a science – it is an art.

## References

Bourdieu, P. and Passeron, J.-C. (1994) Language and the Teaching Situation in Bourdieu, P., Passeron, J.-C. and Saint Martin, M. (eds) *Academic Discourses* Cambridge: Polity

Brookfield, S. D. (1990) *The Skillful Teacher* San Francisco, CA: Jossey-Bass

Brown, G. and Atkins, M. (1988) *Effective Teaching in Higher Education* London: Methuen

*Collins Dictionary of the English Language*

Daloz, L. A. (1988) *Effective Teaching and Mentoring* San Francisco, CA: Jossey-Bass

Dearing, R. (Chair) (1997) *Higher Education in the Learning Society* (Summary Report) London: HMSO

Eble, K. E. (1988) *The Craft of Teaching* San Francisco, CA: Jossey-Bass (Second Edition)

Eisner, E. W. (1969) Instructional and Expressive Educational Objectives in Popham, W. J., Eisner, E. W., Sullivan, H. J. and Tyler, L. L. (eds) *Instructional Objectives* Chicago, IL: Rand McNally

Freire, P. (1998) *Pedagogy of Freedom* Lanham: Rowman and Littlefield.

Gagné, R. M., Briggs, L. J. and Wagner, W. W. (1992) *Principles of Instructional Design* Fort Worth: Harcourt Brace, Janovitch (Fourth Edition)

Hirst, P. and Peters, R. S. (1970) *The Logic of Education* London: Routledge and Kegan Paul

Jarvis, P. (1995) *Adult and Continuing Education: Theory and Practice* London: Routledge (Second Edition)

Jarvis, P. (1997) *Ethics and the Education of Adults in Late Modern Society* NIACE: Leicester

Kidd, J. R. (1973) *How Adults Learn* Chicago, IL: Association Press (Revised Edition)

Lippett, R. and White, R. K. (1958) An Experimental Study into Leadership and Group Life in Maccoby, E. E., Newcomb, T. M. and Hartley, E. L. (eds) *Readings in Social Psychology* New York: Holt

McGregor, D. (1960) *The Human Side of Enterprise* New York: McGraw Hill

Palmer, P. J. (1998) *The Courage to Teach* San Francisco, CA: Jossey-Bass

Peters, O. (1984) Distance Teaching and Industrial Production: A Comparative Interpretation in Outline in Sewart, D., Keegan, D. and Hohmberg, B. (eds) *Distance Education: International Perspectives* London: Croom Helm

Peters, O. (1998) *Learning and Teaching in Distance Education* London: Kogan Page

Pratt, D. and Associates (1998) *Five Different Approaches to Teaching in Adult and Higher Education* Malabar, FL: Krieger

Rogers, C. (1983) *Freedom to Learn for the 1980s* New York: Merrill (Second Edition)

Skinner, B. F. (1968) *The Technology of Teaching* New York: Appleton Century Crofts

West, C. K., Fowler, J. A. and Wolf, P. M. (1991) *Instructional Design: Implications from Cognitive Science* Englewood Cliffs, NJ: Prentice Hall

# Chapter 3

# Teaching styles and teaching methods

*Peter Jarvis*

Few people have written about the educative society, Kidd (1961) being a notable exception and no one, as far as I can discover, has written about a teaching society although the information society contains echoes of it. Teaching has traditionally been associated with the idea that there is a truth proposition (knowledge) or an accepted theory that can be disseminated through the agency of the teacher – but in late modernity the idea that there is a truth or an indisputable theory to be taught is now harder to accept, although there are many people who still hold to the idea that what they are taught is true. Foucault (see Sheridan, 1980) called this a 'will to truth'. Even so, the fact that there are a variety of teaching methods – didactic, Socratic, facilitative and experiential – indicates that teachers have recognised that there are an increasing variety of ways of approaching their task. Nevertheless, this provides teaching with a degree of flexibility that might have become increasingly utilised in the face of the epistemological changes referred to in the previous chapters (see Jarvis, 1995 for a discussion on this).

Over the years, however, there has always been the recognition that some teaching is teacher-centred whilst other is student-centred, although the latter has not been practised in all forms of education as much as it might have been. This distinction has been most well marked in the education of adults, but even in traditional adult education a great deal of the teaching has been didactic. By contrast, student-centred methods presage the learners and their learning and appear more relevant to the idea of the learning society. This is also closer to the ideas about education that emerged in the education of adults, since one of the major differences between the education of children and that of adults is that children tend to be more dependent than adults on their teachers. Children might, but not necessarily will, be more inclined to accept what teachers tell them, so giving it something akin to the status of a truth, while the content of the lessons of teachers of older learners may not be given such status. Indeed, Entwistle (1981) cites Bennett's (1976) study in several places in his book to illustrate the fact that children need more direction in order to learn effectively and this frequently occurred in more formal classroom settings, but many adults criticise teachers for treating them too much like children. In addition, Galton *et al.* (1980) discovered that primary school children were mainly given individual attention in the classroom when the teacher gave information or controlled behaviour.

Teaching methods are frequently taught in courses preparing teachers, both for school and for adult education, but less frequently is reference made to teaching style. Indeed, a number of books on teaching in higher education, for instance, make no reference to teaching styles at all and even the number of the different teaching methods discussed is restricted (see Brown and Atkins, 1988). Yet it is suggested in this chapter that understanding teaching styles is just as important, perhaps even more important, than teaching methods in teaching, and that the education of teachers should focus more directly on teaching style. Indeed, the teachers' style can influence the form of learning that takes place as much, if not more, than the teaching method employed. Brookfield (1990, pp. 12–13), reflecting on his own teaching career, makes reference to this in relation to the fact that the techniques that he was taught in college and in the text-books as 'good practice' just did not work in the classroom, so that he eventually reached the conclusion that many teachers have reached – that those techniques specified as basic for good practice are simply wrong and that they should not relentlessly be applied to practice.

Indeed, teaching style might also influence the learners, even motivate them, much more than do different teaching methods. Even so, there is sometimes a tendency to confuse teaching method and teaching style and merge them into a single phenomenon (see Entwistle, 1981), so that the first section of this chapter examines the differences between them that we feel need to be drawn out and, thereafter, both are examined separately and the final section extends the discussion of the influence of style on learning, with reference to charismatic teaching.

## Part I: teaching methods and teaching styles

Methods focus on the techniques that teachers employ; they are ways of doing it – processes, techniques. There is a sense in which the word 'style' also refers to the way that things are done – its design, and so on. Indeed, style is a much more difficult word to define but it is used here in relation to the manner of 'expression' rather than the actual process of doing. Conti (1990, p. 80) refers to this in terms of the 'distinct qualities' displayed by a teacher. There is a sense in which the teachers' style helps determine the ethos, or the culture, of the situation in which the teaching takes place, although it must be recognised that as individual classes are situated in a school, college or university this also contributes to the ethos.

The distinction drawn between method and style is important here since teaching methods are about the *science* of teaching whereas teaching styles are about the *art* of teaching, as we discussed in Chapter 2. Our concern in this book is to recognise the complexity of teaching – it is both an art and a science, but in the learning society the nature of science itself is being called into question. Teaching methods are about the technical processes of teaching whilst teaching styles are more about the teachers and the way that they conduct themselves during the teaching session, although Morrison and McIntyre (1973, p. 156) point out that personality tests have not been useful in predicting the way that teachers actually teach.

Naturally there is considerable overlap between style and method, since it is the same teacher who usually decides on the methods and who then conducts the teaching process, both of which contribute to the experience that learners have and from which they learn. Entwistle (1981), reporting both on the work of Bennett (1976) and Solomon and Kendall (1979) in the United States, refers to this combination as 'classroom types'. Consequently, this heuristic distinction is made here only to enable us to understand more clearly the processes of teaching and learning.

## Part 2: teaching methods

The science of pedagogics is not an uncommon phrase amongst educationalists from continental Europe, and while we have never referred to education in quite this way in the United Kingdom, there has almost been a belief that once we know the aims and objectives of the lesson and the content to be taught, then the method is self-evident. Indeed many early curriculum studies do not actually include teaching methods at all (Tyler, 1949; Taba, 1962, *inter alia*) as part of their discussion of the curriculum.

The self-evidency of the teaching methods assumes that either teachers will be didactic or that they will use the most efficient methods they know to achieve their specified objectives. Teaching involved the transmission of knowledge/theory or the teaching of a skill – it was an instrumentally rational activity: the outcomes of which can be measured and so the techniques employed can be assessed. This is the science of teaching. Underlying it are certain Enlightenment values – rationality, empirical measurement, universalism (in that the same methods and content could be taught to students of a specified age and level of experience in a course) and the pre-eminence of scientific knowledge. Later in the development of the study of education, more wide-ranging discussion occurred about the different types of technique, although many of these were still basically didactic.

This apparent scientific approach was emphasised in America at this time in a number of studies in instructional design (Gagné *et al.*, 1974; West *et al.*, 1991, *inter alia*). The aim of these works was to provide a rationally consistent basis for the design of certain forms of teaching, to construct systems where teachers were enabled to consider as many eventualities as possible about the programme of teaching that they were preparing. All teachers need to prepare their lessons diligently, and systems certainly help – it was the almost universalistic assumptions underlying this movement that correct preparation would achieve the desired outcomes that are more questionable.

But in the 1960s, as well as this approach to teaching, student-centred methods became more common in schools and colleges; something that had been much more widely practised in adult education for many years. This even led Rogers (1969, p. 103) to claim that teaching was an over-rated activity but then he was also a person-centred therapist, so that he fully endorsed student-centred methods and wrote about facilitation as a method of helping students learn. Indeed, since the 1970s, there has been a wide recognition of different teaching techniques, although even a best-selling book on teaching in further education such as Curzon (1997), which was first published in 1976, still had only a limited section on teaching methods. Other books coming from an education of adults background, however, have concentrated on the wider variety of different teaching methods available (Rogers, 1971 [1989]; Jarvis [1983] 1995; Galbraith, 1990, *inter alia*).

The implications of a science of teaching are that the Enlightenment values mentioned above are valid, something that is questioned here. For instance, the idea that teaching is only designed to achieve specified ends effectively raises questions about the validity of the end and the legitimacy of the means by which the ends are achieved. In other words – does the end justify the means? The idea that we can measure the end-result of a lesson presupposes that the learners stop leaning at the point of the assessment and that what they have learned is measurable, but if they are reflective learners they may continue to learn for a long period after the lesson. Additionally, if they have been motivated by a lesson to continue to study the topic long after the lesson is over when is that measured and is motivation quantifiable? The idea that there is always a best method to achieve ends assumes that 'there is only one way to skin a cat!' The assumption that once the method is right, any competent teacher can achieve the desired ends fails to take into consideration the difference of classes, cultures and teachers themselves.

This approach:

- omits consideration of value rationality, as opposed to instrumental rationality;
- is instrumental and assumes that the achievement of the specified objectives is always a sign of good teaching;
- emphasises outcomes and omits consideration of the unintended learning outcomes;
- is universalistic and downplays social, cultural and individual differences;
- assumes that learning is always measurable, and so on.

While there are many ways in which a scientific approach to teaching is important, too much emphasis on the science of teaching depersonalises the teaching and learning process – something that we see occurring in some forms of distance education, and this does have certain ethical consequences (Jarvis, 1997, pp. 111–120).

A scientific approach to teaching and the wise use of different teaching methods is an important factor in teaching, despite all of the above criticisms. Teaching is still, in part, a technical process. Assessing the competence of teachers to employ certain methods is perfectly justifiable. Indeed, teachers who cannot use a wide variety of teaching methods, who do not evaluate the success of their teaching methods, and so on, are unprofessional. But, as every teacher knows, two teachers using the same techniques to teach the same content will frequently do so in entirely different ways and the outcomes of their lesson will not be the same. Learners know that – they evaluate a teacher as someone who:

- makes it interesting
- lets you find out for yourself
- respects our ideas
- is friendly, and so on.

Basically, these types of evaluation point to the significance of the teachers' style.

## Part 3: teaching styles

In the light of the criticisms of the scientific approach to teaching raised earlier, there is a certain irony that Conti's (1990) discussion on identifying teaching styles focuses upon a quantitative approach to measuring style, based upon the respondents' philosophy of teaching reflected in a Likert-types self-evaluation questionnaire. There is an assumption that if we can measure the teachers' philosophy, personality, and so on, we can know something about their teaching style. Indeed, Eble (1988, p. 64) has suggested that 'style is the image of character'. But Morrison and McIntyre (1973, p. 156) have argued that there does not seem to be a relationship between personality tests and the approach to teaching that different teachers assume. Yet teaching is still about helping others learn, a process in which teachers as individuals still play an important role – but play the role they do, for teaching is an art form as well as a science. Their philosophy may indeed be apparent from the style that they adopt.

Teachers manage their classrooms (Davies, 1971) and many writers have written about management style, and there is clearly some overlap in the literature on style between the two occupations. Perhaps the best known literature common to both is McGregor's (1960) distinction between Theory X and Theory Y. Theory X suggests that managers assume that those with whom they work dislike it so that they have to be controlled, coerced and directed in order to achieve the desired outcomes, whereas Theory Y concentrates on the way that managers focus on the human side of their employees and endeavour to develop them as people. Clearly both of these approaches are very relevant to teaching.

Another classical study on style is that of Lippitt and White (1958) who examined the leadership styles of youth leaders highlighting a threefold typology: authoritarian, laissez-faire and democratic. They found that:

- authoritarian leaders create a sense of group dependence on the leader, that their presence held the group together and that in their absence no work was done;
- laissez-faire leaders achieved little work whether they were present or absent;
- democratic leaders achieve group cohesion and harmonious working relationships whether they are present or not.

Their finding relates to that of Galton *et al.* (1980) who noted how teachers sought to control their classrooms through the use of language. Vygotsky (1978) also raised a significant point about teaching style when he argued that children's understanding was not only developed through their interaction with the physical world but also through their active encounters with others in relation to the world. In other words, the style of the teacher in that interaction helps develop children's understanding.

Other studies have suggested different approaches to examining teaching style, so that teachers are seen as having formal or informal approaches, friendly or distant, humorous or dry, confident or withdrawn and so on. Perhaps the most full discussion on teaching styles is that of Apps (1991, pp. 23–24) who captured different teaching approaches through metaphor:

- Lamplighters – who see to enlighten their students;
- Gardners – who seek to cultivate the mind by nourishing, enhancing and providing the right climate, whilst they also remove the weeds, and then they stand back and let growth occur;
- Muscle builders – who seek to strengthen flabby minds;
- Bucket fillers – who pour information into empty containers;
- Challengers – who question learners' assumptions;
- Travel guides – who assist people along the path of learning;
- Factory supervisors – who supervise both the inputs and the outputs of the process;
- Artists – learning is an aesthetic process;
- Applied scientists – they seek to apply research results about teaching to their own approach;
- Craftspeople – who use a wide variety of skills.

In a sense, however, Apps still sees style in terms of method and content – he (1991, p. 23) suggests that it is 'the sum of everything you do as a teacher'. But I want to point us a little beyond the expert role performance focusing upon certain aspects of the role to the way that the role players perform their role.

Eble (1998, p. 64) suggests that 'Without character, a teacher is more ill-equipped than if he (*sic*) had not mastered particle physics, Shakespeare's tragedies, or harmony and counterpoint'.

The character of the teacher plays a fundamental role in teaching – teachers themselves are their best teaching aids. Emphasis on teaching methods tends to standardise teaching but emphasis on style highlights the individuality of teachers and allows for the recognition that every teaching session is a unique event with the teachers alone being the common element in the different classes that they teach. However, teaching is both an art and a science and so we can combine the two approaches: we can have authoritarian facilitators and democratic didactics, as well as authoritarian didacticism and democratic facilitators. Teachers can be friendly but didactic or friendly but Socratic, and so on. There is no limit to the combinations that can be put together – each class is a unique event: this is what the task of teaching is all about. But it is no easy role, as those of us who do it know only too well, for our teaching style also makes demands on us as individuals, as Parker (1998) beautifully illustrates. The first chapter of this book opens with a sub-heading: *Teaching Beyond Technique*, which tells its own story. Parker reflects upon his own teaching:

> After three decades of trying to learn my craft, every class comes down to this: my students and I, face to face, engaged in an ancient and exacting exchange called education. The techniques I have mastered do not disappear but neither do they suffice. Face to face with my students, only one resource is at my immediate command: my identity, my selfhood, my sense of this 'I' who teaches – without which I have no sense of the 'Thou' who learns
>
> ..........*good teaching cannot be reduced to technique; good teaching comes from the identity and integrity of the teacher.*
>
> (1998, p. 10, italics in original)

His book explores the art of teaching from the perspective or knowing whom we, the teachers, are when we enter relationships with those who learn with us. In it he illustrates that teaching is a personal vocation to be of service to those whom we teach.

## Part 4: the charismatic teacher

In this late modern age, emphasis is increasingly being placed on leadership rather than management – on having that something that encourages and inspires others to reach greater heights than they ever achieved possible. Exceptional teachers may do this with students of whatever age, from the very young to adults and even to older adults, although bureaucratic standardisation (and fear of litigation, etc.) tends to place limits on the outstanding individual teacher.

One of the best known accounts of charismatic teaching remains Kohl's (1967) wonderful account of the way that he taught *36 Children* to learn. In this book, Kohl tells the story of how he worked for with thirty-six children from Harlem, gained their confidence and inspired them to reach beyond themselves to learn and enjoy learning. His style was his own ad he did things that only teachers who open themselves to their children could do. Kohl also recorded that there were other teachers in this very disadvantaged school whose style enabled them to reach the children and gain their trust.

> There were a few who knew and loved the children, who stayed at school heartbroken, year after year, watching the other teachers, being abused by the administration, seeing the children fail and nobody care. I became friendly with one such teacher – he had been at the school for twelve years and all the children there knew him. He knew them too, and was constantly besieged by visitors, kids passed out of the school system returning to talk and feel that some element of the world was constant and available.
>
> (1967, p. 192)

Palmer and Kohl write not about their techniques but about a perspective on teaching that comes from seeking to be caring and understanding, having a personality and a style that made them individuals enabling them to reach their learners and gain their trust. For them style is not a performance, it is a way of living, being and interacting of *being* a teacher.

In this sense, teaching is beyond method, beyond the standardisation of the modern age, it is beyond and the visits to the classroom and the paper chases that the bureaucratic authorities require when then they inspect a school or a department, however necessary those visits are assumed to be by those in authority. Teaching is fundamentally about a concerned human interaction.

## Conclusion

Teaching methods and teaching styles reflect the art and science of teaching; they reflect the modern age of science but point beyond it to the validity of the art, the performance and to the reality of the uniqueness and humanity of teaching. To try to restrict teaching to its methods is to fail to understand the teaching and learning process, to try to restrict it to its art allows for the possibility of irresponsibility and unacceptable eccentricities. To understand the relationship of the one to the other is extremely difficult since each of us who teach engage not only in a time-honoured process but one that is quite unique to the occasion when we are actually teaching when we are always best instrument in the process of teaching. The more we understand ourselves, the more likely we are to understand those whom we are privileged to teach. For style is as important, if not more important, than method in the process of teaching and learning.

## References

Apps, J. (1991) *Mastering the Teaching of Adults* Malabar, FL: Krieger

Bennett, S. N. (1976) *Teaching Styles and Pupil Progress* London: Open Books

Brookfield, S. D. (1990) *The Skillful Teacher* San Francisco, CA: Jossey-Bass

Brown, G. and Atkins, M. (1988) *Effective Teaching in Higher Education* London: Methuen

Conti, G. J. (1990) Identifying Your Teaching Style in Galbraith, W. (ed.) *Adult Learning Methods* Malakar, FL: Robert Krieger

Curzon, L. B. (1997) *Teaching in Further Education* London: Cassell (5th edition)

Davies, I. K. (1971) *The Management of Learning* London: McGraw Hill

Eble, K. E. (1988) *The Craft of Teaching* San Francisco, CA: Jossey-Bass (2nd edition)

Entwistle, N. (1981) *Styles of Learning and Teaching* Chichester: John Wiley

Gagné, R. M., Briggs, L. J. and Wager, W. W. (1974) *Principles of Instructional Design* Fort Worth: Harcourt, Brace and Jovanovich (4th edition)

Galbraith, M. W. (ed.) (1990) *Adult Learning Methods* Malabar, FL: Robert Krieger

Galton, M., Simon, B. and Croll, P. (1980) *Inside the Primary Classroom* London: Routledge and Kegan Paul

Jarvis, P. (1995) *Adult and Continuing Education: Theory and Practice* London: Routledge (2nd edition)

Jarvis, P. (1997) *Ethics and the Education of Adults in Late Modern Society* Leicester: NIACE

Kidd, R. (1961) *18–80 Continuing Education in Metropolitan Toronto* Toronto: Board of Education.

Kohl, H. (1967) *36 Children* Harmondsworth: Penguin

Lippitt, R. and White, R. K. (1958) An Experimental Study of Leadership and Group Life in Maccoby, E. E., Newcomb, T. M. and Hartley, E. L. (eds) (1958) *Readings in Social Psychology* New York: Holt (3rd edition)

McGregor, D. (1960) *The Human Side of Enterprise* New York: McGraw Hill

Morrison, A. and McIntrye, D. (1973) *Teachers and Teaching* Harmondsworth: Penguin (2nd edition)

Parker, P. J. (1998) *The Courage to Teach* San Francisco, CA: Jossey-Bass

Rogers, C. (1969) *Freedom to Learn* Columbus, OH: Merrill (3rd edition – Rogers, C. and Freiburg, H. J. published in 1994)

Rogers, J. (1971) *Adults in Education* London: British Broadcasting Commission (3rd edition (1989) published as *Adults Learning*) Milton Keynes: Open University Press

Sheridan, A. (1980) *Michael Foucault: The Will to Truth* London: Tavistock

Solomon, D. and Kendall, A. J. (1979) *Children in Classrooms: An Investigation of Person–Environment Interaction* New York: Praeger

Taba, H. (1962) *Curriculum Development: Theory and Practice* New York: Harcourt, Brace and World

Tyler, R. (1949) *Basic Principles of Curriculum and Instruction* Chicago, IL: University of Chicago Press

Vygotsky, L. S. (1978) *Mind in Society* Cambridge, MA: Harvard University Press

West, C. K., Farmer, J. A. and Wolff, P. M. (1991) *Instructional Design: Implications from Cognitive Science* Englewood Cliffs, NJ: Prentice Hall

# Chapter 4

# Ethics and teaching
## Exploring the relationship between teacher and taught

*Peter Jarvis*

In recent years there has been a growth in the study of ethics and teaching (Jarvis, 1997; Freire, 1998; Palmer, 1998, Macfarlane, 2004, *inter alia*). In another sense, Levinas' (1991a) study on *Totality and Infinity* is also an ethical study about learning in relationship throughout which he referred to teaching. I want to use some of the ideas in this study to explore an ethical approach to teaching based upon the nature of the relationship between teachers and taught, as I did in *Ethics and the Education of Adults in Late Modern Society* (Jarvis, 1997). Underlying this is Buber's (1959) profound study *I and Thou*. However, using Levinas' terminology I want to divide this chapter into three sections: teaching and the stranger – lecturing; teaching and totalising – managing the system; teaching and infinity – sharing and expanding. Each section contains an ideal type picture of a form of teaching, together with its strengths and weaknesses.

## Part 1: teaching and the stranger – lecturing

In Chapter 2 of this book we used a word picture of a professor performing in a large lecture theatre; the lecturer was far removed from the students and they came to listen to the pearls of wisdom that he uttered from afar. This is not an unusual description – lecturers and the large lecture hall crowded (perhaps) with students wanting to learn the knowledge that is to be presented. Indeed, with the curtailment of funding in higher education in a number of countries, this is a form of teaching that will remain a popular form of knowledge presentation for years to come. Even more so, in distance and e-teaching there is a real possibility that similar forms are emerging in which the lecturers are far removed from the learners and have no personal relationship with them. Lecturing, then, does not only occur in a large lecture hall with the lecturer standing performing before a large audience; it occurs within the much more confined space of the class room. Lecturers are didactic teachers who expound their theme and, having done so, they have completed their task and with clear conscience they can leave the class room. Colin Griffin has dealt with didactic teaching in Chapter 6 of this book and so we need not explore this is great detail here.

Nevertheless, it would be true to say that in lecturing, the teachers can remain true to themselves and to their understanding of the truth. They have had time to think through the information that they present, to know that they have read and studied the latest research on the subject and that what they present is true to their understanding of it. Teaching is about the presentation of information for students to learn. Consequently, two moral elements dominate this approach to teaching: that lecturers should be true to their discipline, and that they should be true to themselves. Indeed, it is a categorical imperative that they do this and to do less is to fall far short of the ethical demands of professionalism in teaching. In this sense, lecturers can present their best understanding of the information and construct their argument in a most logical manner so that the learners can see the validity of what they are being taught. Learners have an opportunity – no, a moral responsibility – to learn what they are taught so that they can use it appropriately thereafter, including in examination settings.

One of the advantages of this approach is that lecturers can prepare their notes, overhead slides or PowerPoint presentations and handouts and present the material in as professional a manner as they know. This reflects the authority and expertise of the teacher. Indeed, it is also a most useful method for novice teachers – all the information is prepared and as long as the lecturers keep to their notes, they are safe. Indeed, when I used to train educators (both school teachers and lectures in all forms of professional and adult education) I used to say to them – if you are not confident of your subject or yourself, prepare a lecture, go into the class room and deliver it and get out before anybody asks you questions that might reveal your ignorance. Lecturing can be the novice teacher's survival kit: but if lecturers are confident then they might be better teaching their subject!

The point about this situation is the social, and sometimes the physical, distance that exists between lecturers and their students. Lecturers are presenting their material without interacting with the students – there is no I-Thou relationship, but an I-It one, where the 'It' is the class or the group. Levinas would see this situation as one in which the lecturers are free, at home in their own world, and they can identify themselves as lecturers simply by their performance. The students do not really disturb the freedom of the lecturer and have no power over them – they are 'strangers'. As strangers, they can make no demands on the lecturers. In precisely the same way, strangers are free; free also from the lecturers, although the students are not free from the demands of the educational system of which the lecturer is a representative. In order to enter relationship but not to destroy the strangers' otherness or self, or the lecturers' own sense of self, they need to enter into conversation with each other and genuine conversation cannot be carefully planned like a lecture presentation; indeed, by its very nature, lecturing is one-way communication devoid of conversation.

Naturally this is an ideal type, but it depicts something about the nature of lecturing but what happens when the strangers seek to enter conversation with the lecturers? Now they impinge upon the freedom of the lecturer and Levinas (1991a, p. 43) writes: 'We name this calling into question of my spontaneity by the presence of the Other ethics'. For Levinas, ethics begins when we experience the other personally and so, in some way, we are no longer totally free, even if we have ever been so. Elsewhere in his work (Levinas, 1991b, pp. 14–15), he suggests that this personal relationship is not merely cognitive but emotive, being vulnerable in relationship with the other. I think that Levinas under-emphasises the ethics of strangers co-existing without entering into relationship. He also under-emphasises the ethics of being true to oneself, like the professional ethics that demands that the lecturers always give their best presentation. Even so, when the stranger becomes a face, a person with whom we can enter relationship through conversation, then different ethical demands are made upon both *ego* and *alter*. Indeed, Levinas (1991a, p. 40) actually goes so far as to suggest that 'the bond that is established between the same and the other without constituting a totality' is religion – but to discuss this here is beyond the brief of this chapter.

In entering a relationship, face to face, each still have to respect the other's sense of being, self-hood and freedom. In the relationship itself there are tremendous challenges and also great potentialities, but they can only be realised in the flourishing and yet respecting the other in the relationship itself. Striving after the richness of this relationship, Levinas claimed, lies at the heart of humanity itself, it is our human desire, and part of the argument of this chapter is that teaching can only occur in human relationship when we can strive to achieve that potentiality but there is a real possibility that we, as teachers, might produce a different outcome if we become totalisers.

## Part 2: teaching and totalising – managing the system

The totaliser reflects the world as we currently know it and this is Levinas' starting point. His question is how can we transcend this world? How can we reach to that something beyond it and embark upon a journey that has no end, which I argue is the ethical ideal of teaching and we will return to this in the next section of this chapter. But first, what is totalising and how does it manifest itself in teaching? The totalisers live in a world dominated by social systems which are objective and rational; it is a world that subordinates the individual (domesticates, is a word sometimes used) and, in one sense, ensures that the stranger will never become a face that can be taken seriously. Wild, in his excellent Introduction to this book, summarises this position:

> To be free is the same as to be rational, and to be rational is to give oneself over to the total system that is developing in world history...All otherness will be absorbed in this total system of harmony and order.
>
> (Levinas, 1991a, p. 15)

This is a system which demands that individuality be subjugated to the group, which is neutral and impersonal, rational and objective. Naturally, this is an ideal type and reflects Wrong's (1961) well-known argument of the over-socialised view of human beings. Wrong argued that humans are not so totally socialised, but the point behind Levinas' argument is that by subjecting human beings to such relationships we fail to recognise their individuality and realise the rich potential of human relationship. While teaching should not be a profession that over-socialises, or indoctrinates (see Wilson, 1964; Snook, 1972), there is certainly more than a danger that totalising tendencies emerge and the human face that sometimes appears is lost in strangerhood as the social system dominates and teachers become too busy for their students, as they have to complete the paperwork or prepare for yet another inspection, or for a variety of other reasons which reflect the type of society to which Levinas is opposed. Wild (Levinas, 1991a, p. 17) writes: 'It is outwardly directed but self-centred totalising thinking that organizes men and things into power systems, and gives us control over nature and other people. Hence it has dominated the course of human history.'

Totalitarian thinking looks to the objective system, to rational means and ends, to power and control and to seeking harmony or conformity with the established procedures and in different ways perhaps we, as teachers, incorporate totalistic thinking in our daily practice. The totaliser takes away the other's freedom, sometimes unthinking, and this can occur through a variety of ways during teaching and learning. I want to suggest just five ways here by way of illustration: the aims and objectives, method, content, assessment of teaching and, finally, by lecturers being over-protective, shepherding or even 'mothering' the students.

### Aims and objectives

The aims of education constitute a major philosophical discussion which is beyond the remit of this chapter but it is worth noting the position adopted by MacIntyre (1964), as a representative of many who would seek to locate education outside the social system in some way or another. MacIntyre wrote:

> I hope it is clear...that the values of rational critical inquiry seem to me to stand in sharpest contrast to the prevailing social values. The task of education is to strengthen the one and weaken the other. Above all the task of education is to teach the value of activity done for its own sake.
>
> (1964, p. 21)

Despite this hope, it is commonly accepted by sociologists that education acts as a means of social and cultural reproduction (Bourdieu and Passeron, 1977), and the more radical Althusser (1972) claimed that education is a powerful state ideological apparatus. The aims of education seem to be at odds with its functions and perhaps we can begin to see the reason why when we look at just one common educational practice – the setting of objectives. Both when a course or module is prepared and when a lesson is prepared, it is commonly expected that the preparation should record the objects of the programme or the session and these are expected to be written as behavioural objectives, for example, 'At the end of this session the students will have learned...'. This is both a false statement and a revealing assumption! The false statement is that prediction is a most problematic concept, especially when it comes to predicting human behaviour. It might be more correct to write, 'At the end of this session, the teacher anticipates covering the following topic(s) ...'. But the revealing assumption is that teachers can not only transmit material but that we assume that the students will learn it in a way that the teachers expect. This suggests an authority of the teacher to control the learning processes of the students and that they will accept what they are taught uncritically. Both of these points need further discussion:

*The authority of the teacher*: The teachers' authority should be as experts in the subject matter being presented and also as experts in the ways in which it is presented – but the teachers do not have the authority over the learners to such an extent that they can control their thought processes. Indeed, that would be indoctrination.

*The students' accepting what they are taught*: Learning is a very complex process (see Jarvis, 2005) in which we learn knowledge, skills, beliefs, attitudes, values, emotions and the senses even though we tend only to assess one or at most two dimensions of this process. Moreover, we often tend to look only for the 'right' answer in that dimension. But to learn critically, creatively, thoughtfully, meaningfully, and so on, is much more complex and if we merely accept what we are told we are in denial of our humanity. Indeed, Nietzsche (Cooper, 1983) suggested that to accept passively what we are told is and act of inauthenticity. But more than this, if teachers expect to create such learning situations they are seeking to take away the students' right to disagree and this is morally unacceptable since it denies their humanity.

Clearly the way that behavioural objectives are used shows that for many teachers, they have not pursued their rationale to its logical conclusion but once we do we can see that underlying them is an untenable ethical position, as well as a completely impractical one. What is clear from this discussion and will become clearer as we develop this chapter is that it is the person who learns (we do not teach education, sociology or mathematics, etc. – we teach students education, sociology, mathematics, etc.) and this is fundamental to our ethical understanding of teaching – if we seek to control, indoctrinate or deny the learners' humanity in any way the students remain strangers with whom we do not really enter into conversation.

Does this mean that we should have no objectives when we teach? Clearly not – aimless activity is not necessarily a good use of time, but we should be more prepared to look at expressive objectives in which the learners assume a much more significant place.

## Teaching methods

Teaching involves conversation, or to put it in a more commonly used jargon – dialogue. There are two forms of dialogue that should follow from good teaching: dialogue between teacher and taught and dialogue between taught and taught, depending on the teaching method being used. Consequently, an initial base line to judge on the ethics of teaching is the extent to which the method chosen encourages dialogue – encourages a situation in which all who speak are listened to.

Now it has to be acknowledged that the teaching role does inhibit this relationship from developing and that even as it does, there is frequently a residue of the authority of the role present in the conversation. But being an authority is not the same as being in authority and if teachers have to utilise the authority of the role in order to teach, then there is a sense in which they need to reflect carefully upon the way that the role is being performed or even their preparation for the role – there may be classes in which role authority is useful but they are fewer than we might assume. There are many books that demonstrate how role authority can be overcome and respect for teachers take its place (see Palmer, 1998, *inter alia*). Being an authority should command the respect of those who seek to learn the topic under consideration.

I am not advocating here that every session should be dialogue all the time and I know that there are many occasions when we want to enter conversation with the learners that the class can be dominated by one or two loquacious students. Yet if we enter a genuine dialogue with the class as a whole, it will often curtail excessive involvement of one or two students. But there is also a place for us to take the talkative learners aside and discuss quite openly with them about their involvement within the group – but it should be done quietly in private, still respecting the personhood of the student. However, this does mean that we need to be quite open with our classes about the methods that we are going to use and discuss with them the advantages and disadvantages, and so on. If we are open and we do enter a dialogue then we must listen to what is said to us and be prepared to learn from it – listening by the teacher is not a façade, but a genuine act of learning on our part.

There are also occasions when we put the students into groups so that we encourage them to talk to and learn from each other. Small group teaching is a very good teaching method when used wisely and well, although there are occasions when it is wrongly used and often students will be aware of it and they can be overheard making comments such as, 'Groups again!' Often when we use group teaching we, as teachers, often wonder between the groups listening to what is going on. However, Brookfield (1990, pp. 194–195) noted that sometimes such visits to the group by the lecturer controlled the group dynamics and so he stopped visiting small groups during teaching sessions. There is a sense in which the residue of the teacher's authority can inhibit genuine discussions in groups, and this should also be avoided because there is a sense in which we might be demonstrating our authority at the expense of the learners. We have to be aware of this possibility.

Indeed, we can all misuse our authority in a variety of way and perhaps Bourdieu's and Passeron's (1977) concept of symbolic violence points us in this direction. Their initial definition is quite broad:

> *All* **pedagogic action** *(PA) is, objectivity, symbolic violence insofar as it is the imposition of a cultural arbitrary by an arbitrary power.*
> (Bourdieu and Passeron, 1977, p. 5
> (*italics* and **bold** in the original))

We might want to dispute the breadth of this definition but the point underlying the definition is the totality of the culture from which we cannot escape, so that they are suggesting that whatever methods are used the learners are still forced to function within a specified cultural framework. However, if we enter negotiation, encourage critical and original thought, we might just overcome the totality of culture, which is a major part of Levinas' argument. It is, therefore, quite ethical to discuss with the class the teaching methods that we are going to employ, even to negotiate with them so that we are sure that we are always trying to enter a genuine conversation with all of our learners.

### Content

It is much more difficult to discuss the content of individual sessions with students since many syllabi are set by the professional bodies or by the validating body and this is both understandable and perfectly acceptable; it is right and proper that students should learn a body of information before they qualify, but there are two points that might be made about this – the first is personal and involves the whole course while the second is much more specific.

From a personal point of view, in the early 1980s I taught a part-time Masters degree course on Adult Education in which all the students were practising adult educators, and one year I discussed with the students an idea that they should choose all the course content and teach each other while I would sit in and contribute occasionally. However, I was far from in-active during this period since each week I prepared a full set of lecture notes on the subject of their choice. The course was a great success from the students' perspective and they enjoyed it very much but the outcome was that I put the notes that I had prepared each week together and published it as a book (Jarvis, 1983) and twenty-two years later that book is still in print in its third edition (Jarvis, 2004). Allowing the students to choose both the content and the method actually proved extremely beneficial and it was ethically acceptable and the students were far from strangers – some are still my friends.

Even if we follow a prescribed syllabus, there is still a place for student involvement in the content for each session. I well remember hearing a colleague once as we came to the end of the academic year coming out of a class and saying – 'Thank goodness, I've covered the syllabus; we had to rush quite a number of things, but I got through it'. The question that might be asked about that exclamation is did he just cover the syllabus or did he teach it? There were many places during the year when he might have discussed with the students which parts they regarded as most vital, whether there were sections that they knew, whether there were some bits they would be prepared to teach themselves, etc., so that he could participate with them in the crucial, new sections, and so on. In keeping them at a distance, they remained strangers who did not interfere with his freedom to choose and whilst he may have felt ethically justified in what he did, there were many other ethical questions that demanded answers.

## Assessment

Assessment is thoroughly discussed in two chapters later in the book but I want to raise two points here. The first comes from Freire:

> On this occasion our teacher had brought our homework to school after correcting it and was calling us one by one to comment on it. When my turn came, I noticed he was looking over my text with great attention, nodding his head in an attitude of respect and consideration. His respectful and appreciative attitude had a much greater effect on me than the high classification that he gave me for my work. The teacher affirmed in me a self-confidence that obviously still had room to grow. But it inspired me to a belief that I too had value and could work and produce results.
>
> (1998, p. 47)

The student was a face, but so often written work is returned anonymously and the students are treated as strangers. But we are not dealing with strangers, we are working with people and so when we assess the work of individuals who are faces to us, then we should enter a dialogue with them in the assessment. We are working with people and it is people who learn and who grow and develop and so that our written comments should be rather like that school teacher cited from Freire's work: we should not just mark things wrong, for instance, so much as to ask why/how they had reached their conclusion; we should write encouraging points and appreciate good and interesting answers, and so on. We are addressing faces not strangers through the written word.

Teaching people takes time! Often we do not have the time. The system demands that we make the faces strangers and get on with other aspects of our work. This too is our temptation, because our work is demanding and time-consuming, but we might actually discuss our difficulties with our students and treat them as faces rather than condemn them to strangerhood. However, there is another way in which we can take away students' dignity and self-hood.

### The over-protective teacher

There are some occasions when teachers gain a following who hang on to their every word, and so on. Sometimes teachers encourage this; it is certainly good for our ego. But if we overstep the mark, as it were, we take from the students something of their freedom and, once again, it is not longer a conversation but an exposition in which the teachers give the students of their wisdom but not from the opposite extreme from stangerhood and we incorporate them into another system – one which revolves around the teachers and their *ego* and this also has many dangers.

In most of our teaching the stranger occasionally emerges as a face and on others the face is condemned to strangerhood. Clearly there are a multitude of factors that create these situations and we are all caught up within the system and its demands and as these demands grow so the potentialities of the face decrease. This does not mean that students will fail – after all they still have the library, the Web and each other, so that there are many other resources. If we treat them as faces, however, we might actually direct them to such resources as we discuss the demands that the system makes on us as teachers. But what does infinity offer?

## Part 3: teaching and infinity: sharing and expanding

Levinas (1991a, p. 52) claims that 'The immediate is the face to face'; it is in this situation that those who interact are open to each other, and it is in conversation that each can inspire the other. Writing from the perspective of the self:

> It is therefore to *receive* from the Other beyond the capacity of the I, which means exactly: to have the idea of infinity. But this also means to be taught. The relation with the Other, or Conversation, is a non-allergic relation, an ethical relation; but inasmuch as it is welcomed this conversation is a teaching...Teaching is not reducible to maieutics; it comes from the exterior and brings me more than I contain. In its non-violent transitivity the very epiphany of the face is produced.
>
> (Levinas, 1991a, p. 51
> (*italics* in original))

Maieutics is the Socratic mode of teaching (see Chapter 7 on the Socratic method) in which Socrates implied that individuals have latent ideas which just had to be brought to the consciousness through questioning. But, Levinas claims that teaching brings something new to the learner through which the learner can grow and develop. In conversation this is a two-way process whereby each enriches the other and continues to do so for as long as the relationship is active. The idea of learning from the students echoes Freire's student/teacher–teacher/student idea – something to which he was to return to throughout his life: 'Only the person who listens patiently and critically is able to speak *with* the other, even if at times it should be necessary to speak *to* him or her' (Freire, 1998, p. 110).

In the Preface, Levinas (1991a, p. 25) suggests that 'infinity overflows the thought that thinks it': it is, therefore, beyond experience. It is growth and development and yet more grow and development since human beings can transcend themselves, and reach towards an infinite capacity and achievement – it is beyond thought itself. Wild (Levinas, 1991a, p. 17) suggests, 'The former (totalisers) seek for power and control; the latter (infinitisers) for a higher quality of life. The former strive for order and the system; the latter for freedom and creative advance.'

There is a folk high school in Tennessee called Highlander and one of the things that I learned from that historic place is my ABC – Any Body Can! It is this hope that lies behind the infinitiser. At this point it might well be asked whether this is not something that most teachers want to do for their students and, to some extent, it is but the point of Levinas' argument is to ask whether we can actually transcend the system and reach to the heights of human creativity and self-hood within it. He leans to the idea that this can only truly happen through conversation in which neither imposes upon the other but each teach the other that enables us to transcend it. It is a truly democratic process.

Clearly, Levinas' argument is open to considerable questioning in some places and in the way it is presented it is certainly centred upon the Self who needs to break away from the social system and transcend it and I do not think that he pursues how the relationship conversational relationship that points us towards infinity sufficiently far. But the ideas underlying his thinking are certainly applicable to the teaching and learning situation, since it points to the:

- all-embracing social and cultural system within which we live and which we take for granted;
- power implicit within the system for the role players (teachers);
- significance of the other (students) as persons (faces);
- importance of the interaction;
- mode of interaction;
- intentions of the participants;
- often untested and infinite capacity of human beings if they can break away from the system.

## Conclusion

There are no directives in striving towards infinity, only hopes and aspirations. These will reflect both the teachers' hopes for their students but also their hopes for the world because in genuine conversation teachers' own beliefs – their own personhood – must be apparent. The more we think along these lines the more fundamental becomes the position which might best be summed up by Freire's condemnation of teaching that just conforms and does not look towards infinity:

> Educative practice is all of the following: affectivity, joy, scientific seriousness, technical expertise at the service of change and, unfortunately, the preservation of the status quo. It is exactly this static, neoliberal ideology, proposing as it does 'the death of history' that converts tomorrow into today by insisting that everything is under control, everything has already been worked out and taken care of. When the hopeless, fatalistic, anti-utopian character of this ideology, which proposes a purely technical kind of education in which the teacher distinguishes himself or herself not by desire to change the world but to accept it as it is. Such a teacher possesses very little capacity for critical education but quite a lot for 'training',

for transferring contents. An expert in 'know-how'. The kind of knowledge this 'pragmatic' teacher needs for his or her work is not the kind I have been speaking of... It is not for me to judge, of course, regarding the value of this knowledge in itself, but it is my duty to denounce the antihumanist character of this neoliberal pragmatism.

(1998, pp. 126–127)

Freire in his more political way concurs with Levinas in his reflections on the self and the world; both point beyond the totality to the infinity or to the utopian dreams of teaching. It was this dream that led Palmer into the movement for educational reform:

I am a teacher at heart, and I am not naturally drawn to the rough-and-tumble of social change. I would sooner teach than spend my energies helping a movement along and taking the hits that come with it. Yet if I care about teaching, I must care not only about my students and my subject but also for the conditions, inner and outer, that bear on the work teachers do. Finding a place in the movement for educational reform is one way to exercise that larger caring.

(1998, p. 182)

Underlying all teaching is a utopian dream, and aspiration towards infinity and the ethics underlying the whole exercise of teaching and learning is that together teachers and learners, who are also learners and teachers, must recognise that it is human beings (faces) who constitute the process and they are always in the process of becoming – growing and developing – and reaching beyond where they are now and the nurturing of this process is human care and concern for the Other.

## References

Althusser, L. (1972) Ideology and Ideological State Apparatuses in Cosin, B. (ed.) *Education, Structure and Society* Harmondsworth: Penguin

Bourdieu, P. and Passeron, J.-C. (1977) *Reproduction in Education, Society and Culture* (trans: R. Nice) London: Sage

Brookfield, S. (1990) *The Skillful Teacher* San Francisco, CA: Jossey-Bass

Buber, M. (1959) *I and Thou* Edinburgh: T&T Clark

Cooper, D. (1983) *Authenticity and Learning* London: Routledge and Kegan Paul

Cosin, B. (ed.) (1972) *Education, Structure and Society* Harmondsworth: Penguin

Freire, P. (1998) *Pedagogy of Freedom* Lanham: Rowman and Littlefield

Jarvis, P. (1983) *Adult and Continuing Education: Theory and Practice* London: Croom Helm

Jarvis, P. (1997) *Ethics and the Education of Adults in Late Modern Society* Leicester: NIACE

Jarvis, P. (2004) *Adult Education and Lifelong Learning: Theory and Practice* London: RoutledgeFalmer (3rd Edition)

Jarvis, P. (2005) *Towards a Comprehensive Theory of Human Learning* London: Routledge

Levinas, E. (1991a) *Totality and Infinity* (trans: A. Lingis) Dordrecht: Kluwer

Levinas, E. (1991b) *Otherwise than Being or Beyond Essence* (trans: A. Lingis) Dordrecht: Kluwer

Macfarlane, B. (2004) *Teaching with Integrity* London: Routledge and Falmer

MacIntyre, A. (1964) Against Utilitarianism in Hollins T (ed.) *Aims in Education* Manchester: University of Manchester Press

Palmer, P. (1998) *The Courage to Teach* San Francisco, CA: Jossey-Bass

Snook, I. (1972) *Concepts of Indoctrination* London: Routledge and Kegan Paul

Wild, J. (1991) Introduction to Levinas E *Totality and Infinity* (trans: A. Lingis) Dordrecht: Kluwer, pp. 11–20

Wilson, J. (1964) Education and Indoctrination in Hollins, T. (ed.) *Aims in Education* Manchester: University of Manchester Press

Wrong, D. (1961) The Over-Socialized Conception of Man reprinted in Wrong, D. (1976) *Skeptical Sociology* London: Heinemann

# Chapter 5

# Radical and feminist pedagogies

*Julia Preece and Colin Griffin*

## Introduction

Radical pedagogy is a theory of practice that specifically aims to empower oppressed groups or challenge traditional forms of social and political oppression. The nature of these aims is changing in the postmodern conditions of society. So whereas it might once reflect, for example, a straightforwardly socialist analysis (Youngman, 1986) or a Marxist analysis (Allman, 1999), radical pedagogy today reflects, as does society itself, a much more complex picture. Consequently, writers are more likely nowadays to contextualise their analysis within the complexity and ambiguity of the postmodern condition rather than within any single critical tradition such as socialism, feminism, or Marxism (Lather, 1991; McLaren, 1995). For writers such as these, the nature both of oppression and of the pedagogical response has changed. Increasingly, radical pedagogy is constructed against a background of globalisation, the risk society, the cultural turn, and so on. In short, what counts as radical pedagogy may no longer be a matter simply of politics, but of critical consciousness or reflexivity, or of a concept of social inclusion or citizenship itself: the issue of cultural power and hegemony has always been at the forefront of the analysis (Livingstone, 1987).

The implications of postmodernism and the learning society for teachers are considerable, since they call into question the traditional concepts of truth, knowledge and authority upon which classroom teaching has hitherto rested. The relativism of knowledge claims, the primacy of learning over teaching, the global possibilities of information technology, demographic changes in the population of learners, all have major consequences for the perceived role of the teacher. In this context, the changing role of the teacher from legislator to that of interpreter

(Bauman, 1987) was introduced in Chapter 2. Critical reflexivity in the learning process means that the authority of the teacher is both challenged and reformulated around the learning process itself. This is what radical or critical pedagogy has traditionally implied. That is, it casts the teacher in the role of empowering learners to bring about social and political change. In the learning society, the role of the teacher in this respect is rendered even more problematic.

This chapter will outline some of the major accounts of radical pedagogy, and place it in the broader context of change which the idea of the learning society stands for. The radicalism of pedagogy may take many forms. Whereas once it seemed an exclusively political or ideological stance, nowadays it is as likely to be associated with the critical reflexivity of learning itself, or with particular kinds of teaching and learning methods. Critical pedagogy may, in other words, take individualistic or collective forms, and it may be concerned with content or method, or the relation between them. In terms of context, it has been used to challenge the perceived failings of the system of public schooling (Kanpol, 1994). More often, it is based on the transformative possibilities for adult education associated with major figures such as Antonio Gramsci or Paulo Freire (Coben, 1998; Mayo, 1999). For these reasons, it is more appropriate to speak of radical pedagogies in the plural, rather than to suggest a single tradition or meaning. Finally, in the context of the risk society (Beck, 1992), we need to extend the concept of critical or radical pedagogies to include the teaching and learning implications of social movements, citizenship, peace, environmental and other such concerns of civil society and the postmodern world.

The chapter provides an overall background view of critical and radical pedagogies, identifying common themes and introducing some of the most important writers, before concluding with an account of some feminist positions and a case study of critical pedagogy in the context of environmental education.

## Part I: background

As has already been stated, postmodern society influences how we perceive knowledge and the role of the teacher. In addition to the opportunities and challenges of technology, increasing student diversity has implications for how and what we teach. Formal teaching has traditionally been based on the notion of a teacher who imparts a particular syllabus to a class of passive participants who are then expected to absorb and reproduce the contents of that syllabus at relevant moments beyond the classroom. Teaching methods in this vein use technology as a tool to enhance and vary the presentation of material, but not necessarily as a means of stimulating new forms of critique. The experience of new kinds of students, such as migrants, the mature, the disabled, and so on, into the traditional classroom has raised the question of whether the teaching environment addresses their practical needs. In some cases these concerns also extend to whether the teaching content acknowledges the experiential background of different students, particularly adult ones. The concept of a learning society does not seem to particularly engage with the teaching experience itself, though there are clearly ideological concepts of how a learning society should function. Coffield (2000) does offer ten models of learning *societies*. These range from models which focus on skills development to social control or individualism to a more reformatory model for structural change. There is nevertheless a contemporary tendency to see *the* learning society in terms of market values, employability and vocationalism (DfEE, 1998).

Radical or alternative pedagogies attempt to move beyond these practical foci for society in that they question the very ideology behind teaching. To varying degrees they all challenge the normative social, political and ideological contexts for teaching and learning. The radical goal is usually to empower the learner and change the educational relationship between student and teacher in order to effect societal change.

There are several labels for such pedagogical approaches; the most common can be linked together into two broad groupings:

- social purpose education
- popular education.

The following categories within these groupings are promoted by organisations such as the WEA and many university continuing education departments (Taylor, 1997):

- conscientisation
- pedagogy for the oppressed
- emancipatory learning
- social action learning
- education for social justice.

The following pedagogies have proved to be the practice basis for the labels in the above groupings, particularly since the 1970s, with a focus on community and non-formal education (Kirkwood and Kirkwood, 1989; Allman and Wallis, 1995; Foley, 1999).

- critical pedagogy
- border pedagogy
- postmodernism of resistance
- post-colonial pedagogy
- feminist pedagogy
- engaged pedagogy.

These pedagogies consist of social visions and practices that are most closely connected to postmodernism. Gore (1993) offers a useful distinction between those who write about such teaching from a philosophical or ideological perspective (Giroux, 1983, 1992; McLaren, 1991) and those who offer practical or instrumental techniques (Freire, 1972, 1976; Shor, 1980), though all writers express an intention to link their ideas with both practice and ideology.

Although the above teaching approaches are not necessarily confined to the post-compulsory education sector, their arguments lend themselves to teaching situations which are free from systems of conformity (which are more likely to happen in the school sector). Moreover, whilst Knowles (1990) is not classified here as someone belonging to the radical pedagogy tradition, there is a sense in which his notion of andragogy (teaching adults) and other adult educators (e.g. Brookfield, 1987; Mezirow, 1990; Thompson, 1997) have influenced how the teacher–learner relationship might be seen as something other than a didactic, one-way process of information giving.

Whilst there are many, therefore, who would claim to belong, at least in part, to a radical concept of emancipatory education, this chapter is confined mainly to a selection of authors who represent radical education from an ideological perspective and those who offer practical ideas for achieving this goal. These are:

- Freire, Shor, Foley
- Aronowitz, Giroux, McLaren
- Feminist educators.

The writers represent various 'takes' on pedagogy, though there is considerable sharing of certain themes.

# Part 2: some common features of radical pedagogies

Radical pedagogies challenge conventional classroom practice. This is perceived as a relationship where the teacher is the knower and the student is the recipient of new knowledge emanating from the teacher. In doing so the teacher perpetuates existing social structures and cultural/political world views towards different social groups. This means that students are encouraged to internalise dominant values about society – which is traditionally blind to gender or other differences. The focus of such teaching is on disseminating pre-defined knowledge whose truth is legitimated through texts, written by established authors with authority to 'know'.

Radical pedagogy teachers assume that conventional teaching perpetuates false consciousness and hegemony (internalised value systems which encourage people to believe in their subordinate position in relation to the status quo). This diminishes oppressed or marginalised people's ability to see how they are being manipulated to accept their oppression.

Radical pedagogies attempt to redress this level of awareness by drawing on theoretical perspectives such as:

- Marxist notions of class and reproduction;
- post-structuralist or postmodernist understandings of discourse and power relations.

Both stances usually take a political position that through education people can use their own self-determination to give themselves individual or collective power and challenge the status quo.

The goal of this approach is to give voice to the unseen, unheard and oppressed and stimulate action for change. This is achieved through a process of criticality – teachers acknowledging their inheritance of being the oppressor but being willing to work with the oppressed. They must recognise their own social situatedness and privilege the concept of difference.

The classroom experience becomes a process of democratic dialogue – with the teacher problematising the status quo and getting students to articulate and theorise what they already know from their own experience. In this context the teacher refuses to be the expert and tries to learn as much as the student – by listening, encouraging critical awareness of the socio-cultural positioning of ideas, beliefs, values. Experiences are shared amongst the peer group and there is an emphasis on exploring themes from daily life.

A postmodernism of resistance slant on these perspectives looks more closely at how oppression functions through power relationships. This includes exploring how certain kinds of truth and knowledge are legitimised by people who have power and authority. In this respect language is regarded as a medium for power and domination. For post modernists truth, meaning and knowledge are relative and based on subjective experiences. Therefore, the goal of radical pedagogy is to legitimate the experiences of the oppressed or marginalised by relating those experiences to wider social influences and by encouraging a theoretical perspective which explains how people give meaning to their world.

There are issues associated with these perceptions of the teacher-student relationship. Brookfield (1987) warns for instance that any attempt to change someone's existing worldview is vulnerable to simply another form of indoctrination. Similarly, even if teachers acknowledge their social situatedness, they inevitably possess their own views. Nevertheless the protagonists claim that continual, self-critical awareness should guard against this.

## Part 3: Freire, Shor and Foley

Freire (1972, 1976, 1978) is generally regarded as the founder of an educational approach which challenges the oppressed to critique their relationship with their oppressors – based on reflection and action. His writings have influenced many generations of educators concerned with social justice. He coined the words 'conscientisation' and 'praxis' (shared critical reflection amongst the oppressed resulting in raised awareness of their oppression followed by group action for change).

Many of Freire's philosophical and teaching approaches are reflected across the different strands of radical pedagogy. For Freire the educator's role is to challenge people's awareness of their situation by encouraging dialogue and developing a permanent critical attitude to their social situation. Freire's goal was to create a teacher-learner relationship which assumed a mutuality: 'A process of knowing with the people how they know things and the level of that knowledge' (1978, p. 25). In other words, a recognition that the learner has knowledge which needs to be legitimised. Freire wanted educators to tread the dual path of recognising their social situation as members of the elite – and therefore potentially the oppressors – but also to steer the learning situation by problematising what might otherwise be accepted as normal and encouraging open discussion: 'The task of the dialogical teacher...is to represent that universe to the people from whom he first received it – not as a lecture but as a problem' (1972, p. 81).

The principal aim of Freire's approach was for all learners to act 'together in unshakeable solidarity' (1972, p. 100). Freire was writing on behalf of Brazilian peasant farmers. His philosophy has underpinned much community education work around the world, though the notion of solidarity is sometimes interpreted more loosely.

Shor (1980) adapted Freire's philosophy within the industrial context of worker education. His focus was on making the link between the internalised psyche and external social relationships in order to enable workers to understand how they were being manipulated by the dominant middle class culture. Shor therefore advocated a dialogic teacher–learner relationship where the classroom subject matter consisted of ordinary, daily life situations which would be critiqued by examining familiar situations 'in an unfamiliar way' (p. 93). 'The teacher surrenders the mystique of power and expertise – while using his or her conceptual understanding of reality to provoke critical consciousness in the students' (Shor, 1980, p. 84).

Shor attempted to promote a form of vocational education which he called 'critical literacy' – a means of combining literacy and political awareness which would empower students to intervene in their own destiny. The teacher's role in this situation is primarily as 'initiator' of questions: 'Raising consciousness about the structured failure built into the system is a key task of the liberatory class' (1980, p. 68).

Griff Foley, another follower of Freire almost twenty years later, claims a teaching goal of working for 'emancipatory action'. By this he means: 'the unlearning of dominant oppressive ideologies and discourses and the learning of oppositional liberatory ones' (1999, p. 4). He emphasises, however, that collective action is not easy to achieve. People's notion of liberation may be complex and contradictory, influenced by 'intra personal, interpersonal and broader social factors' (p. 4). He also picks up the postmodern influences that learners need to develop: 'a critical understanding of how power works in society' (p. 26). Nevertheless he supports the 'enabling conditions' for emancipatory learning which require shared experiences of oppression within a learning group, with the opportunity for reflection and critical thinking that extends the learner 'beyond her current understanding' (p. 105). Foley advocates the use of case study material based on people's every day experiences which can then be critiqued and discussed in relation to their socio-political contexts.

He emphasises that emancipatory learning inevitably requires a critique of capitalism. This is because capitalist systems are seen as based on exploitation and oppression of (usually) the majority for the benefit of (usually) the few.

These positions continue to form the basis of much working class education in the Western world. Their emphases, however, on unified responses to class oppression, with limited recognition of other social structures, mean that for some educators this position alone is untenable in today's more reflexive, pluralistic and risk society. A more elaborate way of interpreting emancipation is required.

## Part 4: Aronowitz, Giroux and McLaren

Gore (1993) claims that these three authors present ideological, rather than practitioner perspectives on pedagogy. They are principally post modernists and as such introduce some new vocabulary into the realm of radical pedagogies. Aronowitz and Giroux talk of critical pedagogy, border pedagogy and a postmodernism of resistance.

Aronowitz and Giroux (1991) start from a similar premise to that of Freire, Shor and Foley. They state that postmodern educators 'need to build upon the tacit knowledge derived from the cultural resources that students already possess' (Aronowitz and Giroux, 1991, p. 15). They see postmodernism as a position which enables them to talk about a world where knowledge is constantly changing and meaning is contingent upon interpretation. It provides a reference point to demonstrate the forever fluid and changing borders of one's identity or 'place in the world' (p. 70).

Aronowitz and Giroux, however, attempt to move beyond a purely postmodern discourse which simply affirms difference without exploring the power relationships which constitute difference and domination:

> Postmodernism fails to link the emphasis on difference with an oppositional politics in which the particularities of gender, race, class and ethnicity are seen as fundamental dimensions in the constitution of subjectivity and the politics of voice and agency.
>
> (1991, p. 80)

By this they mean that people derive their sense of self from the way they are positioned by others. The balance of power defining the sense of difference derives from the sense of authority or dominance of one voice over another. So difference can be seen in multiple ways and so can power and oppression.

It is this perspective which distinguishes the advocates of critical pedagogy from the Freirean notion of collective and unified oppression and collective and unified emancipation. Critical pedagogy therefore, 'respects the notion of difference' (1991, p. 118) and the relations of power which constitute those differences. Knowledge which derives from the experiences of being different forms the basis of the classroom curriculum. Aronowitz and Giroux (1991) call this 'a pedagogy of voice' (p. 100). It explores how students give meaning to their personal experiences and how those meanings help to explain what happens in wider society. In this process it is acknowledged that there is no single position. Indeed, voices are 'multilayered, complex and contradictory' (1991, p. 100). But in order to move the marginalised beyond where they are at, Aronowitz and Giroux argue they must not only interrogate their own experiences but must also use those voices to critically question the 'hegemonic discourses that make up the official curriculum' (1991, p. 128). It is at this point that critical pedagogy becomes 'border pedagogy' or a 'postmodernism of resistance'. Giroux (1992) explains that border pedagogy goes beyond merely the development of a critical capacity to challenge. It examines more deeply how institutions, knowledge and social relations are 'inscribed in power' (p. 28). It is only by understanding fully the processes which cause discrimination and difference that we can begin to understand how to change the social fabric of society. So from a process of dialogue and critical review of text (critical pedagogy) learners can move to a sense of self-determination and individual agency plus action (border pedagogy) – but on multiple levels which have different meanings for different learners.

Usher and Edwards (1994) provide a further interpretation of the emancipatory potential for critical and border pedagogy. They suggest critical pedagogy will 'enable learners to become citizens in a reconstituted pluralistic society' (p. 125); whilst border pedagogy will move citizens to 'become their own agents' in a more political way.

In keeping with some criticisms of Freire, Usher and Edwards suggest that the emancipatory potential of border pedagogy is more ideological than real. They confirm again the danger for teachers of creating a unified, essentialist notion of oppression. They also point out that such dialogue assumes a classroom of absolute trust between all members and underplays the difficulties of rationalising the potentially multiple meanings for difference. There remain, therefore, inherent tensions between the desire of the educator and those of the learners.

McLaren (1991) introduces yet another term 'post-colonial pedagogy'. As its name suggests, this is a pedagogy for anti-imperialism (p. 135) but with a particular emphasis on challenging those responsible for global capitalism. In many respects the goals are similar to those of Aronowitz and Giroux's postmodernism of resistance – to enable the voicing of multiple differences and resistances to the status quo, as defined by imperialists. The focus again is on: 'the self anchored in experience' (p. 140). In this rendering of pedagogy, McLaren spells out all the different aspects of teaching which contribute to either emancipatory or banking education (Freire, 1972) – the curriculum, learning location, institutions, teaching style, social practices and the knowledge–power relationships within the learning culture.

McLaren has drawn upon a postmodern notion of difference (shifting identities and constructions of reality) but taken a strategic oppositional position rather more akin to that of Shor. Capitalism is the prescribed enemy but in a form which enables it to be reproduced to suit the historical moment. Consequently teachers of a post-colonial pedagogy must take this into account. 'The assumptions which guide their work must be analysed in relation to the historical and cultural specificity of its production in the context of classroom relations to reveal both its enabling and disabling effect' (McLaren, 1991, p. 140).

In order to achieve this he proposes the construction of 'border identities'. These are narratives of the self which are critiqued collectively, resulting in deeper understanding of individual histories and their relationship to wider social and cultural contexts:

> Border identities are constructed out of empathy for others by means of a *passionate connection through difference*. This connection is furthered by a narrative imagination which enables connections to be made between our own stories and the stories of cultural others.
>
> (McLaren, 1991, p. 140)

The focus on self, personal histories and an understanding of how dominant cultures manage, through relations of power, to reproduce domination are common themes throughout all these writers. Their differences probably lie in the extent to which they privilege certain forms of difference and engage with the idea that deeper understanding of the self in relation to society can foster individual or group empowerment or action for structural change. As these are often conceptual, rather than evidenced, outcomes it is difficult to know how much the ideology effects actual change, beyond an intellectual level, through practice. The presence of a body of feminist literature within academia perhaps indicates that some structural change is achievable through dialogue and theorising – though it is debatable whether the change is endemic throughout the institution.

## Part 5: feminist positions

A separate strand of critical pedagogies emanates from feminist writers. Gore (1993) has identified distinct locations for this literature – either in schools of education or in women's studies courses. She suggests this location influences whether the issue of feminism or teaching style is forefronted. The curriculum of women's studies courses, for instance, is already a locus for the topic of gender. In schools of education, educational practice is a presumed focus of study – particularly for different social groups of women.

Within these two dimensions this means there are several different feminist positions, ranging from a more liberal, equal opportunities approach to teaching, to the more political position of poststructuralism. All argue for women's space in the curriculum and classroom. This means recognising women role models in texts and women's theoretical perspectives as well as identifying ways in which women's voices are heard in classroom activities. Post-structuralist concepts have strongly influenced these feminist critical pedagogies, focusing the emphasis on validating differences *between* women and their multiple contexts. Gore stresses, however, that feminist literature on pedagogy is largely un-self critical of its own practice and tends to ignore other literature on pedagogy. There is a tendency to define the latter as patriarchal and not linked to women's oppression or a commitment to women's emancipation (Gore, 1993, p. 25).

In spite of these caveats a number of feminist writers have developed more explicit concepts of difference within pedagogy – particularly from gender and race perspectives. Disability within the women's movement is still an under-profiled arena (Morris, 1992). A particular feature of feminist pedagogy is its effort to challenge the patriarchal nature of academic teaching and curriculum. There is an additional focus in that much feminist teaching involves women teaching women. This places a new identity relationship between teacher and learner which is explored by black writers (e.g. Hill Collins, 1990; hooks, 1994).

hooks (1994) takes a black feminist perspective which she calls 'engaged pedagogy'. Here the learner's experiences and life histories become a medium for enhancing the curriculum: 'Linking confessional narratives to academic discussions so as to show how experience can illuminate and enhance our understanding of academic material' (1994, p. 20). Her emphasis, like other writers, is to privilege marginality as 'more than a site of deprivation'. The teaching goal is to shift the experience of marginality to a place for resistance. In other words, learners are encouraged to 'look beyond the limitations of their current condition' and find a way of using that experience to build a different kind of world (Galloway, 1999, p. 226).

There is a sense in which feminist literature gives greater credence to the concept of 'emotional knowledge' than some of the other writers. Hill Collins (1990), for instance talks about the 'insider view' and 'situated knowledge' which is grounded in the black experience of being part of a spiritual community of African Americans as well as articulating the insider experience of racism. The difference for most women's studies courses and courses which adopt an explicitly feminist approach is that the teaching is frequently done by women in an environment of shared identity between teacher and learner. An example of this can be seen in community courses for adults where Muslim Pakistani women may be discussing curriculum content in environments that are specifically designed for their needs:

> They walk into the community centre, at that time there are no male classes, they are all women tutors and it's a real sense of community and belonging and sisterhood and they feel comfortable, they feel that they own that place and they belong there.
> (Fahana, in Preece and Houghton, 2000, p. 83)

Barr (1999) extends this notion of the relationship between emotion and knowledge. She emphasises it is not up to the educator to decide what is really useful knowledge. She claims we 'need to reinvisage the notion of rationality in less exclusive ways – which do not separate emotion from intellect' (p. 12).

For Barr, then, feminist pedagogy includes a critique of narrow forms of rationality and a recognition of feeling as a source of knowledge – as well as the use of collective inquiry to create new knowledge and the recognition of one's social location within those experiences. So from McLaren's exploration of the psyche, feminists move to a more explicit acknowledgement of 'emotion' as contributing to reason and knowledge and therefore as a part of power relationships.

## Part 6: critical pedagogy and environmental education

We have seen in this chapter that some radical pedagogies may reflect ideologies of oppression which are, from a postmodernist perspective, rather essentialist and homogeneous. In other words, they inadequately address the issues such as diversity, complexity, reflexivity, risk, and ambiguity which increasingly characterise contemporary society. For this reason, it is sometimes claimed that the emancipatory potential of radical pedagogies can be more ideological than real. Despite the frequent reference in such pedagogies to critical praxis as envisaged by Freire (1972), there remains the question of the teacher's role. In other words, where is there a practitioner perspective in all this?

In this section we turn to consider the implications for pedagogy and the teacher's role in relation to one of the universal concerns of postmodern or risk society, namely, environmental education.

In a review of critical theory and praxis in environmental education, Fien (1994) has argued that 'Critical theory provides an emancipatory framework for educational practice as it asserts that individuals and groups should be in control of their own lives and be able to determine their own destinies' (p. 21). Environmental education therefore reflects the apparent contradictions in the ways in which environment issues are constructed:

> Why do children generally express positive attitudes to the environment but fail to see the link between their consumer habits and environmental quality? Why does their enthusiasm for the environment dissipate as they grow older? In what ways might our teaching practices contribute, at least in part, to the action paralysis of modern society?
>
> (Fien, 1994, pp. 21–22)

The answers to these questions depend upon distinguishing between three approaches to teaching about the environment:

*1 Education* through *the environment.* Be it in a city street, a beach, a park, a farm, a forest or the school grounds, education through the environment can be used to give reality, relevance and practical experience to learning. Increased awareness of aspects of the environment can be expected from any opportunities for direct contact with the environment. Opportunities to learn out-of-doors can also be used to develop important skills for data gathering, such as observation, sketching, photography, interviewing and using scientific instruments, as well as social skills such as group work, co-operation and aesthetic appreciation. Environmental awareness and concern can also be fostered by linking learning to direct experiences in the environment and allowing learners to become captivated by the complexity and wonder of natural systems or immersed in the values conflict over particular environmental issues.

*2 Education* about *the environment.* Such feelings of concern are not enough, however, if living responsibility and sustainability in the environment is an educational goal. Concern needs to be translated into appropriate behaviour patterns and actions but, for this to happen, it is essential for learners to understand how natural systems work and the impact of human activities upon them. This will include learning about political, philosophical, economic and socio-cultural factors as well as about the ecological ones that influence decisions about how to most responsibly use the environment. Knowledge about the environment is essential if all citizens are to participate in any informed debate aimed at resolving local, national and global environmental issues. There is much that many non-formal avenues of environmental education, as well as formal curriculum areas, including the arts as well as the natural and social sciences, can contribute to providing such knowledge.

*3 Education* for *the environment.* Education *for* the environment aims to promote a willingness and ability to adopt lifestyles that are compatible with the wise use of environmental resources. In so doing, it builds on education *in* and *about* the environment to help develop an informed concern and sense of responsibility for the environment through the development of an environmental ethic and the motivation and skills necessary to participate in environmental improvement. Education *for* the environment may be located within the socially-critical traditions in education because of its concern for social critique and reconstruction (Fien, 1994, pp. 20–21).

All of these approaches to environmental education can result in good teaching practices in relation to methods, curriculum and so on. But whereas education *through* and *about* the environment represent traditional pedagogy, education *for* the environment is intended to identify what Freire (1972) meant by *critical praxis*:

> The issues raised by consciously teaching towards social transformation and ecological sustainability through education *for* the environment pose many challenges to traditional schooling and necessitate a reconsideration of the way critical thinking, environmental values, education and political literacy are addressed...Critical praxis involves the wide range of teaching strategies...including enquiry based learning, value exercises,

ideology critique, community contact, and social action of various sorts. What distinguishes critical praxis from the use of these strategies individually is their integration into a focused programme for conscientization and empowerment.

(Fien, 1994, pp. 47–48)

The above illustration is contexted in schooling, but, as it suggested, whereas children are generally positive towards environmental issues, they often fail in later life to link their lifestyles as consumers with environmental quality: their enthusiasm is 'dissipated' as they grow older.

Clearly, the emergence of new social movements, together with widespread disillusion with traditional ideological politics, is a prominent feature of the learning society. Much lifelong learning theory and policy lays stress on the potential of social movements, informal learning and civil society as themselves major sites of learning.

But it is doubtful whether learning in later life has engaged very much with these developments, or that teachers in post-compulsory education reflect them in their teaching practices. This has recently been observed in the context of adult education:

> The emergence of new social and urban movements since the 1960s has grown…in opposition to the 'old' movements of labour…Such movements have relied more on popular protest and direct action of a 'personal and political' kind in order to create social change. For example, the womens' movement, the peace movement, the environmental movement, to name a few of the more important ones, have had a significant educative impact in the public sphere as well as in the private life of many individuals…We need to learn from these movements. However, adult education is often outside of them and fails to connect with the potential they offer for a collective and critical pedagogy of learning.
>
> (Crowther, 2000, p. 488)

If this is the case, radical or critical pedagogy, and critical praxis in education, would have to be relocated into social movements and not confined to the early years of schooling, if education *for* the environment is to become a reality.

The case of environmental education as radical pedagogy draws attention to the general issue of the *site* of such learning in postmodern conditions, or in the learning society itself. Radical pedagogies are increasingly located in the learning contexts of social movements or civil society as such, more perhaps than in the formal institutional sites of education, which were the site of the radical pedagogies of the past. This does not necessarily mean that the conditions of oppression have disappeared, but only that, in the learning society, the educational conditions of resistance have been transformed.

## Conclusion

Debates about the learning society have created opportunities for experimentation in teaching and learning – both practically and ideologically. Radical educators argue, however, that teaching that effects real change towards more equality in society requires structural change. This means educational systems and the people within them need to problematise what seems normal. Within that the notion of how knowledge is perceived at all needs to be re-examined. This chapter has described and highlighted a range of radical pedagogies that purport to do this. The field is awash with terminology which at first seems to be articulating very similar positions. Such a perception is further complicated by the limited amount of cross-referencing between the different thematic strands. For example, we have seen the failure to connect environmental education in school and in later life. Nevertheless there are some subtle shifts in focus from the idea of a predominantly Marxist and unified class consciousness to a recognition of plurality within the learning experience. An exploration of different radical pedagogies involves awareness of these shifts in meaning to a more specific focus on how the self is constituted within those differences. From here individual as well as collective identities, social situatedness and emotion all need to be considered within pedagogies which strive for intellectual criticality coupled with radical change in society.

## References

Allman, P. (1999) *Revolutionary Social Transformation: Democratic Hopes, Political Pssibilities and Critical Education*, Bergin and Garvey, Westport, CN

Allman, P. and Wallis, J. (1995) 'Challenging the Postmodern Condition: Radical Adult Education for Critical Intelligence', in M. Mayo and J. Thompson (eds), *Adult Learning, Critical Intelligence and Social Change*, NIACE, Leicester

Aronowitz, S. and Giroux, H. A. (1991) *Postmodern Education, Politics, Culture and Social Criticism*, University of Minnesota Press, London

Barr, J. (1999) *Liberating Knowledge: Research, Feminism and Adult Education*, NIACE, Leicester

Bauman, Z. (1987) *Legislators and Interpreters*, Polity Press, Cambridge

Beck, U. (1992) *Risk Society: Towards a New Modernity*, Sage Publications, London

Brookfield, S. (1987) *Developing Critical Thinkers: Challenging Adults to Explore Alternative Ways of Thinking and Acting*, Jossey-Bass, San Francisco, CA

Coben, D. (1998) *Radical Heroes: Gramsci, Freire and the Politics of Adult Education*, Garland Publishing Inc., London

Coffield, F. (ed.) (2000) *Differing Visions of a Learning Society*, ESRC/Policy Press, Bristol

Crowther, J. (2000) 'Participation in Adult and Community Education: A Discourse of Diminishing Returns', *International Journal of Lifelong Education* **18** (6), 479–492

Crowther, J., Martin, I. and Shaw, M. (1999) *Popular Education and Social Movements in Scotland Today*, NIACE, Leicester

Department for Education and Employment (DfEE) (1998) *The Learning Age: A Renaissance for a New Britain* (Green Paper CM 3790) The Stationery Office, London

Fien, J. (1994) 'Critical theory, critical pedagogy and critical praxis in environmental education', in B. B. Jensen and K. Schnack (eds), *Action and Action Competence: Key Concepts in Critical Pedagogy*, Studies in Educational Theory and Curriculum Vol. 12, Royal Danish School of Educational Studies, Copenhagen

Foley, G. (1999) *Learning in Social Action*, NIACE/Zed Books, Leicester

Freire, P. (1972) *Pedagogy of the Oppressed*, Penguin, London

Freire, P. (1976) *Education and the Practice of Freedom*, Writers and Readers Publishing Corporation, London

Freire, P. (1978) *Pedagogy in Process*, Writers and Readers Publishing Corporation, London

Galloway, V. (1999) 'Building a Pedagogy of Hope: The Experience of the Adult Learning Project', in J. Crowther, I. Martin and M. Shaw (eds), *Popular Education and Social Movements in Scotland Today*, Leicester, NIACE

Giroux, H. A. (1983) *Theory and Resistance in Education: A Pedagogy for the Opposition*, Heinemann, London

Giroux, H. A. (1992) *Border Crossings*, Routledge, London

Gore, J. (1993) *The Struggle for Pedagogies*, Routledge, London

Hill Collins, P. (1990) *Black Feminist Thought*, Routledge, London

hooks, b. (1994) *Teaching to Transgress*, Routledge, London

Jarvis, P., Holford, J. and Griffin, C. (1998) *The Theory and Practice of Learning*, Kogan Page, London

Kanpol, B. (1994) *Critical Pedagogy: An Introduction*, Bergin and Garvey, Westport, CN

Kirkwood, G. and Kirkwood, C. (1989) *Living Adult Education: Freire in Scotland*, Open University Press, Milton Keynes

Knowles, M. (1990) *The Adult Learner: A Neglected Species* (4th edn), Gulf Publishing Co, Houston

Lather, P. (1991) *Getting Smart: Feminist Research and Pedagogy with/in the Postmodern*, Routledge, London

Livingstone, D. W. (1987) *Critical Pedagogy and Cultural Power*, Bergin & Harvey/ Greenwood Press, Oxford

McLaren, P. (1991) 'Post-colonial Pedagogy: Post-colonial Desire and Decolonised Community', *Education and Society* **9** (2), 135–158

McLaren, P. (1995) *Critical Pedagogy and Predatory Culture: Oppositional Politics in a Postmodern Era*, Routledge, London

Mayo, M. and Thompson, J. (eds) (1995) *Adult Learning, Critical Intelligence and Social Change*, NIACE, Leicester

Mayo, P. (1999) *Gramsci, Freire and Adult Education: Possibilities for Transformative Action*, Zed Books, London

Mezirow, J. and associates (1990) *Fostering Critical Reflection in Adulthood*, Jossey-Bass, San Francisco, CA

Morris, J. (1992) 'Personal and Political: A Feminist Perspective on Researching Physical Disability', *Disability, Handicap and Society* **7** (2), 157–166

Preece, J. and Houghton, A. (2000) *Nurturing Social Capital in Excluded Communities: A Kind of Higher Education*, Ashgate, Aldershot

Shor, I. (1980) *Critical Teaching and Everyday Life*, South End Press, Boston, MA

Taylor, R. (1997) 'The Search for a Social Purpose Ethic in Adult Continuing Education in the New Europe', *Studies in the Education of Adults* **29** (1), 92–100

Thompson, J. (1997) *Words in Edgeways: Radical Learning for Social Change*, NIACE, Leicester

Usher, R. and Edwards, R. (1994) *Postmodern Education*, Routledge, London

Youngman, F. (1986) *Adult Education and Socialist Pedagogy*, Croom Helm, London

# Part II

# Chapter 6

# Didacticism

## Lectures and lecturing

*Colin Griffin*

Under the heading 'Lectures and Lecturing' can be discovered nearly 100,000 websites. From this we may conclude that the lecture is still with us in some form or another. And yet, for very many years it has been pronounced dead as far as education is concerned, that is, as an effective teaching method.

Thus, a website of Oxford Brookes University reproduces an old paper called 'Twenty terrible reasons for lecturing' (Gibbs, 1981). The arguments reproduced here are acknowledged to be extremely familiar over many decades, but justified in terms of the 'continued prevalence' of lecturing as a teaching method. It seems then that the arguments against lecturing have failed. But have they?

It is certainly the case that the lecture form in *non-educational* contexts remains both widespread and respected. Distinguished scholarly institutions such as the Royal Society or the Royal Society of Arts have lecture programmes at the heart of their communications with a wider public. It might be argued that many seriously educational programmes on TV take a broadly 'lecturing' form. The tradition of a distinguished authority communicating his or her wisdom to a wider public is probably as widely respected as it ever has been.

However, these are not necessarily seen as 'educational', and their object is not the 'teaching' of 'students' but the enlightenment of an informed and receptive audience. So a successful lecture in this context is unlikely to be perceived as didactic, and nor does it *necessarily* fail to be interactive in the ways usually attributed to it.

It is important at the outset, therefore, to distinguish between various contexts of the lecture and lecturing, and to acknowledge that it is only in the traditional education context that the lecture has been regarded as 'dead'. What this means is that it is an ineffective form of teaching and does not result in effective learning on the part of students.

This chapter is concerned only therefore with lecturing in an educational context, and with the arguments concerning its effectiveness. In short, it is concerned with the alleged failure of lecturing to bring about student learning, and with the 'terrible reasons' why it fails yet seems to persist still in the classroom.

Of all the didactic methods of teaching, that of classroom lecturing seems the most obvious. It puts the lecturer in complete control of the learning situation, and seems to cast the learner in an entirely passive role. Nowadays, on the face of it, there seems little scope for the lecture as an appropriate teaching method in the learning society, with its apparent rejection of traditional forms of knowledge and authority, and its focus upon active, learner-centred, self-directed, problem-based and experiential learning. The authority of the lecturer depends upon subject knowledge and the face-to-face teaching and learning situation, whereas the learning society is one in which traditional forms of authority are questioned, and in which communications technology is making possible more and more teaching and learning situations at a distance.

Moreover, lecturing as a teaching method reflects very closely the kinds of institutions and roles associated with the formal education system. But this system is losing its traditional place amongst all the possible sites of learning in the learning society, which are claimed to be the family, the community, the workplace, social movements and so on. Then there are the technical drawbacks of lecturing with which all who have lectured or been lectured to are aware, such as short attention span, the inaudability of the lecturer, dependence upon rote learning through note-taking, the absence of social interaction or effective feedback. In short, the formal lecture would seem to lack almost every pre-requisite for effective learning in the learning society which transcends the classroom. It is apparently a one-way process in which the learner plays little part; there is little scope for reflexivity or for learners to make experiential connections. Above all, the formal lecture provides almost limitless scope for boredom, and also for the irritation which many feel at being 'lectured at' in any situation in life.

And yet it is acknowledged that lecturing remains a major teaching method in all sectors of the post-compulsory education system. 'Lecturer' continues to be the title of the professional role for many in the further, higher and adult sectors of education, and continues to distinguish the role and status of teachers in these sectors from teachers in schools. Student textbooks for prospective lecturers invariably contain theories and practical advice for doing it well and avoiding pitfalls.

The fact that lecturing is a kind of drama played out in 'lecture theatres', and dependent for some of its effectiveness upon the personal or charismatic qualities of the lecturer, also singles it out as a didactic method. Memories of educational experience often invoke anecdotes of enthusiasm or eccentricity which proved powerful stimulants to learning on the part of students. Unfortunately, such charisma is only randomly distributed amongst lecturers as it is amongst everyone else, so it is a matter of chance whether or not our educational memories of lecturing are positive or not. Also, and perhaps unfortunately, such randomness does not lend itself readily to the processes of quality assurance, audit and inspection. So there are aspects of lecturing which are not readily amenable to certain features of the present system, namely, those having to do with public accountability and student success rates in a universal system of formal accreditation. Too much about lecturing comes down to personal qualities which do not lend themselves to control and prediction.

And yet, students continue to value precisely the personal qualities of teachers, which is why mixed-mode teaching and learning systems, incorporating both distance and face-to-face opportunities, seem to prove attractive to many. Moreover, lecturers themselves might draw attention to the fact that a good lecture is more than a charismatic performance addressed to passive students. Lectures may serve as useful overviews of a topic, or to stimulate reflection on contradictions, anomalies or discrepancies, or to suggest further reading and research. In short, a good lecture fulfils support functions: it need not be confined to the conveying of information, but may incorporate a variety of interactive learning opportunities.

This chapter will explore some of these issues raised by teaching as a didactic method, by examining:

- The basis of *didacticism*, or the nature of authority and control in relation to the changing role of the lecturer: three types of authority will be identified, namely, social, subject and professional.
- The *pedagogical challenge*, or the critique of lecturing in relation to effective learning, which reflects issues of professional authority.
- The *postmodern challenge* posed by developments in the idea of the learning society, which reflects issues of social and subject authority.
- The *reconstruction* of the function of lectures and the role of the lecturer in what, for some time now, has been described as 'post-education society'.

## Part I: lecturing as didactic method

Lecturing and teaching are both activities invariably associated with the system of formal education. For some, the era of postmodernism is also the era of 'post-education society' (Evans, 1985). Formal education systems worldwide are said to have failed to bring about the kinds of economic, social and political changes which they were once supposed to help achieve. New policies for lifelong learning are needed in order to bring education more closely into line with the world that is coming into existence. Many international organisations have produced policy proposals for lifelong learning or the learning society, according to which the role of education systems, although still vital, have to be put into much broader learning contexts (EC, 1996; OECD, 1996; UNESCO, 1996).

Didactic methods rely upon forms of authority which are now much more disputed than they were in the age of education, such as the authority of subject knowledge and the social authority of teachers over learners. As was observed at the beginning of this chapter, formal lectures remain, for example, a common public function of learned societies, such as the Royal Society or the Royal Society of Arts. In the education system itself, however, we can distinguish three types of authority which provide the didactic basis of this kind of teaching:

*1 Social authority.* It is possible to speak of being 'in authority' and being 'an authority'. The social authority of the lecturer is constituted by being in control of the *social* situation of the classroom or lecture theatre. For example, maintaining discipline through a combination of charismatic, traditional and rational authority. Charismatic authority refers to the *personal* qualities of the lecturer. Traditional authority might be constituted by the *status* of the lecturer (in the case of younger learners, for example, this might be based upon age and generation). Rational authority is conveyed by the lecturer's instrumental *function* as a means to the end of passing examinations or gaining qualifications.

*2 Subject authority.* It is self-evident that lecturers should be regarded as authoritative in relation to the subject knowledge that they teach. As far as Higher Education is concerned, this generally entails that they should have some direct experience of *research* in their field, although the connection between being an active researcher and an effective lecturer is by no means straightforward. Nevertheless, a lecturer's reputation for having added to the field of knowledge usually constitutes some form of authority in those situations where this is relevant. Thus, it is argued that 'The *unique* contribution of the lecture...derives from the nexus between research and teaching...It is still possible to provide that personal perspective on knowledge, both on the process of constructing and validating knowledge and on interpreting the outcome' (Biggs, 1999, p. 99).

*3 Professional authority.* Whether or not teaching, and hence lecturing, constitutes a professional discipline is open to question: 'there is little sustained analysis of what it is that teachers might have in common with other professionals in terms of the nature of their work' (Squires, 1999, p. 23). Professionalism is constituted by the professional skills which the lecturer commands, and which are the object of training to teach and covered in textbooks written for trainees. They range from voice production to the ability to change bulbs in overhead projectors, from planning and structuring the lecture to preparing visual and other teaching aids to a professional standard. In the past, little or no professional training was required of lecturers, their subject authority being sufficient for their role. But in future all lecturers will be required to have *professional* qualifications to bring them into line with school teachers. Thus there were the original FENTO (Further Education National Training Organisation) standards for lecturers in Further Education, and the ILT (Institute for Learning and Teaching) membership requirements for lecturers in Higher Education, all of which continue to be developed under the government's lifelong learning policies. For lecturers in all sectors of post-compulsory education initial training and continuing professional development have become virtually mandatory.

Bearing in mind these three types of authority which lecturing represents, we can analyse the role of lecturer and functions of lecturing according to the forms of authority which didacticism reflects. As we shall see, *charismatic* authority, or that which relates to the unique personal qualities of the lecturer, seems to constitute a fourth type by virtue of its significance for this particular method.

## Part 2: the pedagogical challenge: what's the use of lectures?

The fact is, that the pedagogical analysis of lectures and lecturing has been almost exclusively confined to the forms of professional authority which these invoke, with surprisingly little reference to the other forms of authority which were distinguished above.

The reason for this is that a technical or commonsense knowledge of what it is to be a good or a bad lecturer has developed, and indeed is now being further extended by the demands of public accountability and competition for accreditation and formal qualifications for lecturing. The question 'what's the use of lectures?' begs the question 'what's the use of teaching?' and it is readily assumed that learning *entails* teaching. But this is precisely the issue that is raised by developments such as lifelong learning, the learning society, and the postmodern challenge to traditional beliefs about knowledge and authority, and, indeed, to the idea of professionalism itself.

Being an effective lecturer, with an appropriate range of skills, therefore continues to constitute much of the content of the training of teachers for further, higher and adult education. Understandably, trainee teachers tend to lay particular stress on their need to develop effective classroom skills as part of their professional preparation.

As a result, there has been a focus in professional training upon:

- *Types* of learning theory (behaviourist, cognitive, social, experiential and so on).
- *Names* of learning theorists (Pavlov, Skinner, Thorndike, Gagne, Dewey and so on).
- *Professional* discourses of learning (objectives, outcomes, styles, support, assessment and so on).

Unsurprisingly, trainee teachers have often failed to make connections between these, except in the most superficial way and unrelated to the actual learning of actual learners.

The pedagogical challenge to lecturing has been constructed in terms exclusively of whether or not lectures are effective in bringing about learning from the perspective of *scientific* knowledge and *professional* skills. In the thirty years since 1971, when Donald Bligh's book *What's the Use of Lectures?* was first published, the general tone of textbooks has been defensive with regard to lectures and lecturing. The conclusion has been that there is still a place for the lecture amongst the repertory of professional skills of lecturers, but that it needs to be put into more learner-centred, reflexive and experiential contexts wherever possible. Since lecturing continues to be a major function of professional lecturers, this is perhaps not surprising. Nor is it surprising that the book continues to exercise widespread influence and remained so long in print (Bligh, 1998).

We will now consider the professional or pedagogic 'post-Bligh' account of lectures in the three contexts where this is the main professional role; further, higher and adult and continuing education:

*1 Further Education.* The Further Education sector is nowadays extremely heterogeneous, accounting for a wide range of types of students and courses and including a proportion of degree and postgraduate provision. The lecture remains a significant teaching method throughout. A typical professional introduction to the method will therefore provide a typology of lectures, stressing those functions for which it is most appropriate, such as an introduction and overview of particular topic. The kinds of objectives which it can achieve are generally described as ranging from the cognitive through affective to attitudes and values. Presentational issues of planning, structure and strategy are discussed, along with issues of the environment, delivery, feedback, lecture notes, and handouts and evaluation (Curzon, 1997). Other textbooks stress more the lecture as a successful 'performance' and the need for 'mastery' of the material (Gray *et al.*, 2000), but issues of planning, structuring and effective presentation styles and materials are universally stressed, together with practical advice about preparation and context.

*2 Higher Education.* There is a much weaker tradition of professional training for lecturers in Higher Education, simply because the research function of the institutions and the profession of 'scholarship' itself have pushed the concept of professionalism here much more into the field of abstract and theoretical knowledge. Also the tradition of elite recruitment to the sector has perhaps led to assumptions about the intellectual autonomy of undergraduate learners, assumptions which with the onset of mass Higher Education systems seem less warranted than they once were. The assumption, typically, was that 'Explaining is at the heart of teaching in higher education just as its obverse, understanding, is at the heart of learning' (Brown, 1978, p. 2). The functions of lecturing in Higher Education are therefore explanation on the part of the lecturer and understanding on the part of students. As the author says:

> There are two major strategies that one can adopt for this purpose. The first is to help lecturers to develop their methods of preparing and giving lectures through ideas and activities which increase their awareness of the processes involved. The second is almost the inverse of the first: it is to help students develop *their* methods of learning from lectures through ideas and activities which increase their awareness of the processes.
>
> (Brown, 1978, p. 105)

Thus, in addition to issues of structure, planning and presentation, students' listening to lectures and note-taking may be supplemented by activities such as buzz groups, research projects or exercises, as well as audio-visual aids.

*3 Adult and continuing education.* In the case of adult students, the straight lecture has generally seemed much less appropriate as a teaching method, and pedagogic or didactic approaches have usually been adapted to the students' adult learning needs. In general, therefore, the lecture has been traditionally associated with opportunities for participation such as discussion and questioning. The attempt to differentiate sharply between the pedagogy of schooling and the andragogy of adult education (Knowles, 1978) has reflected to some extent the disfavour into which lecturing once fell. However, the lecture remains a major method of teaching in adult and continuing education, modified by more interactive and adult-oriented strategies: 'it must still be recognized that it is a useful teaching tool, especially when it is well used, but only for the transmission of knowledge' (Jarvis, 1995, p. 120). This restrictive function of the lecture in the classroom (i.e. to the transmission of knowledge) is one of the distinguishing features of the lecture in educational settings: in the wider public context, of course, a lecture may achieve very much more than 'mere' knowledge, by stimulating curiosity, debate, or a certain value-orientation towards knowledge itself. In other words, a function of the lecture in the public context is that it instructs *and* enlightens. The function of the classroom lecture seems strictly limited to instruction if it is to achieve these narrowly educational aims.

In all of these three sectors of education, the lecture is acknowledged to remain a major teaching method, and to have survived the criticism it fell under since the 1970s: 'It exemplifies the process of "one-way communication" and, as such, has been criticized severely. And yet the lecture persists as a common mode of instruction in colleges of further education and elsewhere.' (Curzon, 1997, p. 314); 'the lecture is still an important part of a teacher's "armoury"' (Gray *et al.*, 2000, p. 94); 'Lecturing is perhaps the most frequently employed teaching technique despite all the criticisms that have been levelled against it at various times' (Jarvis, 1995, p. 117).

In this section, we have considered the functions of lecturing and the role of lecturers in terms of *pedagogy*, that is, as a didactic teaching *strategy*. Much of the pedagogy of lecturing has been conducted in the light of Bligh's influential book. This was based upon a scientific appraisal of the lecture method in relation to effective learning, and was no doubt influential because it focused clearly on techniques and strategies. It also seemed to provide a clear criterion of appropriateness for effective learning:

> The lecture is as effective as other methods to transmit information.
>
> Most lectures are not as effective as discussion to promote thought. Changing students' attitudes should not normally be the major object of a lecture.
>
> Lectures are relatively ineffective to teach values associated with subject matter.
>
> Lectures are relatively ineffective to inspire interest in a subject.
>
> Lectures are relatively ineffective for personal and social adjustment. Lectures are relatively ineffective to teach behavioural skills.
>
> (Bligh, 1998, p. 10)

This pedagogical critique of lecturing seems to leave the lecture with a very limited role in bringing about learning, if scientific evidence about their effectiveness is to be believed. This has constituted the criticism, against which, as we have seen, many continue to defend the method.

But from a learning society perspective, the problem of the pedagogic challenge to lecturing is simply that we have lost any sense of the learner, learning needs and, indeed, of learning itself. Bligh's book does not refer to learning at all; Brown, in the context of Higher Education, says almost nothing about it. Learning features much more prominently in the context of Further and Adult Continuing Education, as would be expected where personal growth and development are more prominent in relation to learning.

Thus, in the pedagogic challenge to lectures and lecturing, which reflects effectiveness, strategy and technique, learning is reduced to a function of instruction, explanation and understanding. This projects a relatively homogenous account of learners and their learning needs. It also leads to the somewhat paradoxical conclusion that if the lecture can only be effective in conveying information, then in a world awash with information technologies, the question 'What's the use of lectures?' seems more rhetorical than ever. To say that lectures need to be supplemented by other, presumably quite different teaching methods, in order to be effective in a wider context than information, simply begs the question itself.

The idea of the learning society, and of lifelong learning, poses a much more fundamental challenge to lectures and lecturing. With the individual learner at the centre of the stage, with formal educational institutions losing their pre-eminence as the sites of learning, with the challenge to 'professionalism' itself, and with a much more inclusive concept of learning than merely explanation and understanding, a more basic question needs to be answered.

## Part 2: the postmodern challenge: what's the use of teaching?

We have seen that the pedagogical challenge to lectures and lecturing is based upon the professional form of authority. It reflects scientific evidence about the appropriateness of strategy and technique, reduces learning to matters of instruction, explanation and understanding, and projects a homogenous view of learners and their learning needs. With the primacy of 'learning' over 'education' in the professional discourse, much wider issues now arise (Jarvis *et al.*, 1998).

The learning society, which is associated with the postmodern view of the world, poses a much more fundamental challenge, not only with respect to didactic teaching methods such as lecturing, but to the whole relationship between teaching and learning (Jarvis, 2001).

In order to begin to understand the nature of this challenge, it is necessary to go back to the basis of didacticism in the typology of authority set out earlier in this chapter, and understand postmodern perspectives as, in part, a series of challenges to traditional forms of authority. The distinction was made between *social*, *subject* and *professional* authority as the basis of the lecturer's didactic role. To this might be added *charismatic* authority, since many textbooks on teaching methods, such as those mentioned above, place some emphasis on the personal qualities of the lecturer as contributing to effective learning, or not.

In the previous section, it was suggested that the pedagogical critique of lecturing, or answers to the question 'What's the use of lectures?' has been conducted mainly in terms of professional authority, with regard to scientific evidence, strategies, techniques and methods. The general conclusion has been that the lecture, alongside and integrated with other and more interactive methods, continues to have its place in the teacher's classroom 'armoury' or repertoire. It is said to be particularly suitable for conveying information but not, on its own, much else. It is still defended as a justifiable teacher-centred method. Above all, lecturing seems to be inescapably linked with the classroom situation of formal educational institutions.

The learning society, stressing as it does the learner-centredness of education, the significance of non-formal, informal, reflexive, experiential and developmental learning, poses a challenge to didacticism in general and lecturing in particular. In other words, the pedagogical critique seems to demonstrate that, apart from conveying information, the lecture is ill-suited to most kinds of learning associated with the learning society.

The learning society, as a postmodern phenomenon, is associated with challenges to traditional forms of knowledge and authority, as well as challenges to the adequacy in such times of traditional structures of educational provision, with their roles and functions such as that of lecturing. It is the professional base reflecting the authority of the role that is brought into question, as the various functions of explanation, instruction, interpretation and legislation are called into question. It is not only lecturing, of course, but all forms of teaching as such which are having to be reformulated.

The issue of how far learning depends upon effective teaching has long been an open one. Learning theorists such as Rogers (1969), Knowles (1978), Tough (1979) and Mezirow (1991) have all argued that effective learning is self-actualising, self-directed, self-planned and self-transformative. Didactic teaching merely reproduces traditional categories of knowledge and forms of authority, and fails to result in 'real' learning as a result.

In order to explore some of these points, the implications of the postmodern challenge will now be briefly described in relation to the various forms which lecturers' and teachers' authority take.

*Social authority.* As was suggested at the outset, this can take a variety of forms, but in the present context it refers to the traditional social status basis of the lecturer, which is that of the professional. The concept of the professional has, however, been rendered much more problematic in conditions of market economics and consumerism. The changes wrought by new forms of information and communications technology have eroded the traditional status of professionals based upon the monopolisation of forms of knowledge and expertise. The fast-expanding possibilities for self-directed or self-planned learning projects, with all their implications for personal growth and development, have forced professionals such as teachers into the market-place. In other words, the authority of the teacher rests much more now upon the capacity to sell knowledge as a commodity in the market-place, rather than the traditional claim to monopolise knowledge itself. Public accountability and quality assurance, rather than traditional criteria of professionalism, now determine the professional role in the public sector. In short, the autonomy of the professional, which the lecturer's role once reflected, has been successfully challenged and considerably eroded in the postmodern conditions of society.

*Subject authority.* From a pedagogical perspective, the authority of the lecturer has been based upon a body of subject knowledge, and the idea that lectures should reflect expertise or 'mastery' of subject matter is one of the most important criteria for success. The concept of the curriculum reflected discrete subjects or forms of knowledge, and lecturers were expected to have mastery of one or more of them. In fact, the social authority or status of the lecturer was reflected in the title of 'lecturer in physics' or 'lecturer in history', or whatever. To some extent too, the status of the abstract knowledge itself also contributed to the subject authority of the lecturer. In any case, clearly lecturers are expected to be authorities or experts in their fields. What counts as knowledge, however, in the learning society, is rather different than that conveyed by the traditional curriculum of 'subject knowledge'. The idea of knowledge as a rather static body of abstract truth is giving way to a much more relative and reflexive one:

> Now technological knowledge is changing minute by minute and second by second. With this rapid change, it is almost impossible to regard knowledge as a truth statement any longer. We are now talking about something that is relative. It can be changed again as soon as some new discovery is made that forces people to change their thinking.
>
> (Jarvis *et al.*, 1998, p. 7)

Although such relativism will be differentially experienced between different subject areas, there is little doubt that the whole concept of the 'subject area' and 'subject knowledge' is becoming problematic, with inevitable consequences for the authority which lecturers and lecturing derive from it.

*Professional authority.* On the face of it, there is an increase in the degree of professionalism which lecturers are expected to display, with new forms of qualifications and licences to practice which have traditionally characterised professions other than that of teaching, such as law and medicine. The standards demanded by frequent inspection and quality audits are nowadays required to be much more transparent than they once were. In this sense, the professional authority of lecturers can be said to be gaining in prominence. But it has to be acknowledged that this access of professional authority is driven by market forces and public accountability, rather than by any increase in the social status of lecturers or any increasing recognition of the expertise or mastery of subject knowledge. It focuses very strongly upon teaching *methods* and *strategies*, and competence in dealing with the bureaucratic apparatus of control, as statutory curriculum principles are imposed not only upon the school sector but the whole of post-compulsory education. In fact, much of the professionalism of lecturers consists of the kinds of form-filling and record-keeping activities which would once have been regarded as essentially secretarial rather than professional. In other words, the new professional authority of lecturers can be regarded as little more than de-skilling in relation to traditional criteria of autonomous professional status: competence, rather than authority, constitutes the professionalism of the lecturer in the learning society.

*Charismatic authority.* This is an aspect of effective lectures and lecturers which is often stressed in the literature of training, so much so that it seems to constitute a fourth type. It is the authority which derives from the personal qualities of the lecturer, and can be traced in other professions, such as law. Charisma, in fact, could be regarded as a typical form which authority in postmodern society takes, with its focus upon the personal qualities and lives of individuals in sport, popular culture and popular media. It cannot be explored in depth here, but it is to be noted because it involves the old issue of whether good lecturers are 'born' or 'made' by effective training. The pedagogic critique of lecturing reflects an acknowledgment of its importance, but whether or not a good lecture is a kind of theatrical 'performance' has always been suspect, since it seems to defeat the purpose of training, especially in those cases of individuals who were apparently not 'born' to teach. Charismatic authority is important for effectiveness, and seems consistent with developments in the learning society, with its stress upon the uniqueness of the individual. However, its basis is anecdotal and experiential rather than anything more systematic.

We are now in a position to compare and contrast the pedagogic and the postmodern or learning society critique of lectures and lecturing:

- The pedagogical critique reflects a view of professional autonomy, whereas the postmodern reflects a view of the lecturer much more in relation to the demands of the market economy and public accountability.
- The pedagogical critique reflects a view of subject knowledge as a body of truths which lecturers 'master' and which constitutes their expertise, whereas the postmodern regards truth in more relative terms, much more experiential and reflexive.
- The pedagogic critique of lecturers and lecturing tended to base professional status on a combination of social and subject authority, whereas the postmodern perspective stresses the primacy of

competence and accountability, and implies a de-skilling of the lecturer's role to some degree.

- The element of charismatic authority, according to the pedagogic view, was a desirable if unpredictable attribute of effective lecturing, whereas charisma in postmodern society stands for its individualism, rather than the pedagogic tendency to homogenise learners and their learning needs.

The contrast between these critiques or perspectives on lectures, lecturers and lecturing permits us now to draw some conclusions about this particular form of didacticism in the learning society.

## Part 3: reconstructing lectures and lecturing

As we have seen, most commentators agree that lecturing remains one of the most important teaching methods in education, and that it is likely to remain the case. Those days are gone when it was fondly imagined that all learners were self-sufficient with respect to their learning needs and autonomous in meeting them. Gone too is the belief that there was no longer any role for teachers and teaching, didactic or not.

However, it is equally true that the learning society has brought with it major implications for these kinds of methods. Apart from the changes in the nature of authority which have been outlined above, there are new contexts in which lecturers and lectures must reconstitute their role and function. Here are some examples:

- The focus now is upon learning, rather than education: this means that learning, and not simply understanding, is the ultimate aim of all teaching methods, including that of lectures.
- The formal system of education, with its institutions, roles and functions, is no longer the main or only site of learning: the learning society comprises non-formal and informal learning on many different sites, such as family, community, social movements and in civil society generally.
- Learning in the learning society is an activity, perhaps work-based or problem-solving, with strong emphases upon experience, reflection and personal growth in all of the sites where it takes place.
- The role of the state in the formal provision of education is retreating in the face of market forces and consumer-led styles of teaching and learning: teachers generally have to accommodate their methods to

developments in consumerism and information and communications technology.

- The status and authority of lecturers, and teachers generally, will depend less upon traditional forms of professional autonomy and more upon competence in meeting the learning needs of learners as consumers, as well as the meeting of externally imposed quality assurance standards.
- Didactic teaching methods, including lecturing, will have to be adapted to a much less homogeneous body of learners and their learning needs to be effective, lectures will have to address individual learning needs and styles much more closely than in the past. This principle in particular is being incorporated into training for Qualified Teacher status and into continuing professional development strategies.
- Developments in information, communications and media technology mean that learners as consumers will have a much wider choice of learning methods than in the past: the face-to-face lecture will have to find its place amongst a range of open and distance learning alternatives.
- Traditional roles of teachers and lecturers will need to be much broader than those concerned with instruction, explanation, understanding and subject knowledge, to include a range of counselling, pastoral, mentoring and facilitative functions.

These are the kinds of conditions in the learning society which will shape the future of lectures and lecturing. On the face of it, the traditional lecture, with its imagery of passive, authoritative and rote learning of information, seems considerably challenged by the developments associated with the learning society. And yet, as has been seen, the lecture remains a major teaching method, for all its didacticism, and seems set to do so for the foreseeable future.

The future of lecturing and the lecture method depend on a reformulation of what is meant by didacticism, and the forms of authority with which this is associated and which have been outlined in this chapter. As we have seen, some of these forms of authority are unlikely to survive the learning society or postmodern challenge.

Paradoxically, the only form of authority which seems even to be strengthened under postmodern conditions seems to be that of charisma. Students choose face-to-face methods because they represent the human face of learning. Once the traditional forms of social and subject authority have been abandoned, then the individual and personal relations of learning may be re-instated. Thus, the learning processes of doubt, reflection, critical thinking, questioning, and the live interaction of discussion, and question and answer, are made possible in ways that distance methods cannot achieve with the same degree of immediacy. Didacticism in the form of social control is abandoned in favour of the acceptance of the self-direction of learners and their individual learning needs.

No doubt, the form of the mass classroom lecture does not permit the kinds of experiential, reflective, critical or interactive learning which seems central to the learning society, but the role of lecturer seems likely to be merged with wider and more learner-centred roles. Thus lecturing becomes just one element in an armoury or portfolio of teacher roles in a learner support context. The nature of the lecture itself may approach much more closely the kind of presentation which is familiar in business and commerce, with its powerpoint and data projection technology. Whether a presentation can be said to be the same thing as a lecture is doubtful, in the light of the broad range of functions which have been introduced in this chapter, and in particular with regard to the increasingly heterogeneous body of learners and their learning needs.

What seems beyond doubt, however, is that the didactic element of lectures and lecturing will need to be adapted to those real-life learning contexts of learners, which comprise the family, community, work and social movements sites of learning, and which the learning society recognises as equally significant as the formal institutions of education itself.

## Conclusion

This chapter has outlined some of the consequences for the roles and functions of lecturers and lectures in the learning society, which is an object of national and international education policies. Didactic teaching methods have been placed in a context of the kinds of authority with which they have been traditionally associated, and the challenge of postmodernism analysed in terms of its consequences for this particular method. As a result, it was suggested that there is no *necessary* contradiction between didactic methods and effective learning. However, such methods need to be re-positioned against a global background of change in thinking about authority and knowledge. These changes lie behind the kinds of social and economic forces which are bringing the learning society into existence.

# References

Biggs, J. (1999) *Teaching for Quality Learning at University: What the Student does*, Society for Research into Higher Education and Open University Press, Buckingham

Bligh, D. (1998) *What's the Use of Lectures?* (5th edn), Intellect, Exeter

Brown, G. (1978) *Lecturing and Explaining*, Methuen, London

Curzon, L. B. (1997) *Teaching in Further Education: An Outline of Principles and Practice* (5th edn), Cassell, London

European Commission (EC) (1996) *Teaching and Learning: Towards the Learning Society* [White Paper on Education and Training] EC, Brussells

Evans, N. (1985) *Post-Education Society: Recognising Adult as Learners*, Croom Helm, London

Gibbs, G. (1981) *Twenty Terrible Reasons for Lecturing*, SCED Occasional Papers No. 8, Birmingham

Gray, D., Griffin, C. and Nasta, T. (2000) *Training to Teach in Further and Adult Education*, Stanley Thornes, Cheltenham

Jarvis, P. (1995) *Adult and Continuing Education: Theory and Practice* (2nd edn), Routledge, London

Jarvis, P. (ed.) (2001) *The Age of Learning: Education and the Knowledge Society*, Kogan Page, London

Jarvis, P., Holford, J. and Griffin, C. (1998) *The Theory and Practice of Learning*, Kogan Page, London

Knowles, M. (1978) *The Adult Learner: A Neglected Species* (2nd edn), Gulf Publishing Co, Houston

Mezirow, J. (1991) *Transformative Dimensions of Adult Learning*, Jossey-Bass, San Francisco, CA

Organisation for Economic Co-operation and Development (OECD) (1996) *Lifelong Learning for All*, OECD, Paris

Rogers, C. (1969) *Freedom to Learn*, Merrill, Columbus, OH

Squires, G. (1999) *Teaching as a Professional Discipline*, Falmer Press, London

Tough, A. (1979) *The Adult's Learning Projects: A Fresh Approach to Theory and Practice in Adult Learning* (2nd edn), Ontario Institute for Studies in Education, Toronto

United Nations Educational, Scientific and Cultural Organisation (UNESCO) (1996) *Learning: The Treasure Within* [Report to UNESCO by the International Commission on Education for the Twenty-First Century] UNESCO/HMSO, London

# Chapter 7

# The Socratic method

*Peter Jarvis*

The traditional image of teaching is 'telling' – the words of the Master communicated to the learners who learn and remember them. Yet even this traditional picture raises quite fundamental questions since, if I communicate information and it is learned, then surely I am a competent teacher, or at least I have taught. However, if I communicate information and it is not learned, does this make me a bad teacher, or have I not taught the learners at all? And so, the question is, is teaching no more than communicating or is it successful communication? This is a nice question, but the follow-up question to this is, need teaching necessarily involve communicating information? Socrates would have said that it did not. He argued that the teacher's job might be to bring to the consciousness latent knowledge with which we are born. In the Meno (Plato, 1956), Socrates argued:

> Thus the soul, since it is immortal has been born many times, and has seen all things both here and in the other world, has learned everything that is. So we need not be surprised if it can recall the knowledge of virtue or anything else which, as we see, it once possessed. All nature is akin, and the soul has learned everything, so that when a man has recalled a single piece of knowledge – *learned* it, in ordinary language – there is no reason why he should not find out the rest, if he keeps a stout heart and does not grow weary of the search; for seeking and learning are nothing but recollection.
>
> (Plato, 1956, pp. 129–130 (*italics* in original))

Socrates then demonstrated his argument to Meno by questioning the slave boy about geometrical problems which the boy answers correctly. Socrates says to Meno:

> Now notice what, staring from this state of perplexity, he will discover by seeking the truth in company with me, though I simply ask him

questions without teaching him. Be ready to catch me if I give him any instruction or explanation instead of simply interrogating him on his own opinion.

(Plato, 1956, pp. 135–136)

Now it is clear that Plato's argument on the immortality and omni-science of the soul is more than disputable in today's world. But this does not rule out that there are things that we have learned that are never brought to our consciousness – what I have called pre-conscious learning (Jarvis, 1987, 2005, *inter alia*) and Polanyi (1967) has referred to as tacit knowledge – unless we have a subsequent experience or are questioned about it. Pre-conscious learning occurs in a very wide variety of situations in everyday life and it would require more space than we have in this chapter to expound it in detail but let me give two examples:

- During our everyday life many things occur at the periphery of our consciousness of which we are partially aware but which are not at the centre of our attention – may of these are learned but never brought to our conscious awareness unless we have a subsequent experience that makes us aware of them.
- In all of our learning we do not only learn knowledge or skills, we also learn attitudes about them, values, beliefs and so. However, we are not tested on our attitudes or values, etc. and so we merely internalise them, reflect them in our general demeanour and assume them – unless we are forced to question them.

Tacit knowledge, on the other hand, is nicely illustrated by Polanyi (1967, p. 4);

We know a person's face, and can recognize it among a thousand, indeed among a million. Yet we cannot usually tell how we recognize a face we know. So most of this knowledge cannot be put into words.

He goes on to note that the police had recently introduced photo-fit methods to help people recall descriptions their tacit knowledge. Indeed, we could also use the illustration of knowing how to ride a bicycle but not being able to tell another person. Indeed, this is probably true with many advanced skills, which wrongly let people to believe that skilled craftspeople were inarticulate, but not being able to bring to the conscious mind or put into words something which is only known tacitly does not make one inarticulate, it is something quite natural and it requires techniques, such as questioning, to help people bring this knowledge to consciousness.

However, in reading the passage in which Socrates asked the questions, it could well be argued that while he was not giving the slave boy instruction or explanation he was leading him logically through an argument and that in responding to each question the slave boy was learning, and it is through the sequence of questions that the boy reached his conclusions.

Consequently, we can already see two distinctly different forms of teaching through questioning: helping learners to recall pre-conscious learning or tacit knowledge and leading learners through a carefully constructed sequence of questions towards a pre-determined conclusion. But then we might also ask, need the conclusion be pre-determined? Might there not be a questioning process that is not so carefully structured so that learners do not follow the thought patterns of the questioner? Of course there can! This leads us, then into yet another element of teaching through questioning.

In addition, we might all use the short question and answer tests to help memory recall. We might run a 'Twenty Questions' at the start of some sessions – but these questions have also to be very carefully structured so that we ask precisely the question that we need to in order to get the answer that we seek.

We are in a position to specify at least four different ways in which teachers can teach through questioning:

- Helping learners to call to mind what they have learned pre-consciously or their tacit knowledge.
- Leading learners through a carefully structured sequence of questions to a pre-determined answer.
- Starting learners on a questioning process which is totally unstructured at the outset.
- Having question and answer tests to aid memory recall.

Underlying this approach, however, is something even more fundamental to our understanding of human learning and that is the nature of the questioning process itself. But when we, as learners, ask questions it is not necessarily connected to teaching, but it is the first stage in the learning process, and it is to this that I want to turn briefly now although I discuss this much more fully elsewhere (Jarvis, 2005), and again in a later chapter.

Have you ever thought about the fact that, after a young certain age (about 4 years), very few of us go around everyday life asking questions much of the time. Maybe this is because we have learned answers to many of our everyday questions and we have learned to take life for granted. Schutz and Luckmann (1974, p. 7) describe this situation:

> Every application within the life-world goes on within the milieu of affairs which have already been explicated, within a reality that is fundamentally and typically familiar. I trust the world as it has been known to me up until now will continue further and that consequently the stock of knowledge obtained from my fellow me and formed from my own experiences will continue and preserve its fundamental validity... So long as the structure of the world can be taken as constant, as long as my previous experience is valid, my ability to operate on the world in this or that manner remains in principle preserved.

This is a situation that we all recognise in which we trust our previous learning and take the world for granted. But what happens when the world has changed? What happens when we cannot take the situation for granted? Immediately we might ask ourselves: What do I do now? Where can I find the answer? and so on. This is a situation which I have called disjucture – a situation when my biography (memories of my past experiences) and my interpretation of a present situation are not in harmony. We are in a disjunctural situation and we do not know what to do. It is this realisation of ignorance that is the beginning of the learning process, when we ask ourselves questions, and so on. Television programmes, like Candid Camera, are based upon this situation – when an innocent person is confronted with an unexpected situation and, often, the outcome is humorous or embarrassing to the innocent person. But the reality is, when we cannot take our situation for granted then we are forced to ask questions. But most of us do not like to live in a dissonant situation and so we try to resolve it. In this sense, the realisation of ignorance is the beginning of the learning process and one of the teachers' jobs is to generate a disjunctural situation – often by asking questions. This moment of disjuncture is a teachable moment!

The confusion generated by Candid Camera was often humorous but it could have been embarrassing and this is important for us as teachers because the last thing that we want to with our learners is to case them embarrassment, especially before their colleagues and so we have to learn the art of creating disjuncture, of asking questions, in such a manner as to preserve the dignity and self-respect our own learners but still generate in them the dissonant situation that motivates them to resolve it. This means that it is unwise to address our question directly to specific named individuals in the session because, if they do not know the answers, they might feel embarrassed, and so on.

However, the art of preparing precise questions is one that we often take for granted. We assume that we can communicate precisely by just posing a question. However, earlier in my career I used to run workshops for examiners, helping them to write good questions for examinations. When I began this I had partially assumed that everybody would be able to do this easily, since all teachers and examiners ask and set questions. Individuals were asked to write questions and also write down the objectives underlying the questions and then the workshop participants were asked if the question and the objectives coincided and, to my surprise, this was rarely the case. Asking questions is a skilled under-taking and we may not be as skilful at it as we presume. This is even more so if we are going to lead a group through a sequence of questions towards a known answer. Unless we deliberately want to set a confused question so that the group will have to engage in analytical thought to try to make sense of it, we do need to be very careful about the wording of questions so that the class is actually discussing precisely what we want it to. There is nothing more embarrassing for a teacher to set a question for group discussion and then discover that a group has found another meaning, topic for discussion, than the one that we intended.

Learning, then, begins when learners ask questions and teachers can facilitate the learning process by gently creating a disjunctural situation in which the learners are anxious to resolve their dissonance. Sometimes, these questioning situations will help bring to our learners' conscious-ness those pre-conscious learning experiences which we have had. This was very apparent in a situation when I was teaching a group of nurse educators and I asked them to write down their definition of learning. This they did. I then said that we would leave this definition aside for a moment and I then asked them, when they were nursing on a hospital ward, if they could sometimes tell the illness of a patient by the odour that came from the bed. They all replied that they could. I then asked them how they had acquired this facility – to which they responded that they had learned it. I then asked them whether any of them had included smell, in any way, in their definition of learning. None had! The point is that for many years we have restricted our definition of learning to knowledge, skills and attitudes, at the most, and forgotten many other aspects of what we learn and so what is learned pre-consciously is never brought to the conscious mind. Socratic teaching can, therefore, serve a most useful purpose in helping students reflect upon their experiences and crystallise their ideas.

There are a number of dangers when we lead sessions through questioning: first, that nobody will answer; second, that we intervene and direct the question at a student in the hope of getting an answer; third, that some one will dominate; fourth, that there will be some who do not participate and we know that if we try to involve them in the discussion through asking them directly, we might embarrass them. Taking each in turn:

- Teachers should not be embarrassed by silence, although when we watch inexperienced teachers we often see that having asked a question if they do not get an immediate response they try to fill in the silence. Students will be aware of this and may not respond deliberately! But classes are not often as cynical as this. Teachers have to find techniques for coping with silence, like going and finding a chair and deliberately sitting down – communicating that we (teachers) have plenty of time to await the answer.
- It is easy for us, as teachers, to overcome this silence by intervening and directing the questions at one or other students. This helps put us at ease but it does not necessarily help the students. In addition, we have to be aware of the ethical issues involved in this, since if we relieve our anxiety at the expense of the students, we are impinging upon their freedom not to answer and this may be a misuse in our authority – it is the authority of office rather than that of the experts who have authority granted to them on the grounds of their own expertise.
- If one or more students dominate the answers then we might have to deliberately direct our questions to another area of the room so that we do not catch their eye, but without isolating another person who might be embarrassed to answer. If this does not work, then we might have to take the student aside privately and discuss with him or her about how we appreciate their keenness to be involved and that we hope that they will always want to answer the questions, but would they also allow/encourage others to participate by restraining themselves.
- In the same way, we might want to discuss with the student(s) who do not respond why this is the case. We might find that some feel that they learn best by reflecting on the process but not by participating in it. Other might be too shy and then we might find ways of helping them participate more fully.

In all of these approaches we, as teachers, can teach without communicating information. But in order to bring this brief chapter to a conclusion I want just to refer to the idea of teaching through inquiry (Bateman, 1990).

Bateman's book provides many illustrations about inquiry-based teaching written from a narrow perspective. Even so, he illustrates how this approach to teaching and learning is based on problem solving and inductive reasoning. We will meet this approach a little more in Chapter 11 when we discuss practice-based teaching and learning. However, this approach to teaching might also be regarded as teaching through research since students are set a problem/project and encouraged to research. Getting students to learn through projects is a means of preparing them for more general research an it is in accord with practitioner research (Jarvis, 1999).

Setting projects involves more than setting the question; now it demands that teachers actually help the students a little by providing opportunities to discuss the way that a project develops, helping students think about the resources (books, people, institutions, Web and so on) that they can employ in undertaking their work, learning something about research methods and even trying help them see that once we undertake practical projects we are dealing with different forms of knowledge – practical and integrated rather than single disciplinary – rather than a single academic discipline and abstract knowledge. In fact, if we do this job thoroughly, our preparation will not doubt take at least as long as it would to prepare a lecture on the subject – but then being a lecturer may well be a different occupation to being a teacher. Perhaps this is a major clue in the difference between teaching and lecturing – the lecturer is concerned primarily with the subject matter and the methods of presentation are subsidiary whereas in teaching the methods of teaching are as important as the content in many instances.

It is not only the method but the style of teaching which is also very important. Eble makes the point that:

> The teacher's general stance can invite or discourage questions. A skilful teacher may need nothing more than a gesture, a turn of the head, a singling out by hand or look, even a pause, to elicit questions.
>
> The art of asking questions, eliciting answers, and moving with both to an understanding is the essential art of those who deal with the discussion method.
>
> (1988, p. 88)

Teaching is an art which we have to learn and we are, in many ways our best tool, but we have to use ourselves well – and the style that we employ, which will no doubt reflect our own personalities unless we are superb actors, is crucial to a good use of the Socratic method.

One other advantage of this approach is that students learn to concentrate on a research question and seek to answer it. If they learn to do this at this level, they will be greatly helped when it comes to writing dissertations and theses at other levels in their educational career. Inquiry-based teaching can, therefore, be a mixed mode approach to teaching, both information giving and, at the same time, encouraging enquiry. But once we recognise that learning begins with the question, it is not hard to see how research is also merely a matter of learning – and, even teaching!

## Conclusion

It is sometimes claimed that Socratic teaching is non-authoritarian but this would not be true. The way that Socrates led the slave boy through the questioning process was quite authoritarian, but it is a useful technique to help students move quickly from one stage to another. These more open and non-authoritarian methods lend themselves to discussion and inquiry, but they often take more time. Often, time appears to be of the essence, although, as I have argued elsewhere (Chapter 4) it may be a bad use of time just to cover the whole of the syllabus. Active learning, being involved in the discussion/research and so on, probably results in learning the topic under consideration much better and more thoroughly than if the learners are just told the answers.

## References

Bateman, W. (1990) *Open to Question* San Francisco, CA: Jossey-Bass

Eble, K. (1988) *The Craft of Teaching* (2nd Edition) San Francisco, CA: Jossey-Bass

Jarvis, P. (1987) *Adult Learning in the Social Context* London: Croom Helm

Jarvis, P. (1999) *The Practitioner Researcher* San Francisco, CA: Jossey-Bass

Jarvis, P. (2005) *Towards a Comprehensive Theory of Human Learning* London: Routledge

Plato (1956) *Protagoras and Meno* (trans: Guthrie, W.) Harmondsworth: Penguin

Polanyi, M. (1967) *The Tacit Dimension* London: Routledge and Kegan Paul

Schutz, A. and Luckmann, T. (1974) *The Structures of the Life-World* London: Heinemann

# Chapter 8

# Facilitation and facilitator style

*Josie Gregory*

> What happens to another person in your presence is a function of who you are and not what you know.
>
> (From Ram Dass, *The Only Dance There Is*)
>
> In my relationship with persons I have found that it does not help, in the long run to act as though I were something I am not.
>
> I find that I am more effective when I can listen acceptantly to myself, and can be myself.
>
> (Carl Rogers, 1961, p. 39)

Facilitation is an ancient art; it had a place in spiritual and monastic traditions in the form of guides, spiritual masters and spiritual directors where it still flourishes. Facilitation is found in many forms of experiential and practical learning such as role modelling, apprenticing and reflective, empirical experimentation. In the twentieth century facilitation re-emerged within progressive or radical education and expanded through the new psychotherapeutic fields such as Gestalt, Psychodrama, therapeutic art and dance and other humanistic personal development approaches. From here it permeated into the adult education field with experiential approaches to learning, particularly in personal and professional development.

The philosophical and psychological orientation, which I outline below, offers a rationale and description of the particular forms of knowledge facilitators engage with. Propositional and practical knowledge are more recognisable within traditional forms of education. This chapter attempts to integrate two other forms of knowledge, experiential and imaginal (Heron, 1992, 1999) as a necessary foundation to propositional and practical knowledge.

In this chapter I will offer a definition of educational facilitation, describe some of the main skills and attributes of a facilitator, discuss the training of facilitators and, finally, describe some implications for practice. The chapter is strongly influenced by Heron's (1989), extensive research and publication on facilitator styles.

## Facilitation

Facilitation literally means 'easing'. Its art is in drawing out the wisdom already embedded and lying dormant in the psyche of the learner. One belief of humanistic education and pragmatic constructivism is that learning is a recovery of or remembering that which we already know. Some believe that this inner knowledge is lost in the plethora of what we are told we should know and from a tendency, it would seem, to forget what we know. Facilitation may thus be seen as re-awakening our latent talents and store of unconscious wisdom. Helping learners realise their capacity to learn is the hallmark of the facilitator, moving education from a delivery of static knowledge to a dialogical relationship where knowledge is co-created. Rogers stated:

> We are, in my view, faced with an entirely new situation in education where the goal of education, if we are to survive, is the facilitation of change and learning. The only man who is educated is the man who has learnt to learn: the man who has learned how to adapt and change, the man who has realised that no knowledge is secure, that only the process of seeking knowledge gives a basis for security. Changingness, a reliance on process rather than upon static knowledge, is the only thing that makes any sense as a goal for education.
>
> (1983, p. 120)

Facilitation is the educational skill of accessing the phenomenological world of the individual, textured in social and cultural variables and helping the learner get in touch with their internal capacities to learn and to make sense of their experiences. The facilitator works with internal constructs and their external manifestation in behaviour, bringing these to conscious awareness, so that they can be looked at anew and developed if useful, or unlearned if inhibiting. Facilitation seeks to understand the frame of reference of self and the other, to reflect on how knowledge is derived from experience through implicit and explicit theoretical lens.

Facilitators are people with the skills to create conditions within which other human beings can, so far as is possible, select and direct their own learning and development. A facilitator is a 'process guide who works with a group to assist it to achieve its self-defining purpose

(Hunter, 1999, p. 118). The facilitators' philosophy informs their approach and is manifested as a concern with the psychological growth of the person. Rogers, who was influenced by Dewey's (1916) progressive education, thought that some teachers would not have the promotion of psychological growth as their educational aim.

Facilitators value experience and make it the premise on which other types of learning, imaginal, propositional and practical occur. This is part of the andragogical tradition (Knowles, 1978, 1985), where experience 'is not just a pedagogical device but more significantly an affirmation of the ontological and ethical status of adults, in particular the mark of their radical difference from children' (Usher et al., 1997, p. 95). Adult educators accept the validity of experience for children as much as for adults and in this sense the splitting of learning models into andragogy and pedagogy is false. The description of how adults learn does not invalidate how children learn, rather it is a reflection of the concerns among adult educators that sprang up in the 1960s as part of creating 'liberating structure' to facilitate adults learning.

The internal homogeneity between progressive education, humanistic education, and experiential learning lies in the belief in the active learner as one who has personal agency in that he or she is self-directing, intrinsically curious and motivated to learn. Harré (1983) states that being an agent means to conceive oneself as a being in possession of an ultimate power of decision and action. This notion can be illustrated by Heron's definition of the educated person:

> An educated person is someone who is self-directing: that is, one who determines and is internally committed to what he conceives to be worthwhile objectives, to acceptable means of achieving them, and to appropriate standards of performance in achieving the objects by those means. Secondly, he is someone who is self-monitoring: he evaluates his own performance in the light of the standards he has set and becomes aware of the extent to which that performance fulfils, exceeds or falls short of those standards. Thirdly, he is someone who is self-correcting: he modifies his own performance, his standards, and means, or his objectives as experience and reflection appear to his considered judgement to require.
>
> (1974, p. 1)

This demonstrates self-agency, commitment to a goal or direction in life and ability to make judgements about ones own self-development needs. These are the motivational forces that are aspired to in facilitation practice. Equally, it is advocated that self-agency is developed with the support of a facilitator and a learning group. The energy and commitment that is put into creating a peer learning community, as discussed elsewhere in this volume) attests to the importance of developing the social self, as well as the transcendental, and rational contingent self. This is contrary to Usher *et al.*'s account (1997, p. 93) that self-agency is part of the humanistic tradition of myopic individualism. Rather self-agency embraces all forms of individual, social and cultural learning and all forms of knowledge as they are useful to the participant or group. To only operate within restricted models such as the 'training and efficiency', or self-directed-learning model, or humanistic education or critical pedagogy, at the exclusion of the other perspectives is to do exactly what holistic education resists, that is splitting into 'good' and 'bad' or 'this but not that'. This splitting-off of the individual from the social and cultural milieu with education portrayed as individual liberation would certainly offer a negative imagery of learning as concerned with individual blocks and barriers and oppressive pedagogy (Usher *et al.*, 1997, p. 94).

These ideological approaches to facilitation emerge out of a particular philosophical framework that espouses the self-directed nature of learning. These values guide and direct intentions that act as a blueprint for facilitator style and interventions as well as for learning outcomes. Heron (1990, pp. 15–16) actually identifies participant qualities towards which the practitioner interventions are aimed, which underpin both facilitator practice and participant ideals. The facilitator works towards:

1   self-direction and co-operation;
2   informed judgement and open communication;
3   self-development and social change;
4   emotional competence and interpersonal sensitivity;
5   self-awareness and social perception;
6   celebration of self and others.

Facilitators act as guides helping participants explore their own self-knowledge, transpersonal (incorporating the spiritual and religious experiences of the person) and social knowledge. Traditional didacticism has its proper place in education where much knowledge is seen to be outside the individual and often exclusively delivered by people who know to those who do not. But it includes only two of the four modes of knowledge – practical and propositional knowing. Theoretical and practical knowledge of science, much of the humanities and technology and so on, are not part of the internal wisdom of the person and to that extent the pedagogical model is valid. Expressive art is an exception as are some forms of practical knowledge, where there is often a significant degree of freedom for individual interpretation and creativity. It is, however, possible to work experientially with propositional knowledge, looking at its application in specific and contemporary contexts, and to that extend such learning can be facilitated. However, other qualities such as emotional competence and interpersonal sensitivity are often not even considered as part of the educational context.

## Skills and attributes of the facilitator

Facilitators help others develop from the inside out, meaning from a values and feelings domain to their expression in behaviour, and facilitation can be explored in terms of both being and doing – what the facilitator 'is' and what the facilitator 'does' or the passive and active aspects of presence and performance. It is difficult to separate these fully because they are intertwined and interdependent. Presence means who the facilitator are – their essence, self-realisation, awareness, attention, charisma, states of being, sub-personalities, and so on. Performance is action, what facilitators do – such as their skills, interventions, intentions, style, techniques and so on (Gregory, 2000). I will first explore what a facilitator is.

Presence is how facilitators use their energy and attention during face-to-face interaction with participants. It is their self-awareness, being centred and grounded in their current state of being and is a function of their self-development and self-management. Being centred means being physically and mentally balanced, adopting an aligned posture combined with a calm mental state, and focusing attention on the present (Tosey and Gregory, 2001). Being grounded means being emotionally competent, so that other people's distress will not throw the facilitators off balance. Nevis defines presence as:

> the living embodiment of knowledge: the theories, the practices believed to be essential to bring about change in people are manifested, symbolised, or implied in the presence of the consultant.

And later:

> living out of values in such a way that in 'taking a stance', the intervenor teaches these important concepts. That which is important to the client's learning is exuded through the consultant's way of being.
> (1991, p. 2)

Nevis, who comes from a Gestalt orientation, makes a clear distinction between presence, personality and style. He suggests that a part of the facilitators' task is to provide the kind of presence which may be lacking in the client system to enable learning to occur. Heron (1987, p. 59) provides a more esoteric view of the nature of presence as outlined in the following extract:

> These three things – commitment of soul, charisma and bearing – all go together to make up presence. The result is a transfiguration of human expression in this world by potency in another world. It is *as if* the person is living, breathing, being and moving in two worlds at once; is in conscious command of their expression in physical space and in ka space at the same time. Hence the sense of a visitor, an entrant from the other world into this. Ka space means the non-physical, non-subjective realm. Ka is derived from the Egyptian concept of the Ka soul, set free from the human body at death to enter the future world.
>
> (Heron, 1987, p. 1)

This view of presence is based on the notion that as individuals we are capable of mediating various types of energy/presence from another dimension (e.g. the spiritual or cosmic dimension) and simultaneously manifesting these energies in the here and now. This is an important admixture in the performance of the 'charismatic facilitator' (Heron, 1999) and includes physical presence, in posture, facial expression, gaze, touch, sensory perception, gestures and relative position in relation to others. It includes intrasensory perception that is, an apprehension of the other's phenomenological world. When combined with sensory perception this creates an empathic energy field that allows attunement, resonance and deeper communication between self and the other.

An important aspect of presence is self-esteem which develops with the growth of competence, achievement and recognition. Many practitioners find their competence and achievement blocked by a negative self-concept. Our presence is determined by both our self-portrayal and what we believe ourselves to be. Authenticity, which might be defined as being true to self is closely related to self-esteem, as Carl Rogers, in the quotation at the beginning of this chapter, emphasised. Pretence is another enemy of authenticity and presence. He goes on to make similar points about self-acceptance and being oneself all the time.

Presence is related to our states of attention: it promotes learning through what might be called free attention. Normally in our lives our attention is held by internal states of anxiety, distress, pleasure or fascination and by external events from the spectacular and sensational to mundane personal interest. Being able to free our attention from the various distracting forces and direct attention to issues through aware and intentional choice is an essential skill in any facilitator role. This is all the more important in experiential settings where the potential for distraction and deflection is enormous. The following is one way of mapping a scale of facilitator states of attention:

1   Facilitator shows no interest or empathy in participant or subject matter – submerged in his/her own internal anxiety and concerns.
2   Facilitator is fascinated by the subject, their own distress or the participant, to the exclusion of all else.
3   Facilitator's attention is distracted, goes off in directions irrelevant to work at hand.
4   Facilitator displaces their own distress, confusion or conflict on to student by attacking, withdrawing, blaming, denial, complaining, etc.
5   Control of attention energy: some attention for task in hand while remainder is buried, displaced, distracted, etc.
6   Full attention directed to task in hand encompassing both own and participants, needs.
7   Attention for work in context, encompassing past and future, but immersed fully in task at hand.
8   Attention for work in context at the engaged participant level and also at the disidentified witness/monitoring level.

The last states of attention (6–8) are obviously likely to be more effective in facilitating the learner than the earlier ones.

Finally, presence as disclosure and self-presentation entails a recognition that while we are in the presence of other people, we are making constant disclosures about ourselves both verbally and non-verbally, intentionally and perhaps unintentionally. For instance, our general appearance, the way we initiate contact and maintain it and the forms of communication we chose all give others information about us. Facilitators may or may not disclose something of their background, knowledge, attitudes, goals and personal needs. Disclosure may help or inhibit the learning process and the building of the relationship necessary for facilitative interventions to be effective. Being aware on the impact of our presentation on others and appropriately choosing what to disclose and how and when to disclose all enhances facilitation.

Developing personal presence is an essential attribute of the effective facilitator. Presence can be enhanced by a variety of methods, for example, disidentification with personalised and narrow perspectives; cultivation of internal and external awareness by transcending perceptive barriers; developing personal functional capacities, increased self-knowledge, charismatic training and grounding in and preparation of your subject matter; and development of a positive self-concept, self esteem, self-presentational capacities, or evocation of the Higher 'self' and I list below some specific personal qualities Heron (1999, p. 20) believes the facilitator needs to have:

- *Authority*: being able to hold and use authority (both positional and expert authority) without displacing your personal distress on to others.
- *Confrontation*: to confront supportively, work with projections and defence that emanates from the group.
- *Care*: ability to show compassion, are genuine and empathetic in your work.
- *Range of methods*: effectively deal with deep regression, catharsis and transpersonal aspects of group life, and have a wide repertoire of techniques and exercises for personal and interpersonal development.
- *Orientation*: you can provide clear conceptual maps as required.
- *Respect for persons*: you respect the autonomy of the person and the rights of individuals to choose when to change/grow.
- *Flexibility of style*: you move deftly and flexibly as the situation demands, between interventions in one dimension, between dimensions and between modes so that the group dynamic and individual learning can flourish.

Not all the above qualities are necessary for all facilitators nor for all facilitated events. Much depends on the type of facilitation required but they are all listed above to demonstrate the breath and depth of facilitation skills. The proviso is always that the facilitator does not, ever, offer facilitation in areas of personal, interpersonal and transpersonal exploration in which they have not been trained, are not competent nor have experienced for themselves as a client or participant. Even the most innocent facilitation of personal development will touch on emotional, spiritual, and imaginal levels if one is working holistically. The skill of containment of emotional expression, (Stapley, 1996) containment of fear of getting it wrong, or being vulnerable in front of others all require a nurturing, yet respectful detachment from the group agenda. Heron highlights this point:

> The enemy of presence is anxiety. Actors often have a lot of fear before going onto the stage. It usually goes once they are out front, with the secure content of rehearsed lines which they can fill with presence. But extempore speech in everyday life may often generate a lot of subtle anxiety.
>
> (1987, p. 9)

For some facilitators this hurdle can be overcome by rehearsal or by deep relaxation exercises but for others some significant personal development work may need to be done before presence in the face-to-face situation can be consistently achieved. Hence emotional competence (Heron, 1992; Postle, 1993) is one of the central planks on which facilitator presence sits alongside other attributes presented here. Roger Harrison (1995, p. 37) refers to emotional competence as 'being open about feelings, expressing vulnerability and uncertainty, supporting, caring and the like'.

## The facilitator–participant relationship

Heron (1999, p. 1), one of the first modern developers and writers in this field, states that 'a facilitator is a person who has the role of empowering participants to learn in an experiential group'. This role is seen as legitimised by the participants, who voluntarily accept the facilitator in this role. Unsolicited facilitation is an infringement on the participants' right to self-determination, so that there is a presupposition of a formal contract between learner and facilitator which must be in place before facilitators can act.

Both parties in the relationship, the individual participant (or group) and the facilitator metaphorically, sit side-by-side rather than face-to-face; both look out onto the same world and have a conversation about what they are experiencing and how they are making sense of their experience. For such a relationship to be effective, a degree of openness and honesty, of shared vulnerability to disclose self and the ability to articulate such disclosures are essential. Even the use of the word participant rather than learner denotes the different relationship, that is that both teacher and learner are participating in learning with a balance of power that strives to be more equal than usually found in traditional education. Such a relationship is different from teaching. While both types of relationships have their place in education, learning is most effective when there is flexibility for different forms of knowledge to be engaged with using different methods of teaching and facilitative relationships as appropriate. In the latter, a human relationship is established between the facilitator and participant, both are equal in this relationship, one is contracted by the other to share their knowledge and general worldview, in so far as it is relevant, and both share of themselves emotionally, behaviourally, spiritually and cognitively. The principle of holistic education is central to both parties in facilitation. 'An holistic approach to the person embraces and affirms complexity, inclusion and diversity and resists reductionism' (Clarkson, 1989 p. 8).

Facilitation is associated with student-centred learning. The teacher-student relationship is also a contract, usually of the type where students sign up for a programme and expect to be offered some form of tuition and to have their work fairly assessed towards some academic award. Depending on the nature of the programme the teaching may be teacher-centred or the programme may run by independent study and all shades in between. There will be an implicit contract which is mostly unconscious and only experienced by one or both parties if the contract is deemed to be broken. Many students have learned through their initial education to expect variation in the different types of relationships they have with teachers. It may seem like a lottery to students as they experience having little influence over whether teachers will like them or not. Such relationships seem emotionally driven and often unpredictable, others driven by results and high grades. The implicit contact is called the 'psychological contract' and is the main driving force underpinning relationships (Gregory, 1996). While it is seldom labelled as such, to sit and listen to students tell of their treatment at the hands of lecturers' shows that the students are aware of a psychological contract, because it has been broken. As a result, students become disenchanted or desensitised. This desensitisation does not mean that the psychological contract is not needed nor that it does not exist, it exists if people feel unheard, rejected and treated as objects, an 'I-it' rather than an 'I-thou' relationship (Buber, 1958). The effect of a broken psychological contract is that students do not believe that the teacher or lecturer has their interests as heart, so they withdraw a major part of themselves from the relationship, do not give of their best and their learning is impeded. The psychological contract is based on (often) unexpressed expectations that are not fulfilled. However it is also based on espoused promises that are not carried through.

Researching the concept of facilitating interpersonal skills within the health profession I found that facilitators ignore the psychological contract

**Facilitating 'Learning about Self'**

*Facilitator*

Mutual self-disclosure of feelings, values and beliefs
competent in facilitating experiential learning
role model intentional therapeutic behaviour
good understanding of group dynamics
valuing/respecting the individual
creating interactive group learning
supporting personal development
appropriate hierarchical power
appropriate expert power

↓

**THE PSYCHOLOGICAL CONTRACT**

**Participant/Group**

↑

psychologically 'safe'
feeling free to take risks
more aware of group process
transferability of learning to work
more self-directed autonomous learners
emotionally competent with self and others

↓

*Learning outcomes*

*Figure 8.1* Aspects of the psychological contract (Gregory, 1996).

at their peril (Gregory, 1996). The psychological contract is seen as paramount when facilitating others to learn about themselves. Figure 8.1 shows what is required for the psychological contract to be in place. The hourglass is analogous to a top-down filtration, which needs to be initiated by facilitators and it lays the foundation for a conducive learning environment. It also reflects a positive feedback loop when the qualities of good facilitation filtering through to participants via an explicit psychological contract are reflected bake to the facilitator from the participants.

For example, having appropriate expert power will not automatically create psychological safety for the participants, but if facilitators feel psychologically grounded in themselves, with strong self-esteem and use their expert power appropriately, it is likely to create psychological safety. Consequently, facilitators need to be competent in all the attributes they want students to acquire through the educative experience. This is the essence of the psychological contract. In line with the philosophy of facilitation there are two other educational processes that are congruent with facilitation: collaborative assessment and co-operation with peers. Both of these are the subject of other chapters in this volume.

As facilitators acknowledge that people are able to identify their own goals, they offer a way of negotiating how they may be met through some form of learning contract which is made either formally or informally at the beginning of the learning experience. Equally, as goals are usually related to the participant's central needs or values their relevance is respected and given due consideration. Believing that the participants have all the resources and wisdom within them to meet their own needs and goals, facilitators are tentative about defining the 'correct path' the participant should take, preferring to act as a sounding board while the participants discuss options and make choices that best suit their particular worldview. To impose solutions on a participant, which are unsolicited, is considered degenerate, incompetent or unskilled (Heron, 1999). Yet, paradoxically, facilitators need to exercise diagnostic skills and offer these skills to participants so that they can confront distorted perceptions and limiting patterns of behaviour. A substantial part of the learning contract is the identification of learning needs and what needs to be unlearned if the individual is to develop greater self-awareness and personal and professional competence. Often what needs to be examined are socially constructed perceptions of self that are experienced as inhibitive. Critical reflection using Bateson's (1973) levels of learning, Argyris (1994) single and double loop learning with Watzlawick's (1990) notion of first and second-order change are all seen as useful models to aid critical reflection.

## Facilitation as a teaching and learning style

Having examined presence and performance and the facilitator-participant relationship, I now want to summarise and discuss some of the significant functions of the facilitator.

Rogers (1983) suggests that they enact the following broad role-sets:

- setting the initial mood or climate of a group's experience;
- eliciting and clarifying the purposes of individuals as well as the more general purposes of the group;
- regarding themselves as a flexible resource;

- responding to expressions they accept both intellectual as well as emotional attitudes, endeavouring to give each aspect the appropriate degree of emphasis which it has for the individual or group;
- taking the initiative in sharing him/herself with the group – feelings as well as thoughts – in ways which do not demand or impose but rather represent simply a personal sharing which participants may take or leave;
- in facilitating learning they endeavour to recognise and accept their own limitations;

Facilitators are often process facilitators, helping a work or learning group recognise the psychological agendas that might be impeding the group's effectiveness. They are not necessarily technical experts, and their process expertise rests on understanding the personal, interpersonal and group dynamics operating at social, psychological and existential levels of human relationships. Part of their expertise is to understand how individuals and groups learn and change.

When training facilitators we focus on twelve main themes (Mulligan 1992 cited in Gregory, 2000): some I have already mentioned. I list them all here for the sake of completion. They are divided into four broad headings:

| Headings | Themes |
| --- | --- |
| Practitioner | Presence, qualities, values and beliefs, knowledge and subject expertise |
| Client | Diagnostic skills, assessment and evaluation of client outcomes |
| Interventions | Intentions, guiding models and theories, interventions, channels of communication |
| Environment | Dynamics of relationship, organisational context |

Experience, as we have said, is a platform for learning; it is an integrated form of knowing. This does not mean that all experiences participants bring are unproblematic. Many of the experiences which created problems for learning in the past are brought to the new educational experience, consciously and unconsciously. These will have the effect of inhibiting learning, re-stimulating low self-esteem or, conversely, over-confidence, all of which will be brought to the surface. The former prevents self-directed learning while the latter focuses on some dimensions of the academic or commercial at the expense of the human or the spiritual, which Habermas (1974) calls distorted or constraining constructs. These constraints, developed as part of the socialisation process, need to be critically assessed for their usefulness and validity as part of the emancipatory processes of adult education. Much of the training of facilitators focuses on helping trainees recognise in themselves the distressed patterns they bring to experiential learning from prior schooling and training and providing them with skills to help them unlearn the distorted and compulsive behaviours they bring to new learning. From this learning they are in a better position to facilitate the same processes in others.

Participants in facilitated experiential learning groups often seek a holistic learning experience which may focus on personal and or professional issues. In order to achieve this, the facilitator of a workshop will intentionally ask for voluntary interactive participation and will offer some guidance or ground rules which may answer the question often asked of the group, 'What do you need to feel safe to work and learn here?'

The facilitator mode of working is both related to the learning contract and to the educational or social context. It is also in part dependent on the facilitator's own preferred style. Heron (1999) offers a model of facilitator style, discussed below.

## The dimension of facilitator style

The model describes three political modes: hierarchy (autocratic or consultative), co-operation (negotiation or consultative) and autonomy (functional or contractual). They refer to the power relationship between facilitators and participants and address the questions about decision making in the group learning context. The six dimensions are:

- The Planning dimension – goal orientated, aims, ends and means.
- The Meaning dimension – cognitive understanding of experience.
- The Confronting dimension – raising awareness to individual and group resistance.
- The Feeling dimension – addressing emotional competence and incompetence.
- The Structuring dimension – methodology of structuring experiences.
- The Valuing dimension – creating a support climate that celebrates individuals.

Combining each mode with each dimension provides a framework whereby facilitators might both plan and evaluate their own performance. This is the basis of Heron's analysis of facilitator styles. But they might also form the basis of guidelines for personal development, since they help facilitators reflect on their own identity, on the limitations of their own competences and on the types and techniques with which they can work, and so on.

## Conclusions

In summary, the main factors influencing facilitation are the internal cultural environment or group context, the social and psychological contract, the wider culture, both institutional and environmental, the facilitator style and the model of facilitation. The reframing of experiential learning theory into theories of pragmatic constructivism and critical science addresses some of the postmodern critique about personal autonomy being disassociated from the social self. Within the educational theory and practice espoused here, the self is understood as socially constructed, personal and spiritual development having validity and essence in relationship. Buber's (1958) – I-Thou versus I-It. It is the former construct through which people come together for the purpose of living and learning. All experiences are constrained as well as enhanced within the social and cultural milieu in which we act. The challenge in higher education and accredited programmes is to bring together theories of teaching and learning that take account of the individual and collective needs, the need for different forms of knowledge and how these might be facilitated, the institutional requirement for programme specifications and assessment within a philosophy that is ethical in its treatment of the person.

## References

Argyris, C. (1994) *On Organizational Learning*. Oxford: Blackwell Business.

Bateson, G. (1973) *Steps to an Ecology of Mind*. London: Paladin, Granada (new edition 2000).

Buber, M. (1958) *I and Thou*. New York: Scribner and Sons.

Clarkson, P. (1989) *Gestalt Counselling in Action*. London: Sage.

Dewey, J. (1916) *Education and Democracy*. New York: The Free Press.

Gregory, J. (1996) *The Psycho-Social Education of Nurses*. Aldershot: Avery.

Gregory, J. (2000) *Facilitating Interventions: One-to-One*. Module 5. MSc in Change Agent Skills and Strategies. Guildford: School of Educational Studies, University of Surrey.

Habermas, J. (1974) *Theory and Practice*. London: Heinemann.

Harré, R. (1983) *Personal Being*. Oxford: Basil Blackwell.

Harrison, R. (1995) *Consultant's Journey*. London: McGraw-Hill.

Heron, J. (1974) *The Concept of a Peer Learning Community*. Guildford: Human Potential Research Project, University of Surrey.

Heron, J. (1987) *Confession of a Janus-Brain*. London: Endymion Press.

Heron, J. (1989) *The Facilitator's Handbook*. London: Kogan Page.

Heron, J. (1990) *Helping The Client: A Creative Practical Guide*. London: Sage.

Heron, J. (1992) *Feeling and Personhood. Psychology in Another Key*. London: Sage.

Heron, J. (1999) *The Complete Facilitator's Handbook*. London: Kogan Page.

Hunter, D. (1999) *Handling Groups in Action*. Aldershot: Gower.

Knowles, M. (1978) *The Adult Learner-A Neglected Species* (2nd edition). Houston: Gulf.

Knowles, M. (1985) *Andragogy in Action*. San Francisco, CA: Jossey-Bass.

Mulligan, J. (1992) *Facilitating Interventions: One to One*. (Module 5 Study Guide: MSc in Change Agent Skills and Strategies). Guildford: University of Surrey, School of Educational Studies.

Nevis, E. (1991) *A Gestalt Approach to Organisational Consultancy*. New York: Gardener Press.

Postle, D. (1993) Putting the Heart Back Into Learning, in Boud, D., Cohen, R. and Walker, D. (eds) *Using Experience for Learning*. Buckingham: Society for Research into Higher Education and Open University Press, pp. 33–45.

Rogers, C. (1961) *On Becoming a Person*. Boston, MA: Houghton.

Rogers, C. R. (1983) *Freedom to Learn for the 1980's* (2nd edition). Columbus, OH: Merrill.

Stapley, L. (1996) *The Personality of the Organisation: A Psycho-Dynamic Explanation of Culture and Change*. London: Free Association Books.

Tosey, P. and Gregory, J. (2001) *Dictionary of Personal Development*. London: Whurr Publications.

Usher, R., Bryant, I. and Johnston, R. (1997) *Adult Education and the Postmodern Challenge*. London: Routledge.

Watzlawick, P. (1990) *Muenchhausen's Pigtail or Psychotherapy and Reality: Essays and Lectures*. New York: W.W. Norton and Company.

# Chapter 9

# Principles of experiential education

*Josie Gregory*

This chapter focuses on the theoretical principles of experiential teaching and learning showing that it has its genesis in the philosophy of progressive and emancipatory adult education. The determination of some educators to value and account for adults' learning through life experiences has lead to a growing literature on exactly how people learn what they learn through experience and from experience. The epistemological concerns raised in such studies can be found under such broad headings as emancipatory education and transformative learning (Mezirow, 1981, 1999), experiential learning in higher education (Weil and McGill, 1989; Boud *et al.*, 1993) criticality (Brookfield, 2000) Habermas' (1974) critical social science, and personal and spiritual development (Rogers, 1983; Postle, 1988, 1993; Heron, 1992; Rowan, 1993). The debate spans many pedagogical issues within the education of adults from teacher training to the life long learning agenda and raises some tantalising questions about how people learn from experience, to how experiential learning be effectively facilitated. It also offers a critique on the educational environments that foster such learning. This chapter surveys some of important principles of experiential teaching and learning with a view to highlighting some of the main contemporary ideological and practice issues. The main focus is the purpose of all learning, that is the acquisition of knowledge and how this might be acquired through aspects of experiential learning. A description and discussion of experiential teaching and learning methods themselves is covered elsewhere in this volume.

## Context of experiential education

Experiential methods of teaching and learning have existed from ancient times. Meditation, awareness exercises, 'personality' profiles such as the Enneagram, story telling, visualisation and much more can be found associated with wisdom traditions such as Christian mysticism, Sufism, yoga and Buddhism (Rawlinson, 1997).

What is new is not so much the discovery of the methods themselves, but of their acceptance in mainstream contemporary education. The formal educational agenda in modern Western society has typically been dominated by the acquisition of cognitive knowledge, and to a lesser extent by vocational preparation, and sports education aside, has either neglected or actively repressed the education of body, emotion and spirit.

Exceptions tend to have stood out. There was a wave of radical and counter-cultural thinking in the 1960s and 1970s, through figures like Rogers (1983), Heron (1974) and Knowles (1978). In fact, the modern philosophical base which gave rise to experiential learning practice in higher education since the 1970s has its origin in Dewey's (1938) progressive education. Progressive education was adopted as a central tenet of humanistic psychology and the Human Potential Movement in the 1970s and continues to influent humanistic adult educators (Carr and Kemmis, 1986; Brookfield, 2000). According to Dewey (1938, p. 20):

> We shape all knowledge by the way we know it. (subjectively) *(and)*: I take it that the fundamental unit of the newer philosophy is found in the idea that there is an intimate and necessary relation between the processes of actual experience and education. If this is true, then a positive and constructive development of its own basic idea depends upon having a correct idea of experience.

Yet radical or progressive educational ideas appear to have had little widespread influence on formal education, despite the common rhetoric of educating 'the whole person'. Their impact has been felt more in the personal development workshops of the 'growth movement', and to some extent in areas of professional development. It is rare to find experiential learning underpinning a curriculum, rather than being used as an occasional leavening or confined to promulgating Kolb's (1984) experiential learning cycle. The idea that formal (traditional) education might concern itself with the emotional and inner life of the person remains a curious and potentially risky idea to many.

Traditional education often termed 'education from above' (Jarvis, 1985) is seen as more politically/socially controlling of learners and inhibitive to individual creativity (Dewey, 1938) whereas progressive education is seen as the 'education of equals' (Knowles, 1978). In fact

Durkheim's (1972 cited in Williamson, 1979, p. 4) definition of traditional education emphasises the sociological perspective:

> Education is the influence exercised by adult generations on those that are not yet ready for social life. Its object is to stimulate and develop in the child a certain number of physical, intellectual and moral states which are demanded of him by the political society as a whole, and by the particular milieu for which he is specifically destined.

Contrary to the aforementioned and particularly when working with adult learners, Knowles asserts that the education of equals is based on the following premises:

*Changes in self-concept*: As the person voluntarily moves, in terms of self-concept, from dependency to increased interdependency (in learning), he becomes psychologically adult. He then no longer wants to be controlled by others and displaces this in resentment and resistance.

*The role of experience*: As the individual matures he accumulates an expanding reservoir of experiences that causes him to become an increasingly rich learning resource, and at the same time provides him with a broadening base to which to relate new experiences. To a child, experience is something that happens to him; to an adult his experience is who he is. So in any situation in which that experience is being devalued or ignored, this is not just a rejection of the experience, but of the person himself.

*Readiness to learn*: Adults are more ready to learn. It is not the case of learning what they 'ought to learn' as with children, but what they think they need to learn as relevant to their life, career and so on. The critical implication of this assumption is the importance of timing learning experiences to coincide with the learners' developmental tasks.

*Orientation to learning*: Adults tend to have a problem-centred orientation to learning. The reason for this is the timing of the learning to relevant here and now application. (Adapted from Knowles, 1978, pp. 58–59.)

Such philosophical premise and educational values are best expressed through a curriculum that places experiential learning as pivotal to the educational process. For if personal experience and personal knowledge is valued and built on the learning is more likely to mirror the four outcomes expressed above. Such outcomes have formed the bases of many adult liberal educational programmes as well as Continuing Professional Development.

Economic pressures of contemporary education appear to militate against experiential learning and personal development in the undergraduate and most postgraduate curricula apart form some vocational degrees. Moves towards distance learning improve access for some, but reduce face-to-face contact and the encounter of human beings to a minimum. Modularisation of programmes, that grand rationalist project designed to maximise student choice, often means that 'learning communities' are so transitory that students have little chance to bond, affiliate, and identify with their peers or their programmes. Funding for, and research into, educational innovation is often restricted to technological developments. Increasing student numbers means that large cohorts are the norm, and while these do not exclude the use of experiential methods they test the ingenuity and competence of educators to the limit. Professional development in 'large group teaching' continues to emphasise the lecture above all other methods. The idea of understanding and utilising large group dynamics is rarely found outside Organisational Development methods such as 'future search' (Weisbord, 1987), the Tavistock Institute's 'Leicester conference', and Open Space Technology.

Even so, a significant number of educators continue to believe in the value of experiential learning and holistic development. While these principles and practices, quite rightly, have to respond to contemporary critique (e.g. Burgoyne and Reynolds, 1997) they are also re-emergent, as in the UK Lifelong Learning agenda. For example, the theme of emotional competence (e.g. Postle, 1993) has been prominent in the educational agenda of the Human Potential movement for many years, without ever becoming a mainstream idea. But this is very close to the concept of emotional intelligence (Goleman, 1996), which has exploded onto the organisational training scene and is in danger of being seen as a panacea for all the psychological and economic ills of society. It seems that personal development is a strongly interdisciplinary field, a shared territory in which, for example, educators and organisational consultants embrace psychotherapeutic models of change, educational theories of learning, spiritual notions of human potential and more. Whether one regards this as a welcome post-modern eclecticism or an ethically questionable slippage is, of course, another debate.

## Principles of experiential education

Experiential methods usually relate to a cluster of educational principles. At times they may be regarded as stand-alone components that can be slotted into any educational process, and as such represent a valuable resource for educators. They are more likely to be potent, however, in an integrated approach to curriculum design in which experiential learning and personal development are the core, rather than peripheral in the design.

Experiential learning is a complex process involving theory and practice, action and reflection. Boud *et al.* (1993, p. 1) say:

> Most of what is written about learning is from the perspective of teachers or researchers who assume that there is a body of knowledge to be taught and learned. What is missing is the role and relevance of learning from experience no matter where it occurs. Learning involves much more than an interaction with an extant body of knowledge; learning is all around us, it shapes and helps create our lives – who we are, what we do. It involves dealing with complex and intractable problems, it requires personal commitment, it utilises interaction with others, it engages our emotions and feelings, all of which are inseparable from the influence of context and culture.

They go on to list five propositions about learning from experience (Boud *et al.*, pp. 8–16):

1   experience is the foundation of, and the stimulus for, learning;
2   learners actively construct their experience;
3   learning is a holistic process;
4   learning is socially and culturally constructed;
5   learning is influenced by the socio-emotional context in which it occurs.

These propositions are very similar to Carl Rogers principles and were very likely developed out of his work. Rogers emphasised that education should be 'person-centred'. He coined the phrase 'person-centred counselling' and spread the concept to education. The assumptions underlying experiential learning Rogers (1983, pp. 278–279) identified were:

1   Human beings have a natural potentiality for learning.
2   Significant learning takes place when the subject matter is perceived by the student to have relevance for his own purposes.
3   Much significant learning is acquired through doing.
4   Learning is facilitated when the student participates responsibly in the learning process.
5   Self-initiated learning, involving the whole person of the learner, feelings as well as intellect, is the most pervasive and lasting.

6   Creativity in learning is best facilitated when self-criticism and self-evaluation are primary, and evaluation by others is of secondary importance.
7   The most socially useful learning in the modern world is the learning of the process of learning, a continuing openness to experience, an incorporation into oneself of the process of change.

This list of assumptions of the characteristics of the adult learner while humanistically based is almost identical to Mezirow's description of adult learners in contemporary cultures. Mezirow's (1999) Transformation Theory sits within post-modern cultural relativism and some of his assumptions underpinning a comprehensive learning theory will be discussed later in this chapter.

From the above list of assumptions it can be seen that experience is central to learning, therefore any educational process that claims to foster the creation and assessment of experiences will need to fulfil this criterion. It can also be seen that this type of learning bridges the fields of personal and professional development and academic education, in that by its holistic nature experiential learning actively embraces all four functions of thinking, feeling, intuition and sensing which humans have of being in contact with the world, and acquiring knowledge. Heron (1992, pp. 14–15) expands on these four modes of functioning in the following way:

1   affective-embracing feelings and emotions;
2   imaginal-comprising intuition and imagery;
3   conceptual-including reflection and discrimination;
4   practical-involving intention and action.

These four modes are placed here to illustrate the holistic nature of humanistic learning theory which can be applied to learning processes whether in a therapeutic, educational or social and health care setting. Experiential education, Dewey's 'educative experiences' (1938, p. 28) implies engaging all modes of functioning if learning is to be an integrative experience for the individual. As Heron (1989, p. 13) states:

> Experiential knowledge is knowledge gained through action and practice. This kind of learning is by encounter, by direct acquaintance, by entering into some state of being. It is manifest through the process of being there, face-to-face, with the person, at the event, in the experience. This is the feeling, resonance level of learning.

There is also Kolb's definition of learning as 'the process whereby knowledge is created through the transformation of experience' (1984, p. 38).

The reason for the choice of experiential methods as a way of manifesting the philosophy of adult learning can be summed up in Heron's (1999, p. 1) description of group experiential learning:

> By an experiential group, I mean one in which learning takes place through an active and aware involvement of the whole person, as a spiritual, energetically and physically endowed being encompassing feeling and emotion, intuition and imaging, reflection and discrimination, intention and action.

Certainly if experiential learning as described by Heron is to be holistic as well as expanding knowledge it needs to move through the face-to-face encounter to the other levels; the imaginal, conceptual and practical. To map such knowledge progression Heron (1999) has developed a useful model which he calls a manifold or multi-modal learning. This has four dimensions, the experiential, the imaginal, the propositional/ conceptual and the practical. These four dimensions form a pyramid or up-hierarchy with the affective/experiential dimension at the base and the imaginal, the propositional and the practical levels following upward. Thus the model suggests that experience is the most primary form of knowing; that our experience is typically translated next into presentational knowing (using images, metaphors, fantasies); that conceptual or propositional knowing is a further stage; and that altogether these create the possibility of practical knowing, that is of using knowledge in action.

The current emphasis on the 'education of the affect', that is, developing emotional competence or emotional intelligence, means having the ability to 'manage one's own emotions awarely in terms of the basic skills of control, expression, catharsis and transmutation' Heron (1992, p. 131). This raises questions for some educators about the nature of the boundary between education and psychotherapy. For the purposes of this discussion, I believe that the boundary is by no means rigid if one adopts a humanistic perspective and if one defines psychotherapy in a non-clinical, growth oriented activity, 'an intentional and committed process of personal development' (Rowan, 1993, p. 98).

Further principles of experiential education are those of self-directednesss, empowerment and autonomy. These have been criticised (e.g. Burgoyne and Reynolds, 1997) for representing an individualised, psychologistic, non-political perspective, although this does not negate their concern to counter education that is other-directed, disempowering and alienating (see Habermas, 1974). Self-directedness is the principle that learners, rather than teachers or trainers, take charge of their own learning. It also refers to the process by which learners diagnose their needs, define learning goals, identify resources and methods and assess their progress. Key writers contributing to the concept of self-directed learning are Stephen Brookfield, Cyril Houle, Malcolm Knowles and Allen Tough (see Jarvis *et al.*, 1998, pp. 77–87).

Empowerment has become something of a slogan, especially in the business world where talk of 'empowering' people entails the idea that some external authority is capable of enabling others to become 'empowered'. Rather like learning, empowerment may be spoken of as if it were a universal good. Christine Hogan, a humanistic educator and facilitator from Australia, has written about empowerment from a personal development perspective. She cites a definition of empowerment by Hamelink:

> a process in which people achieve the capacity to control decisions affecting their lives. Empowerment enables people to define themselves and to construct their own identities. Empowerment can be the outcome of an intentional strategy which is neither initiated externally by empowering agents or solicited by disempowered people.
>
> (Hamelink, 1994, pp. 132–133, cited in Hogan, 2000, p. 12)

Finally in this review of principles, experiential approach will often entail a notion of power sharing or reflect a form of 'peer principle'. In Heron's (1999) model of facilitator styles, the peer principle implies mutual aid and support between autonomous people who are at the same level, politically. In adult education learners, particularly in professional and personal development and experiential groupwork, combining peer learning with benevolent hierarchy allows participants to see each other as a rich learning resource and not become solely reliant on the facilitator. This is an essential pre-requisite for a peer learning community.

## Application – forms of knowledge acquisition

Dewey's educational philosophy comes alive with the use of Kolb's (1984) and Heron's (1989) experiential learning cycles. Both cycles require the learner to move through an inquiry process of experience, reflection, generalisation (or conceptualisation) and testing (or practice) (after Kolb, 1984). Both models advocate learning with others for the purpose of the encounter, assistance with reflection and feedback on practice.

This educational process is considered facilitative in that it follows the definition of a helping relationship where both the self and peers have the intention of promoting the growth, development, maturity, improved functioning, improved coping of life of each other (Gregory, 1996).

Learning is holistic if it offers opportunities for engagement of all seven capacities the individual (Mulligan, 1993) brings to experience for the purpose of acquiring knowledge. These are thinking, imaging, feeling, memory, intuition, sensing and will. Curriculum design and development that focuses exclusively on the cognitive and or practical levels of knowledge will not succeed in providing 'whole person' education just the same as those who focus on offering emotional and imaginal experiences without engaging the other functions will not succeed either regardless of what they espouse. However different capacities will be in the foreground depending on the type of learning involved and a model of these relationships is offered here.

The four modes of knowing are:

- The world of presence      Experiential knowing
- The world of appearance    Presentational knowing
- The world of essence       Propositional knowing
- The world of existence     Practical knowing

In summary form, according to Heron (1992, pp. 157–160) there is:

- Experiential knowing, dealing with the *world of presence*, where imaginal and affective modes play an important part, with the affective the dominant parent. This is the world-view of the mystic and visionary. Presence refers to the unique impact of that particular being, its distinct signature.

On its own this could be seen as the subjective reality of the individual that includes visionary experiences, and process-engaged participatory perception sometimes of an archetypal form (p. 158). However, it also allows for a suspension of prejudged beliefs and knowledge so the experimenter (learner) can create their own categories and interpretation to their experience.

- Presentational knowing focusing on the *world of appearance*, where the imaginal and conceptual modes conjoin with the conceptual mode being the stronger parent. 'The world view of the artist, poet, phenomenologist and discriminating observer' (p. 159).

The imaginal mode of intuition and imagery is primary where interaction with reflection and discrimination yields discernment about patterns and phenomena and their interconnections (Heron, 1992, p. 159). Here phenomenological concerns are relational, forming patterns and moving between Buber's (1958) 'I-it' to the 'I-Thou' forms of knowledge. If facilitated accurately it will flow from grounded experience and offer independent analysis of events. Learning is situated and contextualised.

- Propositional knowing as the *world of essence* where reflection and intention pair as the conceptual and practical modes. The world-view of the inquiring intellect. The conceptual or intention mode is the dominant parent. This world-view stems mainly from reflection and discrimination, and is focused on the essences of, or universal ideals, which we use in various combinations to define the nature of things' (p. 158).

This combination can be viewed as scientific and technical and if isolated from the previous two modes could be labelled 'scientism' (Habermas, 1974). In combination however, it becomes a powerful means of critically examining underlying assumptions, personal and cultural.

- Practical knowing; the *world of existence*. The practical and affective modes engender the world of existence. The world-view of the doer. 'Intention and action are primary, and together with emotion and feeling, create a lived world of enterprise and endeavour, in which deeds encounter what exists' (p. 159).

This combination can be seen as the creation and fostering of social structures and interpersonal relationships when the heart and will work in unison. It can also be the technical or practice world essential for action research type experimentation necessary to live responsibly in relation to our environment. Again if this combination excludes the propositional and imaginal, it could be considered conceptually superficial and dull.

In experiential education, working with the internal world of participants we need to be alert to consistencies between the aforementioned modes or their discontinuities. At any one time one of the modes will be in the foreground while the others will be tacit, falling into the background. According to Heron (1992) an integrated fourfold, simultaneous multi-world view is the characteristic of the educated person.

So far in this chapter learning has been viewed as individualistic through the explanation of the internal capacities of the individual, and the imposition of a holistic frame of reference which is both humanistic and therapeutic (Rogers, 1967; Rowan, 1998) yet I have also said that experiential learning is essentially emancipatory within progressive education. Emancipatory implies a need to feel liberated, but liberated from what? One form of liberation advocated by Mezirow (1999, p. 2) is 'to create new experiences deliberately to expose our mindless frames of references that rely on past forms of interpretation and action, or previously established distinctions and categories without questioning their underlying assumptions'. Mindful learning on the other hand implies an openness to making sense of new experiences using new categorisation on that experience and using more than one perspective in interpretation.

Habermas, when developing his theory of critical social science in opposition to 'scientism' spoke of three 'knowledge-constituitive interests; the technical, the practical and the emancipatory' (Carr and Kemmis, 1986, p. 135), the first of which is mainly instrumental, scientific knowledge and fits loosely with Heron's propositional knowledge, 'a knowing what and why'. Practical knowledge is viewed as an iterative hermeneutic process, a dialogical process, where shared meaning through language develops into an interpretive science, 'a knowing what, how and when' and is similar to Heron's practical knowledge. The cornerstone of emancipatory knowledge is based on Habermas's proposition that there is:

> a basic human interest in rational autonomy and freedom which issues in a demand for the intellectual and material conditions in which non-alienated communication and interaction can occur. This emancipatory interest requires going beyond any narrow concern with subjective meaning in order to acquire an emancipatory knowledge of the objective framework within which communication and social action occur. It is this emancipatory knowledge that critical social science is essentially concerned.
>
> (Carr and Kemmis, 1986, pp. 135–136)

My experience of offering experiential education over the last twenty years, allows me to be convinced that learning from and by experience needs to have this critical reflective science to have educational value. The emancipatory emphasis is about moving beyond imposed restrains about how we acquire knowledge, constraints that are both internal and external that deal with the experience and the interpretation of experience.

Equally it is about taking the cultural and social fabric of society into our reflective frames when we seek to learn by and from experience. Psychotherapeutic education often focuses on the former subjective emphasis while Habermas, Mezirow and followers of critical social science (Carr and Kemmis, 1986) insist on using the latter as a theoretical lens within which the binding of the subjective with the interpersonal and environmental realities are all accounted for in understanding what impinges on the individual's sense of self. This form of emancipation interest Habermas calls critical sciences. The medium used is power. Power within educational relationships occupies the minds of post-modern thinkers. The debate about which knowledge is valid in society, who holds this knowledge, who is best to impart knowledge and assess the legitimacy of another's knowledge are central to critical social sciences and transformative theory. Usher and Edwards (1994, p. 223) ask: 'if emancipation and knowledge are chimeras deployed in the exercise of an omnipresent power, what point is there in challenging dominant practices.' Most education imparts established knowledge without a critique of its relevance or an examination of the underlying assumptions. Usher and Edward's belief is that experiential learning comes closest to post-modern thinking than other forms of teaching such as classroom instruction. However this is predicated on experiential teaching and learning giving equal if not stronger emphasis on the critical reflection of the experience as much as the experience itself. Here is where the essential question of who facilitates experiential learning arises and how is it different from teaching. Teachers who only impart established knowledge are not experiential facilitators, equally educational and organisational trainers who offer tasks and experiences to learners for the purpose of showing them one right way of doing things, or one right way of behaving in social and organisational setting (such as 'good team work'), may be doing an excellent job, but they are not experiential facilitators. The characteristics of facilitators is discussed at length in Chapter 8 of this volume. The essential point to make here is that experiential facilitators are expected to be competent critical reflectors who can hold lightly a multi-perspectival view, will be experienced in working at the different levels of critique, subjective, social and cultural and who do not believe in one truth outside the individual, they live with uncertainty as the norm, wishing only to critically examine beliefs to liberate self and others from the oppressive bondage of imposed interpretative structures.

The experiential learning cycle offers opportunities for the student to voluntarily enter an experience, an encounter, for the purpose of understanding something about him or herself and something about the context and content he or she is engaged with. A typical experience offered as part experiential learning is a psychosocial experience such as learning about group dynamics. This is done by asking the group to engage with some form of groupwork where the task is to understand what goes on in groups at a social, psychological and existential level. Frequent exposure to this type of experience allows students to learn an enormous amount about their behaviour, feelings and thinking in group settings, which is atheoretical at this point. Using the experiential learning cycle, they can move through the encounter, to varying degrees of deep personal reflection about their own intrapsychic world. This often results in students sharing with each other previous family group dynamics and work team dynamics that appear to be similar or very different to the present experience. This phase is often experienced as deconstructive of old polarised interpretations and how to behave in the world. It is sometimes accompanied by a sense of instability which needs competent facilitation. From this encounter they move to conceptualising about group theories and testing new ways of relating to others in the group. Ways that are more congruent with the present than the past. The reflective stage often expands from self-reflection and self-understanding to the social and cultural environment based on the belief that humans are relational and learned behaviour has strong historical and ecological influences. There is therefore a concern to check what behaviours are distorted and constrained by social conditions beyond the individual's control.

Mezirow (1981, p. 6) writes of 'the emancipatory process of becoming critically aware of how and why the structure of psycho-cultural assumptions has come to constrain the way we see ourselves and relationships'. Habermas advocates that such social constraints must be made transparent and if seen to be affecting the individual's right to freedom and rational autonomy, that a theory is found to explain how the constraints are distorting, with the intention of eliminating them. By distilling the historical processes, which have caused subjective meanings to become systematically distorted, the person can work towards liberation. The method for doing this is by critique, through a process of 'relentless criticism of all existing conditions' (Marx cited in Carr and Kemmis, 1986, p. 138), including the power base of learning and educational and social knowledge. Experiential learning in group settings allows for this critique of personal and group forms of established ways of thinking to be witnessed, critiqued and dissolved so that new constructions are co-created which are grounded in the shared experience rather than ideology or compulsive distorted interpretations of others.

## Conclusion

Learning through and from experience requires the recognition of what is subjective, what is social and what is ideology being lived out by the individual and by the group. The emancipatory process needs to address all three levels. Rogers' belief that man is goal oriented and seeks ways of meeting these goals may seem to be negating the social environment and its constraints. There is a criticism of humanistic psychology that it is too individualistic, believing that the power to change and create one's own reality resides in the individual. Habermas (cited in Carr and Kemmis, 1986, p. 138) however, argues that:

> Social groups are prevented from achieving a correct understanding of their situation because, under the sway of ideological systems of ideas, they have passively accepted an illusionary account of reality that prevents them from recognising and pursuing their common interests and goals.

Through an understanding of how ideological forces generate inaccurate self-understanding such frames of references are striped of their power to influence and the person is free to ground their knowledge in the collective experiences and needs. Humanistic education under the heading of pragmatic constructivism and aligned to post-modern critique is very concerned with the social and the political dimension, it always has been, hence its identity with progressive and emancipatory education, with its hallmark that people do not 'move from a false belief to a true one but from an unexamined to a critically examined belief' (Mezirow, 1999, p. 3).

## References

Boud, D., Cohen, R. and Walker, D. (1993) *Using Experience for Learning*. Milton Keynes: SRHE and Open University Press.

Brookfield, S. (2000) Contesting Criticality: Epistemological and Practical Contradictions in Critical Reflection. *2000 AERC Conference Proceedings*. http://www.edst.educ.ubc.ca/aerc/2000/brookfield1-web.htm

Buber, M. (1958) *I and Thou*. New York: Charles Scribner Sons.

128   Josie Gregory

Burgoyne, J. and Reynolds, M. (eds) (1997) *Management Learning: Integrating Perspectives in Theory and Practice*. London: Sage.

Carr, W. and Kemmis, S. (1986) *Becoming Critical: Education, Knowledge and Action Research*. London: The Farmer Press.

Dewey, J. (1938) *Experience and Education*. New York: Macmillan Publishing Co.

Goleman, D. (1996) *Emotional Intelligence*. London: Bloomsbury.

Gregory, J. (1996) *The Psycho-Social Education of Nurses*. Aldershot: Avery.

Habermas, J. C. (1974) *Theory and Practice*. London: Heinemann.

Heron, J. (1974) *The Concept of a Peer Learning Community*. Guildford: University of Surrey, Human Potential Research Project.

Heron, J. (1989) *The Facilitators' Handbook*. London: Kogan Page.

Heron, J. (1992) *Feeling and Personhood. Psychology in Another Key*. London: Sage. http://zeus.sirt.pisa.it/icci/partknow.htm

Heron, J. (1999) *The Complete Facilitator's Handbook*. London: Kogan Page.

Hogan, C. (2000) *Facilitating Empowerment*. London: Kogan Page.

Jarvis, P. (1985) *The Sociology of Adult and Continuing Education*. London: Croom Helm.

Jarvis, P., Holford, J. and Griffin, C. (1998) *The Theory and Practice of Learning*. London: Kogan Page.

Knowles, M. (1978) *The Adult Learner – A Neglected Species* (2nd edition). Houston: Gulf.

Kolb, D. A. (1984) *Experiential Learning – Experience as the Source of Learning and Development*. London: Prentice-Hall.

Mezirow, J. (1981) A Critical Theory of Adult Learning and Education. *Adult Education*, 32(1), pp. 3–27.

Mezirow, J. (1999) *Transformation Theory – Postmodern Issues. 1999 AERC Conference Proceedings*. http://www.edst.educ.ubc.ca/aerc/1999/99mezirow.htm.

Mulligan, J. (1993) Activating Internal Processes in Experiential Learning. Chapter 3 in *Using Experience for Learning*. Boud, D., Cohen, R. and Walker, D. (eds). Milton Keynes: The Society for Research into Higher Education and The Open University Press.

Postle, D. (1988) *The Mind Gymnasium*. London: Macmillan/Papermac (digital edition available in 2001 at: http://www.mind-gymnasium.com/).

Postle, D. (1993) Putting the Heart Back into Learning. Chapter 2 in *Using Experience for Learning*. Boud, D., Cohen, R. and Walker, D. (eds). Milton Keynes: The Society for Research into Higher Education and The Open University Press.

Rawlinson, A. (1997) *The Book of Enlightened Masters*. Chicago, IL: Open Court.

Rogers, C. R. (1967) *On Becoming a Person*. London: Constable.

Rogers, C. R. (1983) *Freedom to Learn for the 80's* (2nd edition). Columbus: OH: Merrill

Rowan, J. (1993) *The Transpersonal: Psychotherapy and Counselling*. London: Routledge.

Rowan, J. (1998) *The Reality Game* (2nd edition). London: Routledge.

Usher, R. and Edwards, R. (1994) *Postmodernism and Education: Different Voices, Different Worlds*. London: Routledge.

Weil, S. and McGill, I. (1989) *Making Sense of Experiential Learning: Diversity in Theory and Practice*. Milton Keynes: The Society for the Research into Higher Education and Open University Press.

Weisbord, M. R. (1987) *Productive Workplaces: Organising and Managing for Dignity, Meaning and Community*. Oxford: Jossey-Bass.

Williamson, B. (1979) *Education, Social Structure and Development*. London: Macmillan Press.

# Chapter 10

# Experiential methods of teaching and learning

*Paul Tosey*

This chapter offers a compendium of experiential methods of teaching and learning, drawing on methods relevant to adult learning in educational, personal development and management development contexts.

Defining the scope of 'experiential methods' is somewhat problematic, as are notions of experience and experiential learning themselves (e.g. Boud *et al.*, 1993). The approach here is to focus on methods that might be appropriate to the 'concrete experience' stage of Kolb's (1984) experiential learning cycle.[1] In other words, while observation, reflection and planning are all aspects of experience, this chapter concerns itself with methods through which the material that can be observed, reflected upon and planned for, is actually encountered in the 'here and now'.

For this reason I have not included a wide range of practices that support experiential learning and which are likely to be prominent in any experientially based curriculum. These include ideas about reflection, the use of learning contracts and so on. Also, because they are dealt with elsewhere in this and other volumes, I have not addressed principles of enquiry-based or problem-based learning, which are fundamentally experiential, or of work experience.

The chapter's purpose is primarily to indicate the array of experiential methods and processes available for use within educational programmes (see also Tosey and Gregory, 2001). The selection here reflects a cross-fertilisation between fields such as management development, adult learning, and counselling and psychotherapy, therefore the particular use of experiential methods needs to be adapted to the purposes of the specific educational context. The categories adopted here – which represent a somewhat arbitrary grouping of ideas and is neither definitive nor mutually exclusive – are as follows:

1   attention and presence: methods intended to enhance states of being and awareness;
2   creative thinking and accelerated learning;
3   the gymnasium principle: tasks, enactment and expression;
4   encounter: increasing self-awareness;
5   groupwork;
6   the imaginal: using imagination and intuition for inner exploration.

## Part 1: attention and presence: enhancing states of being and awareness

Personal development will often lead to enhanced sensory awareness and emotional sensitivity (see Stevens, 1971). Awareness was, and remains, a central feature of the 'curriculum' of ancient disciplines such as t'ai chi chuan (a form of graceful, rhythmic, meditative exercise originating in China), yoga and Zen Buddhism. In contemporary personal development, Gestalt in particular (e.g. Clarkson, 1989) emphasises the value of present-time, sensory awareness, of what we sense and feel in the 'here and now'. In Gestalt it is suggested that people spend much of their existence thinking about the past or the future.

The idea that 'mindfulness' in everyday awareness can transform our experience is a frequent theme. Rowan (1998, pp. 161ff) advocates the development of a particular form of awareness or consciousness, less focused than usual, and a whole-body rather than intellectual awareness. He likens this to Freud's 'free-floating attention' and calls it 'listening with the fourth ear'. In Neuro-Linguistic Programming (NLP) (Bandler and Grinder, 1975; O'Connor and Seymour, 2003) a related distinction is found between a defocused, expanded peripheral vision and foveal (focused) vision.

These and related disciplines also attend to the development of states of being and presence. This may extend to interest in 'altered' states of consciousness, for example, the trance modes or states of attention found in autogenics and in some methods accelerated learning (see below). Modalities such as NLP take the view that everyday consciousness consists of varying states, and that it may be misleading to mark out some as extraordinary through the label 'altered'.

In the self-help technique of co-counselling (see the website of Co-counselling International, which includes manuals that have many experiential exercises), attention means deep listening to the cues of what another is saying and doing. It may involve all the five senses, kinaesthetic, auditory, visual, tactile and olfactory. Giving full attention means that the counsellor listens attentively without interrupting and without non-verbal interference apart from a steady gaze, setting aside their own interpretations, concentrating on the other person's story and their needs, and letting go of any need to take action.

There are copious methods of developing states of relaxation (in which the person is free of unnecessary emotional and physical tension), particularly in programmes concerned with stress reduction. Many self-help sources exist, for example, the 'Relaxation and Stress Reduction Workbook' (Davis *et al.*, 2000). Methods include Autogenics ('self-generating'), which is based on self-hypnosis. Using simple mental exercises, according to the British Autogenic Society website, the person attains a 'passive concentration', a state of 'alert but detached awareness', which is considered helpful for stress management and many stress-related conditions.

Most meditation practices (e.g. Gunaratana, 2002) are claimed to be calming and to lead to an internal silence, so that new insights and understandings develop. Contemporary Western interest in meditation has been prompted by exploration of Eastern religions, though is often practised mainly for stress management and relaxation.

In Zen, and in Buddhism generally, meditation begins by awareness of breathing, observing our own mental events non-judgementally. The quality and rhythm of breathing is significant in many other modes of development. Breathing is a primal experience. Rowan notes (1993, p. 192) that breathing works on physical, emotional, intellectual and spiritual levels. It has a significant role in voice work, as well as therapeutic modes involving regression (see Hendricks, 1995).

Bodily awareness may be enhanced through movement (see below) and through massage, forms of which exist throughout the world. Applications range from the use of touch for health and relaxation to specialised methods of healing, such as Shiatsu and acupressure, and therapeutic and developmental modes of bodywork. These specialised forms require the practitioner to be properly trained. Touch is a universally important human experience, as well as one around which many taboos exist. Using touch is common in humanistic approaches and personal development workshops. For example, an icebreaker may encourage people to make some form of physical contact and energising activities may involve brief massage. But where touch is not explicitly a working medium, and not explicit in the educational contract, practitioners need to take care with use of touch so that is not experienced as invasive, sexual or otherwise inappropriate.

## Part 2: creative thinking

Many methods of creative thinking are related to the idea that the two hemispheres of the brain have different functions (see Sperry, 1964; Ornstein, 1972). The typical associations are that the left brain is logical, sequential, rational, analytical and objective; the right brain is intuitive, holistic, synthesising and subjective. Researchers (e.g. McCrone, 1998) have challenged the somewhat simplistic and romantic nature of the distinction. If treated as a metaphor rather than as a matter of scientific truth, the left brain-right brain model is a useful, aid to 'thinking about thinking' even if it does not explain the workings of the brain.

Brainstorming is a creative problem-solving process whereby a person or group generates ideas without censoring or evaluating them (see Buzan, 2003), akin therefore to the psychoanalytic practice of free association. The principle is that by 'turning off' the judging, censoring part of the mind (i.e. typically the 'left brain') people can freely produce creative, apparently nonsensical ideas which they might otherwise dismiss as irrelevant or stupid. Often these provide useful connections or new ways of perceiving a problem. A brainstorming session may last a set length of time (e.g. 10 minutes), or until the flow of ideas has dried up. Participants then move on to exploring and evaluating the brainstormed ideas.

Mind Mapping is a note-taking and note-making technique, also associated with Buzan (Buzan and Buzan, 2003), who argues that notes based on spontaneous patterns that are developed around a central topic or theme are much more conducive to recall than those prepared in the traditional (within Western societies) linear form. Pattern notes (mind maps), utilising key words, images and colour have, suggests Buzan, the benefit of engaging both sides of the brain.

'Lateral thinking' is a related practice devised by de Bono (1990). This refers to non-linear, non-logical thinking, the purpose of which is to make creative associations.

Synectics is a creative problem-solving methodology developed by Gordon (1961). It makes use of metaphor and analogy to break free from constraining assumptions or mind-sets – essentially, by making the strange familiar, or by making the familiar strange. He believed that the emotional and irrational components of creative behaviour are more important than the intellectual, but need to be understood and used as tools in order to increase creative output. Synectics is used in business, education, and other settings (e.g. Nolan, 1989).

## Rehearsal

Mental, imagined rehearsal of a performance is another form of creative method ('live' rehearsal of interpersonal skills is addressed under 'enactment'). Mental rehearsal relates to our ability to practise a process or activity in our minds (Dilts, 1998). In NLP, it is used to strengthen or improve behavioural performance, cognitive thinking patterns and internal states. When applied to behavioural performance, mental rehearsal involves creating internal representations, in the form of images, sounds and feelings, of some behaviour or performance we desire to enact or improve. Mental rehearsal – a slight misnomer, as the rehearsal is by no means purely cognitive – is used extensively in sports psychology. It is reckoned by some that mental rehearsal can be as effective as actual practice.

Visualisation is a mental process using 'the mind's eye' as a way of accessing imagery and internal information. It deals with inner events through visual rather than verbal thought and may be done consciously (remembering or imagining) or unconsciously (dreaming). Visualisation is relevant to mental rehearsal and also to the imaginal realm (see section below). The assumptions behind such techniques as 'creative visualisation' (Gawain, 1995) and 'imagework' (Glouberman, 2004) are that it is possible to bring about what people want to create in their lives.

Also relevant here is the notion of positive thinking. Peale (1953) was one of the first to write about this and he expounded the view that it is more constructive to focus on the positive (what we want), than on the negative (what we wish to avoid). This principle has been used in personal development applications, (e.g. in the NLP practice of imagining personal goals or outcomes). Goleman (1996, pp. 86–87) comments on the importance of hope and the real effects of one's expectations, but if overdone, positive thinking can become unrealistic.

## Accelerated learning

Meier (2000) refers to a variety of methods that claim to engage faster or more efficient learning, such as speed reading.

Educational Kinesiology was developed initially by Paul Dennison[2] to help people with learning difficulties, but is available generally to enhance learning, creativity and enjoyment. Its emphasis is on the relationship between body movement and brain functioning. Bodily co-ordination and integration are significant not only physically but also mentally, and educational kinesiology uses movement to enhance neural pathways. For activities see, for example, Smith (2002).

Suggestopedia is a process that enables the learning of, for example, language through unconscious processing. Hooper-Hensen (1992, p. 197) says, 'Suggestopedia is the creation of a doctor and psychiatrist, Georgi Lozanov from the University of Sofia, Bulgaria. The method was developed in the 1960s and began as an experiment to induce enhanced memorization in schools'. Hooper-Hensen notes that the term 'suggestopedia' is misleading, and has unwanted connotations. Lozanov now uses the term 'desuggestive learning', and eschews the use of any form of hypnosis. The Society for Effective Affective Learning (SEAL) was founded in 1983 to promote Lozanov's work.

## Part 3: the gymnasium principle: tasks, enactment and expression

Much experiential learning involves the gymnasium principle (Postle, 1988), where the programme or workshop provides a safe practice ground for trying out behaviours and skills, and for expressing emotion. There are multitudinous exercises of this kind in sources on lifeskills training, interpersonal skills development, and counselling (see, for example, Heron's six category analysis[3]). A similar approach may be taken to interpersonal skills in areas of assertiveness, listening, interviewing, negotiating and so on.

### Tasks and simulation

Real-time tasks, games and simulations are significant forms of experiential learning method. All kinds of tasks and projects can engage learners in here-and-now experience that provides rich material for reflection. Games can be very effective because in play, people are most likely to be spontaneous, uninhibited and expressive.

Simulations generally place participants in specified roles within a simulated action arena in order to experience the dynamics of a 'real' situation within an educational setting. Simulations can range from individual activities to full-scale events simulating organisations, communities and so on. Many simulations also make use of computer technology.

A variant on this theme is outdoor education,[4] including outward-bound training. This differs in that the experience is contrived but not simulated. It takes participants out of the classroom and, typically, into rural, adventuring setting where, activities such as abseiling, orienteering, and outdoor survival become the source for learning (see, for example, Snow, 1997). Outward-bound training is often used as a team development format, as issues of interpersonal relating are heightened by dependence on other people for success and even survival (Huczynski, 1983). Needs for physical and psychological safety become very important in these situations and effective facilitation should provide for these aspects during the experience, as well as for extensive debriefing through which participants can reflect on their experiential learning.

## Enactment

A key figure here is J. L. Moreno (1889–1974), the originator of psychodrama (an 'action method of group psychotherapy', Holmes and Karp, 1991, p. 7). He is recognised as a pioneer of humanistic, existential therapeutic practice. Psychodrama is a method of dramatic (re)-enactment of human encounters. It is used as a therapeutic modality and as a working method in personal development workshops.

The principal emphasis of role-play, which is derived from psychodrama, is on behavioural performance in simulated, training-type settings, where participants take specified roles to rehearse or act out an interaction; to practise particular skills (e.g. assertiveness); to explore interactions from others' perspectives and to explore options for handling a given scenario. Thus it may lead to attitudinal and/or behavioural change, as well as promote self-awareness. A practical guide is Bolton and Heathcote (1999). In practice, people often feel uncomfortable with role-play's performative aspects and apparent artificiality – it is a powerful tool for experiential learning that needs careful preparation and sensitive facilitation.

Behavioural change and skills development may be assisted by coaching, a notion imported from sport. Coaching is usually, and primarily, a process in which a facilitator – often an external trainer or consultant – assists a manager to perform better (see Whitmore, 2002). As well as improving skills and developing new behaviour, coaching also involves reflective, verbal sessions. A variant is the Zen-influenced, inner game approach (Gallwey, 2002).

The emotional dimension of enactment is emphasised more in methods such as co-counselling, where the focus is on the cathartic release of distress in order to reach insight. Co-counselling has many exercise formats that enable the person to 'act into' emotions or types of behaviour.

## Creative expression

Experiential methods often involve creative expression, or make use of art forms or media (painting, drawing, music and sculpting), common in specific modes of development, like Psychosynthesis (Assagioli, 1975).

Creative writing (Hunt and Sampson, 1998), including biography, poetry, short stories and so on, is a valuable medium for self-expression. In experiential workshops, exercises such as that of writing one's own obituary encourage individuals to review their life and gain a different perspective on the present. Torbert (Torbert and Fisher, 1992) has used autobiographical writing as a personal, and management or leadership, development tool.

Story telling is used in education and in therapy (Gersie and King, 1989). More recently, story telling has been introduced into organisations as a way of acknowledging, capturing and working expressively with people's experience of work. Story telling is a traditional form of communication with many possible functions – entertainment, myth-making, oral history and more. The notion of the 'teaching story' is particularly associated with the Sufis. Idries Shah has introduced this form to the West, and has published several volumes of wonderful stories about the Mullah Nasrudin, the Sufi 'wise fool' (e.g. Shah, 1973).

Dance and movement of many kinds are a prime form experiential method. Movement is utilised in numerous modes of development (e.g. NLP) and also has many specific forms and practices (e.g. the Alexander technique; Dance Movement Therapy; Feldenkrais; eurythmy). An example that is conducive to general educational use is circle dance which seeks to give people in groups a sense of pleasure and purpose in 'moving together', reflecting solidarity in their community. In contemporary applications, teams can debrief dancing together as models of how they operate at work – are they all, for example, 'dancing to the same tune'? The metaphor of 'being in step with each other' is also powerful.

Voice work is another expressive mode. It is essentially a whole-body and whole-person activity, as voice production depends on breathing, posture and movement, is directly linked to emotional expression, and has a spiritual dimension too. Some practitioners have a background in music or singing, and draw on traditions from around the world including Tibet, Mongolia and more. Others have had a primary interest in the psychological and emotional significance of voice, and experience an enhanced ability to sing as a delightful added benefit. 'Voice Movement Therapy' is a particular mode of expressive arts therapy.

## Part 4: encounter and self-awareness

This category concerns using encounter between people. Encounter is in 'real time' – between people being themselves, rather than performing a role or enacting an exercise. This distinction is not hard and fast; psychodrama, for instance, also embraces encounter.

Educating oneself or learning to relate to others on an emotional level has to involve some self-awareness, which is a dimension of most methods, particularly those in the previous category of 'enactment'. Self-awareness refers to our own nature and behaviour, and seeing ourselves as others see us. It encapsulates what is expressed by, for example, the exhortation inscribed above the Delphic oracle ('know thyself'); and by Robert Burns' poem, 'To a Louse' ('O wad some Power the giftie gie us To see oursels as ithers see us!').

### The human encounter

Buber (1958) identified the polarities of 'I - Thou' and 'I - It' as the two forms of meeting that human beings can experience in relation to each other and the world in general. An 'I - Thou' meeting is characterised by a genuine interest in the other person, valuing the 'otherness' of the person whose humanity is perceived as being an end rather than a means to an end. In an 'I - It' meeting, the other person is seen as an object and is utilised primarily as an end. In reality, we experience a rhythmic alteration between the two. Interpersonal dialogue is a therapeutic approach developed by Hycner (1993) and others that is based on Buber's concept of I - Thou, which is also the basis of 'Enlightenment Intensives'. Rowan (1993, pp. 148–149) regards the latter as having the potential for discovery of the 'real self'.

Elements of encounter that we take for granted in everyday life may be placed, as it were, under the microscope in educational settings. For example, Heron worked with 'the phenomenology of the gaze'. In this he considered eye-contact through the mutual gaze to be a primal experience, a deeply significant human encounter.

Encounter also typically involves disclosure, sharing with others aspects of our internal world. Disclosure can have many forms, such as self-assessing attitudes and competence before soliciting feedback from others in self and peer assessment,[5] or sharing our own worldview and experience with others. The aim of disclosure is usually to be transparent (Jourard, 1971), better understood and authentic.

Research shows that people need to feel a strong sense of trust, in an environment of empathy and understanding, to self-disclose

(Gregory, 1996). Workshops often involve trust exercises. These require, and thereby aim to build, a sufficient level of trust between participants to enable disclosure and honesty. A well-known trust exercise is the blind walk. In pairs, one partner is blindfolded and the other is the guide who must assist the blindfolded person to explore their world safely.

The Johari Window, which was developed by Luft and Ingram (1967) (which they called the Johari Window by conflating their first names, Joe and Harry), is a two-by-two matrix with dimensions of self-disclosure, and seeking feedback. This creates four sections or panes (the public arena; the hidden arena; the blind spot; and the unknown arena). The internal sectional dividers are movable so that the window panes can open further depending on the degree of disclosure and amount of feedback.

### Feedback for self-awareness

Encounter methods aim to enhance participants' self-awareness through drawing attention to their behaviour and their impact on others. It is also promoted through a very wide range of feedback formats which do not necessarily involve the type of encounter described above. But they may be used as a basis for discussion between the respondent and a facilitator or peers. These include methods as diverse as the Enneagram (Palmer, 1995), the Myers-Briggs Type Indicator (Briggs-Myers and Myers, 1995), and myriad other forms of profiling, including psychometric testing.

In management, 360° feedback has been in vogue for some years (Ward, 1997). The intention of this is to ensure that managers are sensitive to their impact upon, and the views of, those other than their boss. Used well this can be a powerful developmental experience. Various sources list guidelines or rules for giving and receiving feedback (such as that it is specific, timely and actionable). Handled unskilfully, feedback may do more harm than good (e.g. the person who interjects with 'let me give you some feedback'...and launches into unsolicited criticism).

## Part 5: groupwork

Experiential learning often takes place in a group format. There is not space here to outline the knowledge base that any facilitator of groups should have to hand, but see Benson (2001) or Jaques (2000). Suffice it to say that there are many theories and models of group dynamics, and related trainings. An educator using a group format should be familiar with some models of group dynamics (e.g. Bion, 1961), group roles, group stages or phases (e.g. Tuckman and Jensen, 1977) and the need for ground rules (a process of contracting), discussed elsewhere in this volume.[6]

First, there are techniques that might be used in any educational group. However, just about all the methods and activities described here can be used in groupwork, and the techniques described below only scratch the surface of the formats and processes available in groupwork.

A 'check-in' is a period of time at the beginning of a group session for participants to arrive and prepare for the group's task. This allows participants to 'park' issues that are on their minds; to declare what is 'on top' for them (i.e. uppermost in their awareness); or to share news and to focus on the here and now.

An 'ice-breaker' is literally an exercise designed to 'break the ice', in other words to help participants overcome the anxiety and social difficulty at the beginning of the event. For example, participants may be asked to spend a few minutes in pairs telling each other something about themselves. Depending on the nature of the event, the 'ice' may be seen as something to avoid or to break through as swiftly as possible, or perhaps as a vehicle for drawing attention to group dynamics.

'Energisers' are exercises that raise or increase the level of arousal. These are usually physical activities employed to change the level of attention and arousal in a workshop. An example is where participants stand in a circle giving themselves a brief massage by brushing themselves down with their hands, as if brushing off anxiety or tension, starting with the head and moving downwards to the feet.

A 'buzz group' is a small group convened in the middle of a workshop or lecture to discuss and respond to workshop or lecture content. This changes attention and format; the 'buzz' comes from the sound of several groups in discussion.

A 'fishbowl' typically involves a selection of participants in some activity in the centre of the room, with other participants observing or witnessing in an outer circle. Those engaging in the activity are the 'goldfish'. This format has the advantage that those looking in on the goldfish can also engage in the activity. First, they can observe and be charged with giving feedback to participants. Second, there can be provision for a 'tag' system whereby an observer changes places with a goldfish.

Another option is to use this as a dialogical format, with an inner circle and an outer circle. This can be an alternative to a presentation. Those in the outer circle are attuned more to listening, and need to make a conscious decision to move in order to enter the dialogue. Those in the inner circle are typically less anxious about airing their questions, and can address concerns in a more conversational way. The facilitator can attend during the process to the limited number of participants in the needs of the inner circle. This is a little different from a goldfish bowl, which in any case is a somewhat cold, hard and wet metaphor, so I call it a 'campfire'.

There are also many specific forms of groupwork, for example: Sensitivity Training started in 1946 at the New Britain Teacher's College Connecticut (see, for example, Back, 1972). It was designed to explore the use of small groups as a vehicle for personal and social change. The goal of Sensitivity Training is change through self-expression, rather than self-expression for its own sake. As in encounter, the experience tends to be emotionally intensive.

'Encounter group', (Schutz, 1971) and 'basic encounter', operating on person-centred principles and developed by Carl Rogers (Bozarth, 1986) are two specific forms of this. Schutz's practice of 'open encounter', originating at the Esalen Institute at Big Sur, California in the 1960s, works by facilitating encounters between participants in the here and now. It is often associated with a confrontational style – encouraging people to voice their irritation, anger, disappointment and so on – with others in the room to become authentic. Encounter groups are, according to Schutz and others, capable of achieving great intimacy and releasing joy; but they can be anxiety provoking and potentially destructive to those who feel insecure.

Another variety is the 'T-group', which stands for 'training group'. The T-group method is used for personal and/or team development and was a core method of Organisation Development in the 1960s. According to Aronson (1994, p. 183), 'the first T-Group was an accident that happened when participants in a workshop conducted by Kurt Lewin asked to sit in on the observers' debriefing sessions. The result was a lively and exciting debate, and the practice continued'. Participants are supported in exploring their interpersonal relationships, and the facilitator may intervene in group process or interpersonal conflict, but does not structure or lead the group. Often a T-group will have no task other than to study its own process.

## Part 6: the imaginal

The imaginal world is 'the world we enter when we make up stories or see visions, or hear internal music, and so on' (Rowan, 1993, p. 53): it is a rich inner world of imagery, symbols and myths, and many modes of personal development (e.g. Psychosynthesis) encourage it. The main distinction from the 'creativity' category is that the imaginal is concerned with people's inner worlds and often with the transpersonal (Rowan, 1993) dimension of development. Such work typically has its roots in a combination of Eastern and Western mystical traditions, modern psychology, and psychic and spiritual development.

Affirmation is common in new age sources but is a long-established practice.

> There are many practical applications of the principle that what we affirm and program into the unconscious belief system, we tend in subtle ways to bring about... The basic principle has long been a core idea in the esoteric inner-core understandings of the world's spiritual traditions.
>
> (Harman, 1988, p. 77)

The process of affirming an image makes it stronger and more effective by activating the creative energies needed to achieve the outcome.

The history of visualisation includes its use in early religions and philosophies as a tool for personal growth and transformation, while shamanic healers visualised going on a journey into a person's world in order to restore them to health (Samuels and Samuels, 1975). Guided fantasy is a method for enabling people to access their creative imagination and for enabling inner experience to be brought to conscious awareness. It has been defined in various other ways, for example 'creative visualisation' (Gawain, 1995), 'interactive daydreaming' or 'active imagination'. Guided fantasy can have many different applications. Its basic *modus operandi* is that the person is encouraged to become relaxed and is given some basic, fairly general information about a situation, place or journey; they are then encouraged to supply the detail from their own imagination. The guide or facilitator prompts them from time to time with further very open-ended suggestions or questions, and as the corresponding detail is added by the subject's imagination, or symbolic memory, the whole experience deepens. Subsequently the person may be encouraged to draw, paint, act, talk about or model the detail of their imaginative experience. This can bring fresh insight, an altered mood or a different perspective.

The notion of the heroic quest is that, rather than seeing each person as developing towards some standard ideal state, we can see each person's life as a quest or journey. This idea is present in myths throughout the world (Campbell, 1985, p. 161) and focuses on the idea of gaining self-knowledge through journeying into the unknown and facing and overcoming ordeals. The outward journey of the hero myth is paralleled by the inward journey of psychic development. Several ancient symbol systems are thought to represent this journey; for example, the symbol of the labyrinth (Dawes *et al.*, 2005); the chakras (Myss, 1997); the tarot; and the tree of life. The tarot is one of many symbol systems that can be used in personal development as a symbolic representation of development, or as an aid to reflection and meditation (see Greer, 2002).

## Notes

1  Cross-reference to Chapter 9 that describes Kolb's cycle.
2  Trademarked as Brain Gym, see http://www.braingym.org/, accessed 16.7.2005.
3  Refers to Heron (1990).
4  See, for example, http://www.outdoored.com/, accessed 16.7.2005.
5  Cross-reference to Chapter 15.
6  Cross-reference to Chapter 13.

## References

Aronson, E. (1994) 'Communication in sensitivity-training groups', in French, W. L., Bell, C. H. and Zawacki, R. A. (eds) (4th edn) *Organization Development and Transformation*, Burr Ridge, IL: Irwin

Assagioli, R. (1975) *Psychosynthesis; A Manual of Principles and Techniques*, Wellingborough, Northants: Turnstone Press

Back, K. W. (1972) *Beyond Words: The Story of Sensitivity Training and the Encounter Movement*, New York: Russell Sage Foundation

Bandler, R. and Grinder, J. (1975) *The Structure of Magic: A Book About Language and Therapy*, Palo Alto, CA: Science and Behaviour Books

Benson, J. (2001) *Working More Creatively with Groups* (2nd edn), London: Routledge

Bion, W. (1961) *Experiences in Groups*, London: Tavistock Publications

Bolton, G. and Heathcote, D. (1999) *So You Want to Use Role-Play? A New Approach in How to Plan*, London: Trentham Books

Boud, D., Cohen, R. and Walker, D. (1993) *Using Experience for Learning*, Buckingham: The Society for Research into Higher Education and Open University Press

Bozarth, J. D. (1986) 'The basic encounter group: an alternative view', *The Journal for Specialists in Group Work*, 11(4), 228–232 (website): http://personcentered.com/group1.htm, accessed 16.7.2005

Briggs-Myers, I. and Myers, P. B. (1995) *Gifts Differing*, Palo Alto, CA: Davies-Black Publishing

The British Autogenic Society (website): http://www.autogenic-therapy.org.uk/, accessed 16.7.2005

Buber, M. (1958) *I and Thou*, New York: Charles Scribner's Sons

Buzan, T. (2003) *Use Your Head*, London: BBC Books

Buzan, T. and Buzan, B. (2003) *The Mind Map Book: Radiant Thinking – Major Evolution in Human Thought*, London: BBC Books

Campbell, J. (1985) *Myths To Live By*, London: Paladin, Granada

Clarkson, P. (1989) *Gestalt Counselling in Action*, London: Sage

Co-counselling International (website): http://www.dpets.demon.co.uk/cciuk/index.html, accessed 16.7.2005

Davis, M., McKay, M. and Eshelman, E. R. (2000) *The Relaxation and Stress Reduction Workbook* (5th edn), Oakland, CA: New Harbinger publications

Dawes, J., Dolley, J. and Isaksen, I. (2005) *The Quest: Exploring a Sense of Soul*, Winchester: O Books

de Bono, E. (1990) *Lateral Thinking*, London: Penguin

Dilts, R. (1998) *'Harnessing the Imagination'* (website): http://www.nlpu.com/, accessed 16.7.2005

Gallwey, T. (2002) *The Inner Game of Work*, London: Texere Publishing Ltd

Gawain, S. (1995) *Creative Visualisation*, California: New World Library

Gersie, A. and King, N. (1989) *Storymaking in Education and Therapy*, London: Jessica Kingsley

Glouberman, D. (2004) *Life Choices, Life Changes: Develop your Personal Vision through Imagework*, London: Hodder & Stoughton

Goleman, D. (1996) *Emotional Intelligence*, London: Bloomsbury

Gordon, W. J. J. (1961) *Synectics; The Development Of Creative Capacity*, New York: Harper & Row

Greer, M. (2002) *Tarot for Your Self: A Workbook for Personal Transformation*, New Jersey: New Page Books

Gregory, J. (1996) *The Psycho-Social Education of Nurses*, Aldershot: Avery

Gunaratana, B. H. (2002) *Mindfulness in Plain English*, Somerville, MA: Wisdom Publications

Hanson, P. (1973) 'The Johari window: a model for soliciting and giving feedback', in Pfeiffer, J. W. and Jones, J. E. (eds) *Annual Handbook for Group Facilitators*, La Jolla, CA: University Associates

Harman, W. (1988) *Global Mind Change*, Indianapolis: Knowledge Systems Inc.

Hendricks, G. (1995) *Conscious Breathing*, New York: Bantam Books

Heron, J. (1990) *Helping the Client*, London: Sage

Heron, J. (1999) *The Complete Facilitators Handbook*, London: Kogan Page

Holmes, P. and Karp, M. (1991) (eds) *Psychodrama: Inspiration and Technique*, London: Routledge

Hooper-Hensen, G. (1992) 'Suggestopedia: a way of learning for the 21st century', in Mulligan, J. and Griffin, C. (eds) *Empowerment Through Experiential Learning: Exploration of Good Practice*, London: Kogan Page, pp. 197–207

Huczynski, A. A. (1983) *Encyclopedia of Management Development Methods*, Aldershot: Gower

Hunt, C. and Sampson, F. (eds) (1998) *The Self on the Page: Theory and Practice of Creative Writing in Personal Development*, London: Jessica Kingsley Publishers

Hycner, R. (1993) *Between Person and Person: Towards a Dialogical Psychotherapy*, New York: Gestalt Journal Press

Jaques, D. (2000) *Learning in Groups*, London: Routledge Farmer

Jourard, S. (1971) *The Transparent Self*, New York: van Nostrand Reinhold Company Inc.

Kolb, D. (1984) *Experiential Learning: Experience As The Source of Learning and Development*, New Jersey: Prentice-Hall

Luft, J. and Ingram, H. (1967) *Of Human Interaction: The Johari Model*, Palo Alto, CA: Mayfield

McCrone, J. (1998) *Going Inside: A Tour Around a Single Moment of Consciousness*, London: Faber

Meier, D. (2000) *The Accelerated Learning Handbook*, San Francisco, CA: Berrett-Koehler

Myss, C. (1997) *Anatomy of the Spirit*, London: Bantam Books

Nolan, V. (1989) *The Innovator's Handbook: The Skills of Innovative Management – Problem Solving, Communication, and Teamwork*, USA: Penguin

O'Connor, J. and Seymour, J. (2003) *Introducing NLP Neuro-Linguistic Programming*, London: Harper Collins

Ornstein, R. (1972) *The Psychology of Consciousness*, Harmondsworth: Penguin Books

Palmer, H. (1995) *The Enneagram in Love and Work*, San Francisco, CA: Harper and Row

Peale, N. (1953) *The Power of Positive Thinking*, London: Cedar Books, Heinemann

Postle, D. (1988) *The Mind Gymnasium*, London: Macmillan/Papermac (available as digital edition via http://www.mind-gymnasium.com/, accessed 16.7.2005)

Rowan, J. (1993) *The Transpersonal*, London: Routledge

Rowan, J. (1998) *The Reality Game* (2nd edn), London: Routledge

Samuels, M. D. and Samuels, N. S. (1975) *Seeing With the Mind's Eye: The History, Techniques and Uses of Visualization*, New York: Random House

Schutz, W. C. (1971) *Joy: Expanding Human Awareness*, London: Souvenir Press

Shah, I. (1973) *The Exploits of the Incredible Mulla Nasrudin*, London: Picador

Smith, A. (2002) *Move It: Physical Movement and Learning*, Stafford: Network Educational Press Ltd

Snow, H. (1997) *Indoor/Outdoor Team Building Games for Trainers: Powerful Activities from the World of Adventure-Based Team Building and Ropes Courses*, London: McGraw-Hill

The Society for Effective Affective Learning (SEAL) (website): http://www.seal.org.uk/, accessed 16.7.2005

Sperry, R. (1964) 'The great cerebral commisure', *Scientific American, Jan.*, pp. 142–152, offprint no. 174

Stevens, J. O. (1971) *Awareness: Exploring, Experimenting, Experiencing*, Moab, Utah: Real People Press

Torbert, W. R. and Fisher, D. (1992) 'Autobiographical awareness as a catalyst for managerial and organisational learning', *Management Education and Development*, vol. 23, part 3, Autumn 1992, pp. 184–198

Tosey, P. and Gregory, J. (2001) *A Dictionary of Personal Development*, London: Whurr

Tuckman, B. W. and Jensen, M. A. C. (1977) 'Stages of small group development revisited', *Group and Organizational Studies*, vol. 2, pp. 419–427.

Ward, P. (1997) *360-Degree Feedback*, London: Chartered Institute of Personnel and Development

Whitmore, J. (2002) *Coaching for Performance*, London: Nicholas Brealey

# Chapter 11

# Practice-based and problem-based learning

*Peter Jarvis*

Like Socratic teaching (Chapter 7) both problem- and practice-based learning are teaching methods which use certain forms of self-directed learning and group learning in order to enable individuals and groups to learn in practice situations. Despite their names, practice-based and problem-based learning are facilitative and experiential teaching methods which are becoming very popular in the professions; the former has always been undertaken in apprenticeship systems and through practice placements during training but the latter has perhaps gained its popularity a result of the innovations introduced in health sciences education at McMaster University in Canada. The reasons for its growth lie with the fact that it is also practice-oriented and it is about integrated knowledge rather than the disciplines. Underlying this chapter is the idea that the place of learning is a practice setting rather than a traditional classroom. Schön (1987, p. 37) called these practicums:

> a setting designed for the task of learning a practice. In a context that approximates the practice world, students learn by doing, although their doing usually falls short of real-world work...(it) is a virtual world, relatively free of pressures, distractions, and the risks of the real one to which, nevertheless, it refers.

Even so, a great deal of practice-based learning actually occurs in the real-world, under slightly sheltered conditions.

This chapter, therefore, starts by examining the notion of practical knowledge and, thereafter, looks at both practice-based and problem-based learning, and it concludes with a few critical comments.

## Part 1: practical knowledge

Traditionally institutions of education taught the theory underlying practice and then students went out into their practice in order to apply theory to practice. However, the idea that 'there is nothing as practical as a good theory' is something that seems rather artificial nowadays. I well remember, when I was a teacher in a College of Education preparing school teachers, how the bored students would return to college after their teaching practice quite excited about what they had been doing, but telling us that what we taught barely resembled the realities of their teaching experience. I can also remember an experienced teacher telling the students to forget what they had learned in college because now was the time when they would start to learn to be a school teacher. So what was wrong with our understanding of what we were doing? Some claimed that there is nothing as practical as good theory and therefore either our theory was wrong, or the students had not learned it correctly or, perhaps, theory is not to be applied to practice.

Basically a number of things were wrong, and they revolved around the higher status of theory and the lower status of practice, but theory:

- tends to be abstract and general but practice is specific and unique;
- tends to assume that practice is static but practice changes with the passing of time, so that theory becomes historical;
- divided the knowledge into different disciplines but practice does not divide into a little bit of psychology and a little bit of ethics, and so on;
- tended to assume that things were not learned in practice but were learned in the classroom and applied;
- is cognitive but practice is both integrated and practical.

The students were implying all of these things although they did not articulate it quite so precisely. However, the idea that theory was applied to practice was quite destroyed with Schön's (1983) seminal study, *The Reflective Practitioner*. Schön (1983, p. 54) suggests that professionals:

- know how to carry out actions spontaneously;
- are not always aware of having learned to do these things;
- are usually unable to describe the knowing which the action needs.

More recently, I (Jarvis, 1999) have argued that theory follows practice and that we learn in the doing and when we reflect upon it, especially if what we do works on several occasions, then begin to internalise it and take it for granted.

Now it was recognised widely that learning did occur in practice and that the idea of applying theory to practice was merely another formulation of instrumental rationality. The instrumentalism of Modernity was really called into question and gradually it was recognised that the assumptions about knowledge itself had to be re-examined, which was something Lyotard (1984) and Foucault (1972) had already undertaken.

Indeed, this was a problem with which Ryle (1963) was wrestling long before this. Ryle (1963, p. 50) suggested that in practice individuals are both bodily active and mentally active: that it was one activity that required more than one kind of explanatory description. In a sense, Ryle was still caught up with instrumental rationality and the discussion of knowledge rather than learning. Even so, his is an insightful and early analysis of these problems. He rightly discussed *knowing how* and *knowing that*, although knowing how might more usefully have been sub-divided into *knowing that this is how* and *having the skill to do*. But practical knowledge is actually more profound than this since *knowing that* might more usefully be called *content knowledge* in as much as it deals with the discipline(s) to be practised and *knowing that this is how* might be called *process knowledge*, which is integrated knowledge.

More than an element of subjectivity becomes apparent as we pursue this analysis and, indeed, the more frequently individuals practise a certain skill, procedure or behaviour the more likely they are to habitualise their processes and internalise their knowledge. This led Polanyi (1967) to discuss another dimension of subjective knowledge – tacit knowledge. Experts internalise their procedures and the knowledge that related to these procedures so deeply that they take them for granted. This taken-for-grantedness of tacit knowledge is described by Nyiri (1988, pp. 20–21), quoting Feigenbaum and McCorduck (1984), thus:

> One becomes an expert not simply by absorbing explicit knowledge of the type found in textbooks, but through experience, that is, through repeated trials, 'failing, succeeding, wasting time and effort, getting a feel for a problem, learning when to go by the book and when to break the rules' Human experts thereby gradually absorb 'a repertoire of working rules of thumb, or "heuristics" that, combined with book knowledge, make them expert practitioners'. This practical, heuristic knowledge, as attempts to simulate it on the machine have shown, is 'hardest to get at because experts – or anyone else – rarely

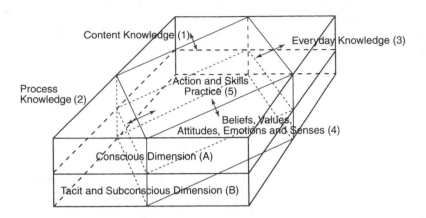

*Figure 11.1* Knowledge and skills.

have the self-awareness to recognise what it is. So it must be mined out of their heads painstakingly, one jewel at a time.

Tacit knowledge is clearly a major dimension of practical knowledge, but practitioners are not automatons – they have their own beliefs and values and it is hard, nigh on impossible, to prevent these playing a significant role in practice and, therefore, they form a fourth dimension of practical knowledge.

We all learn in our everyday life and so we gain *everyday* knowledge (Heller, 1984), and we also use this in our practice of teaching. We acknowledge that sometimes we find it difficult to utilise all our learning in every teaching situation, but we do not deliberately neglect some aspects.

Finally, knowing *that this is how* is not the same as *having the skill to do* so that this element is also a major dimension of practical knowledge, which may be depicted in Figure 11.1.

The double arrows between action and skills and the other dimensions illustrate the fact that we learn in all situations and, at the same time, our knowledge, attitudes, beliefs and values, etc. affect our behaviour. However, we can only actually learn how to do things when we actually practise them. Consequently, we have seen the development of many forms of action learning.

Practical knowledge, then, is:

- learned in practice situations;
- practical, and not merely the application of some 'pure' academic discipline to practical situations;

- dynamic, in as much as it is only retained for as long as it works;
- integrated, rather than divided up by academic discipline;
- not an academic discipline in the same way as the sciences or the social sciences.

The problem confronting teachers now is how can this complex formulation of practical knowledge be taught and learned.

## Part 2: practice-based learning

In the preparations of individuals for a number of the professions the practical placement is quite crucial. We have to devise ways whereby students, whether full-time or part-time, may learn more from their practice than merely by doing it which, in turn, means that they need to have had preparation before they actually begin that practice – induction sessions, visits, discussions with other practitioners and so on. As a result, we have to change our mode of teaching away from the didactic and towards the Socratic (Chapter 7) and the facilitative. Additionally, we have to recognise that those already in practice might act as mentors and so on for our students. In this way, teaching becomes a team exercise, with each member having specific expertise.

Through this approach, we need to encourage learners to generate their own data from practice, through writing learning journals and participating in peer learning communities. The students might never have experienced writing learning journals or participating in peer learning communities, so that it is important that, prior to their practice placement, they are taught the rudiments of journal writing and that peer learning communities are created. Journal writing is more than merely keeping a diary. It is useful in as much as it:

> may help adults break habitual modes of thinking and change life direction through reflective withdrawal and re-entry.
>
> (Lukinsky, 1990, p. 212)

Jasper (1999), however, did point out that some students keeping reflective learning journals found this a threatening process and consequently, the introduction of such teaching and learning methods should be undertaken with some degree of sensitivity.

The journal serves two reflective purposes. First, it helps students to become reflective learners, both on-action and in-action, recording data about reading, study habits, attitudes. Students are also invited to write about their own personal development – recording data about increasing knowledge, increasing ability to identify and articulate issues, and reflecting upon important decisions that they have taken since they enrolled in the programme and so on. Second, it is possible to get students to examine their own self-development and their own feelings of empowerment and he cites the work of Prawat (1991) to demonstrate this. Morrison (1996, p. 328) notes that when reflective practice prospers 'it is seen as by many students as a major significant feature of their development in all spheres'.

Bush (1999) records how he kept a journal whilst teaching adult student nurses 'spirituality in nursing practice'. His entries, which were made within six hours of teaching and re-examined within two days, illustrate how he was grappling with both the teaching of the subject and the mature learners whom he was teaching. He recorded his thoughts about the teaching and the participation of students in this rather emotive but significant topic. Bush (1999, p. 26) concluded that:

> The keeping of a journal provided the educator with an opportunity to connect thoughts, feeling and action and relate them to what was happening now, as opposed to writing about what has already happened.... It encouraged the author to trace the development of any emerging interest and provided a personal account of any growth with a factual reference, that was repeatedly examined in order to create some personal meaning.

As a result of his experiences Bush (1999, p. 25) has decided that in future courses he will also ask students to keep their own journals of the programme. Jasper (1999) in a research project, using grounded theory, on the use of journaling discovered that all the students who used it thought that they changed and developed as people as a result. However, she also discovered that it could not be assumed that students knew how to write a reflective journal and that these skills had to be taught. Once acquired, however, such skills led to both journal writing as a learning strategy and that it became an instrument for both personal and professional growth.

Thereafter, the teachers' role becomes both Socratic helping learners to interrogate their own journals and facilitative in as much as we might facilitate the peer learning community.

We, as teachers, may play a larger part in helping students to reflect on their practice; this is not book knowledge but practical knowledge. However, this is not a stand-alone method and students should still be encouraged to continue their learning from theory and books, etc. and integrate this into their own personal theory, which is then tried out in practice again. In another sense, we are encouraging students to become self-directed learners.

Practice-based learning can take a number of forms, as we shall see below, but in each case the learner is involved in activity, so that another form is action learning which was used in organisations and business since it was designed to produce 'real-life' solutions (Revens, 1982).

Finally, we have to devise new ways of assessing practical knowledge, recognising that this is pragmatic, generated in the practice setting and always changing in the light of new experiences. Consequently, we cannot test 'knowledge' in quite the same way – although we might want to retain some of the more traditional ways of testing that knowledge which is taught in the classroom. We may have to test the ability to analyse, to understand why certain actions should be taken, the ability to reflect and evaluate, and so on. This means that we need to get students to prepare reflective and evaluative assignments on their practice placement through which we endeavour to understand what students have learned and why they performed their roles in the way that they did, which is more than just thinking on their feet but also relating what they did to the teaching and reading that they have undertaken. In a sense, there is now no 'right' or 'wrong' answer, only reasoned statements and it is these that we assess – in a sense we are preparing and assessing reflective practitioners.

## Part 3: problem-based learning

In 1969 the new Faculty of Health Sciences was established at McMaster University and its intention was to let the real issues of practice rather than the theoretical demands of the academic disciplines guide the curriculum. In a sense, learning rather than teaching was placed at the centre of the curriculum, although the teachers are still present as tutors rather than providers of new knowledge. Boud (1985, p. 14), quoting from Barrows and Tamlyn (1980) summarises the principles underlying problem-based learning:

- The problem is encountered first in the learning sequence, before any preparation or study has occurred.
- The problem situation is presented to the student in the same way it would be presented in reality.
- The student works with the problem in a manner which permits his [sic] ability to reason and apply knowledge to be challenged and evaluated, appropriate to his level of learning.

- Need areas of learning are identified on the process of work with the problem as uses as a guide to individualised study.
- The skills and knowledge acquired by this study are applied back to the problem, to evaluate the effectiveness of the learning and to reinforce the learning.
- The learning that has occurred in the work with the problem and in individualised study is summarised and integrated into the student's existing knowledge and skill.

Kwan (2000, p. 137) summarises problem-based learning in medical education in the following manner:

> In the traditional curriculum, preclinical disciplines, such as anatomy, biochemistry, physiology and pharmacology are a prerequisite for proceeding to paraclinical subjects and clinical specialities. They are mainly knowledge-based and usually taught didactically by experts in given disciplinary areas, often as large group classes in lecture theatres. In contrast, PBL (problem-based learning) curriculum, health care problems (HCP) are used as a guide to direct learning from an integrative perspective. Knowledge...(from the disciplines)...will all come into place as long as they are of sufficient relevance to achieving the learning objectives of a given HCP as defined by the students.

Not only do the students define the problem, they control the pace and work out the solutions to the problems in their syndicate groups. Naturally this is a big jump from traditional teaching methods and several 'watered-down' variations have been developed, such as having the disciplines taught didactically before the problem-solving is undertaken, teaching *the knowledge that* and the *knowledge how* in parallel; teaching about the problem before it is discussed by the students, and so on. These versions of problem-based learning are quite familiar with many educators in the professions and can be classified as forms of practice-based education that we discussed above (see Boud and Feletti, 1991).

Many professions have now identified ways in which problem-based learning initiatives can be utilised in their professional preparation and even some of the more traditional disciplines, such as economics (Courvisanos, 1985). But it may be seen that any form of study that starts from a practice situation might start with practical problems rather than theoretical considerations. Such approaches are consistent with experiential learning theory (Jarvis *et al.*, 1998, pp. 46–58).

In addition Hoon-Eng Khoo *et al.* (2000, pp. 143–154) point out that the students regarded this approach to learning as fun and that their research skills had improved considerably and the library was also extremely well used. Even so, it takes a great deal of courage to move away from traditional approaches to such innovative ones and whatever form these take, the innovators are usually confronted with varieties of objections, some more valid than others. Amongst those raised in this instance are that some student groups do not relate well with each other, that the whole of an academic discipline is not covered properly and that the 'big picture' is not fully understood (Leong, 2000). Leong actually practises problem-based learning, agrees that the emphasis on student learning is commendable but she cannot accept that problem-based learning is a sufficient stand-alone technique. Instead, she has proposed a hybrid model with some problem-based and some problem-solving in which the teachers, as facilitators, use their own expertise in working with the students as they examine the problems.

## Conclusions

In the contemporary learning society, where education is becoming more vocationally orientated, it needs to place more emphasis on practical pragmatic knowledge, but what becomes clear from the experiences reported by some of those who have used these approaches, that they are not sufficient in themselves. There is still a place for theoretical perspectives but the nature of theory has changed slightly – now it is no longer to be applied to practice but tested out by the practitioners in practical situations to see whether it works. Theory can only be legitimated in practice situations if it is useful to the practitioners who use it and we can rephrase the old maxim 'There is nothing as practical as good theory' thus 'Theory is only good if it is practical'.

## References

Barrows, H. and Tamblyn, R. (1980) *Problem-Based Learning: An Approach to Medical Education* New York: Springer

Boud, D. (ed.) (1985) *Problem-Based Learning in Education for the Professions* Sydney: Higher Education Research and Development Society of Australia

Boud, D. and Feletti, G. (eds) (1991) *The Challenge of Problem-Based Learning* London: Kogan Page

Bush, T. (1999) Journalling and the teaching of spirituality in *Nurse Education Today* Vol. 19, No. 1, pp. 20–28

Courvisanos, J. (1985) A problems approach to the study of economics in Boud, D. (ed.) *Problem-Based Learning in Education for the Professions* Sydney: Higher Education Research and Development Society of Australia

Feigenbaum, E. and McCirduck, P. (1984) *The Fifth Generation* New York: Signet

Foucault, M. (1972) *The Archaeology of Knowledge* London: Tavistock

Heller, A. (1984) *Everyday Knowledge* London: Routledge and Kegan Paul

Hoon-Eng Khoo *et al*. (2000) Preliminary impressions of PBL: survey by medical students in Wang, C., Mohanan, K., Pan, D. and Chee, Y. (eds) *Teaching and Learning in Higher Education Symposium* Singapore: National University of Singapore, pp. 143–148

Jarvis, P (1999) *The Practitioner Researcher* San Francisco, CA: Jossey-Bass

Jarvis, P., Holford, J. and Griffin, C. (1998) *The Theory and Practice of Learning* London: Kogan Page

Jasper, M. (1999) Nurses' perceptions of the value of written reflection in *Nurse Education Today* Vol. 19, No. 6, pp. 452–463

Kwan, C.-Y. (2000) Problem-based learning in medical education: from McMaster to Asia Pacific Region in Wang, C., Mohanan, K., Pan, D. and Chee, Y. (eds) *Teaching and Learning in Higher Education Symposium* Singapore: National University of Singapore, pp. 135–142

Leong, S. K. (2000) Problem-based learning – my critique in Wang, C., Mohanan, K., Pan, D. and Chee, Y. (eds) *Teaching and Learning in Higher Education Symposium* Singapore: National University of Singapore, pp. 173–178

Lukinsky, J. (1990) Reflective withdrawal through journal writing in Mezirow, J. and Associates (eds) *Fostering Critical Reflection in Adulthood* San Francisco, CA: Jossey-Bass

Lyotard, J.-F. (1984) *The Postmodern Condition* Manchester: University of Manchester Press

Morrison, K. (1996) Developing reflective practice in higher degree students through a learning journal *Studies in Higher Education* Vol. 31, No. 3, pp. 317–332

Nyiri, J. (1988) Tradition and practical knowledge in Nyiri, J. and Smith, B. (eds) *Practical Knowledge* London: Croom Helm

Polanyi, M. (1967) *The Tacit Dimension* London: Routledge and Kegan Paul

Prawat, R. S. (1991) Conversations with self and conversations with settings: a framework for thinking about teacher empowerment in *American Educational Research Journal* Vol. 28, pp. 737–757

Ryle, G. (1963) *The Concept of Mind* London: Peregrine

Schön, D. A. (1983) *The Reflective Practitioner* New York: Basic Books

Schön, D. A. (1987) *Educating the Reflective Practitioner* San Francisco, CA: Jossey-Bass

# Chapter 12

# Mentoring
## The art of teaching and learning

*Gill Nicholls*

The particular focus of this chapter is on mentoring. It is becoming increasingly clear that the quality of education, training and learning will depend crucially on the work of tutors and lecturers in the role of mentor both in the post-compulsory sector of education and in the world of work. Work-based learning has established itself as a means for organisational change and learning in the workforce. First the issues related to the role of mentoring are discussed followed by models of mentoring that can be used and adopted within the teaching and learning situation.

What the role is or should be and what 'mentoring' means, are far less clear. One can go back to classical roots to appreciate what a mentor might be, Homer's wise mentor and his relationship with his protégé Telemachus offers an attractive and thought provoking model of the teacher and educators of tomorrow. One that highlights values such as role model, teacher, an approachable counsellor, a trusted adviser, a challenger and an encourager, hence mythology suggests that a mentor would appear to need qualities of leadership and wisdom, as well as skills and knowledge.

The term mentor has rapidly become a word used for a variety of roles and occupations in the last ten years. Most recently in Britain it has be linked to the guidance given to students in their initial training, particularly in the field of teacher education and in the health service sector. The term mentor has been imported to education from a diversity of other occupational contexts, changed to suit the educational contexts and as a result has caused some confusion as what a mentor is and the role they should play. Jacobi gives a good account of the variety of context and uses literature to demonstrate her point. She states that:

> Although many researchers have attempted to provide concise definitions of mentoring or mentors, definitional diversity continues

to characterise the literature. A review of these varying definitions supports Merriam's (1983) contention that:

The phenomenon of mentoring is not clearly conceptualised, leading to confusion as to just what is being measured or offered as an ingredient in success. Mentoring appears to mean one thing to developmental psychologists, another thing to business people, and a third thing to those in academic settings.

(1991, p. 169)

Wrightsman (1981) also noted the diversity of definitions of mentoring within the psychological research literature and discussed the problems that resulted from the lack of consensus:

With respect to communication between researchers. ...there is a false sense of consensus, because at a superficial level everyone 'knows' what mentoring is. But closer examination indicates wide variation in operational definitions, leading to conclusions that are limited to the use of particular procedures.... The result is that the concept is devalued, because everyone is using it loosely, without precision. (pp. 3–4)

(Taken from Jacobi, 1991, pp. 506–508)

These statements make it clear that there is no consensus as to what mentoring is or the role of the mentor. It also begs the question about what can mentors in the teaching learning situation do best? What are the advantages and disadvantages of using a mentoring system? These question form the basis of the discussion in the second section of this chapter.

Supervision on the other hand brings to mind other concepts and roles for those in educational settings. What do we mean by supervision, what is its role and how is it placed within the educational context?

## Part 1: mentoring

### Concepts and contexts of mentoring

In the introduction to this chapter mentoring was associated with Homer's epic poem, *The Odyssey*. The account given of the mentor suggests that first and foremost that mentoring is an intentional process, second, that mentoring is a nurturing process which fosters the growth and development of an individual. Third, mentoring is an insightful process in which the wisdom of the mentor is acquired and applied by the protégé. Fourth mentoring is a supportive, protective process and finally mentoring is about being a role model. The above assumptions about the mentor and the role of the mentor need to be placed in context of modern times and the expectations of mentors and their mentees. It would be very surprising if the classical mentoring relationship as described above, which existed between Mentor and Telemachus were readily found in modern organisations. With the passage of time and with the changing demands of the learning situations in which mentoring occurs, adaptation of the mentor-protégé has taken place. In order for a constructive discussion to take place a working definition of mentoring needs to be considered. The type of definition that allows inquiry into the role of a mentor as well as giving insight into how the role of a mentor may be developed. Carmin (1993, pp. 10–11) gives such a definition:

> Mentoring is a complex, interactive process, occurring between individuals of differing levels of experience and expertise which incorporates interpersonal or psychosocial development, career and/or educational development, and socialisation functions into the relationship... To the extent that the parameters of mutuality and comparability exist in the relationship, the potential outcomes of respect, professionalism, collegiality, and role fulfilment will result. Further, the mentoring process occurs in a dynamic relationship within a given milieu.
>
> (Cited from Carruthers, 1993)

This definition gives a context and concept of a mentor and the possible skills related to mentoring. The essential attributes of nurturing, role model, the focus on professional/personal development and a caring relationship underpin all aspects of mentoring. Nurturing implies a developmental process in which the mentor is able to recognise the ability, experience, strengths, weaknesses and psychological maturity of the individual that is being nurtured and can provide appropriate developmental and growth tasks that engage the individual. Nurturing also implies providing an environment in which the individual can grow and how best to chose that environment.

Anderson and Shannon (1995) concurs with Camin but suggest that the five areas of mentoring need to be contextualised if they are to help in understanding what mentoring is. These include:

- Teaching
- Sponsoring
- Encouraging

- Counselling
- Befriending.

For Anderson *teaching* means the basic behaviours associated with teaching, including; modelling, informing, conforming/disconforming, prescribing and questioning. In the context of mentoring, these behaviours are guided by principles of adult education. *Sponsoring* means a kind of guarantor, and involves three essential behaviours: protecting, supporting and promoting. *Encouraging* is the process that includes the behaviours of affirming, inspiring and challenging. *Counselling* relates to the problem-solving process and includes behaviours such as listening, probing, clarifying and advising. *Befriending* involves two crucial elements that of accepting and relating (Figure 12.1).

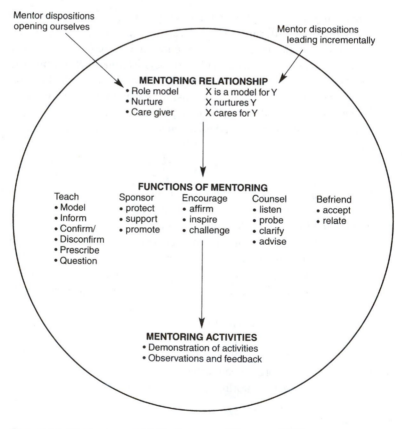

*Figure 12.1* Mentoring model (Anderson and Shannon, 1995).

The five identified functions of a mentor should be seen as mutually inclusive, that is a mentor should be able to demonstrate and engage with all five aspects as and when required. A key function is that of an on going caring relationship as Levison *et al.* (1978) assert that the essence of mentoring may be found within the kind of relationship that exists between the mentor and protégé than in the various roles and functions denoted by the term, 'mentoring'. Figure 12.2 summarises the elements of mentoring. It highlights that basic to mentoring is a relationship that views the mentor as a role model, who cares and nurtures.

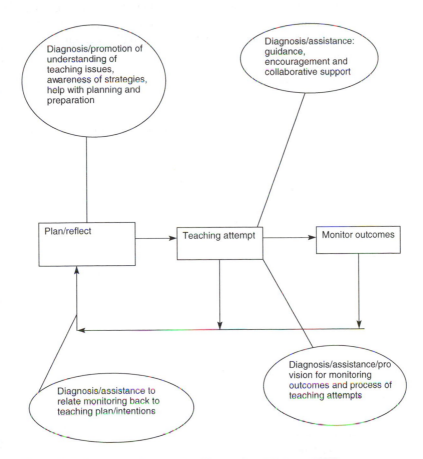

*Figure 12.2* Functions of mentoring (Maynard and Furlong, 1995).

## Part 2: models of mentoring

Anderson's concept of mentoring is based on a caring/nurturing approach. Other models such as that put forward by Rothera *et al*. (1995) suggest a process model. In such a model of mentoring the individual that is mentored will in due course, through experiential learning, internalise the values of the mentor, participates in problem-solving and eventually becomes independent of the mentor. The process model identifies characteristics of mentors through considering professional competence, humanistic traits and functions. Table 12.1 shows the classification and ordering of attributes and roles as identified in a process model of mentoring.

The key areas of this model relate to attributes such as personal and positional qualities. Within these two broad areas mentors need to be able to demonstrate their legitimacy and credibility, quality of relationship and personality as well as being able to offer constructive criticisms.

*Table 12.1* Classification and ordering of attributes and roles related to mentoring

| Professional competence | 'Personal' Attributes (qualities) | 'Positional' Roles (categories) |
|---|---|---|
| | Humanistic traits | Functions |
| Constructively critical comments | Approaches | Adviser |
| Knowledgeable | Encouragement | Object of trust |
| Conversant with requirements of the role of mentor | Helpful | Role model |
| Conscientious | Supportive | Assessor |
| Explaining subject | Gives time willingly | Confidant |
| | Sympathetic | Counsellor |
| | Caring | Friend |
| Gives praise | | |
| *Instrumental* (cognitive) | *Expressive* (affective) | *Repertoire of roles* (typology) |

Source: Taken from Rothera (1995).

### The apprenticeship model

This model has its origins in Aristotle whereby some skills, including many that are difficult, complex and of high moral and cultural value, are best learned 'by the emulation of experienced practitioners and by supervised practice under guidance' (Hillgate Group, 1989). In cases of such skills they suggest that apprenticeship, should take precedence over instruction. The role of the mentor in this model is one where the mentor gives first hand experience in real situations, for example trainee teachers need to experience real students, teaching situations, classroom strategies and subject matter. As Maynard and Furlong suggest:

> In the early stages of teacher training the purpose of that practical experience is to allow them (trainees) to start from concepts, schemas or scripts of the process of teaching. But in order to begin to 'see', trainees need an interpreter. They need to work alongside a mentor who can explain the significance of what is happening.
>
> (1995, p. 79)

In the apprenticeship model the trainee works alongside the mentor taking responsibility for a small part of the work, gradually gaining confidence and skill so that the reliance on the mentor becomes less as the mentee becomes for competent.

### The competency model

This model starts from the premise that the skills that have to be learnt for a given profession are a set of pre-defined competencies that each individual has to master and show competence in. The mentor takes on the role of a systematic trainer, observing the trainee, with a pre-defined observation schedule and then provides feedback to the observed. The mentor can be considered as coaching the trainee on a list of agreed behaviours that form part of the list of competencies specified by others, whether this is a professional body or an organisation. Increasingly competency models are emerging in many of the professions including the training of nurse practitioners and teachers.

### The reflective model

Supporting trainees in reflective process of learning requires a shift in role by the mentor. To facilitate the process of reflection the mentor needs to be able to move from being a model and instructor to being a co-enquirer. Other aspects of their role as described in the other models may well continue, but in order to promote critical reflection a more equal and open relationship is required. Thinking critically about a process or set of skills demands an open-mindedness and involves confronting beliefs and values.

## Part 3: effective mentoring

Effective mentoring is a difficult and demanding task and those performing the role need time and training in order to perfect their mentoring skills. It may be seen as a complementary means to extend training through traditional rotes, whether this is higher education, further education or work-based learning. It is increasingly being used as a support and development activity. Mentoring can be thought of as a multi-faceted concept incorporating personal support and the more rigorous notion of professional development leading to enhanced competence. As a conclusion it is possible to conceptualise mentoring in three successively more complex ways. McIntyre suggests that:

> At its most basic, mentoring involves a personal relationship in which a relative novice is supported by a more experienced peer in coming to terms with a new role. At a second level, mentoring also involves active guidance, teaching and challenging of the protégé by the mentor, who accordingly needs to claim some expertise, wisdom and authority; and this may make it more difficult to maintain the necessary supportive personal relationship. At a third level, mentoring additionally involves the management and implementa- tion of a planned curriculum, tailored course to the needs of the individual.
>
> (1996, p. 147)

## Part 4: using mentoring as a form of professional learning

Educational institutions have for a long time been thought of as the place where students learn. It is only more recently however, that educational institutions have begun to be thought of as places where teachers' profes- sional learning can also take place. Teaching is one of the loneliest professions, with teachers rarely having the opportunity to work with a colleague in a collaborative way so that they can learn more about the teaching learning process. Mentoring in one form or another is a means by which teachers can brake down their isolation and support professional learning in ways that focus on the daily work of teachers and teaching learning situations.

Professional learning about teaching is not simply a matter of propositional knowledge or knowing about a range of strategies. Information bout new approaches to teaching may come from reading, workshops, conferences, etc. but for information to become understanding in a conscious way needs the individual to interpret and transform that knowledge into practice. Professional learning about teaching is a complex process that requires the putting of knowledge and understanding into practice. Part of the problem of translating teaching ideas into practice lies in the tacit nature of ones knowledge about what one is currently doing in their teaching. Mentoring can play a fundamental role in institutions and organisations, which aim to be a professional learning community.

Knowledge about our teaching is in our actions, but the routines and habits of practice mean that the complex decision-making world of the classroom we do not, as a rule, make our knowledge about teaching and learning explicit to ourselves (Carmin, 1988). In the busy world of teaching there appears no need to perform such a function. However, to make a new teaching approach understood in action terms requires the individual to make their current teaching practice, and the theories and beliefs that underpin such practice, explicit so that new approaches can connect with what the individual knows and holds tacitly.

Mentoring can greatly enhance the process of making tactic knowledge explicit. Through the mentoring process the individual is allowed to interrogate their practice, reflect and then reappraise the values, theories and aspirations attached to their individual theories of learning and teaching. What is interesting to understand here is that meaningful learning and development will not occur simply through being involved as a mentor or mentee in itself, this would not be enough. The kind of relationship the individual has with their own learning and the community in which the mentor perceives themselves to be mentoring for professional learning requires active contribution to knowledge and experience respecting new and innovative approaches and recognising as well as understanding how their contribution fits with their own purpose and the support that is expected of them.

The current interest in mentoring for professional development stems from the belief that mentoring, coaching and preceptorship are a way in which individuals and institutions can learn and develop. Mentoring can also be, and is often viewed, as a means for assisting change in organisations. So what is it that mentorship offers teaching and learning? In an increasingly divers and ever changing educational setting, organisations look to see how change can be sustained from within. Mentoring is seen as one such system to facilitate professional learning and thus create change.

The central premise of mentoring as a form of professional learning stems from the belief that individuals may best learn through observing, doing, commenting and questioning, rather than simply listening. The intern, initial teacher trainee or student nurse can be described as someone who is 'initiated into the traditions, habits, rules, cultures and practices of the community they are to join'. Understanding these habits, rules etc., requires the learning of specific language, conventions, know-ledge and patterns. The type of learning Schon calls knowing-in-action. Its form this premise that mentoring of initial and post service individuals is gaining acceptance and ground as a significant method for professional learning.

Mentoring for professional learning emphasises guidance, development and the use and enhancement of individual abilities. Preparation for the role of mentor is key in facilitating the learning of the mentee. The ultimate aim of training and development is to improve teaching and learning environments by adding the necessary value of competence and confidence to both the mentor and the mentee. Mentoring as professional learning can then be considered as a means of enhancing learning competence in such a way that the mentor, mentee and organisation acquire specific competence and then apply them with confidence through performance in the work place.

At the centre of this type of learning is the notion that professional learning requires systematic conversation and dialogue about the actions of teaching and learning, and being able to share experiences of the action. This is a crucial point for the development of understanding regarding the intellectual act of teaching and how this can be enhanced and as a consequence of such enhancement improves student learning. When a mentor and mentee work in co-operative supportive and trusting environments it is possible to make values and beliefs about teaching and learning explicit, both for the mentor to themselves and their mentees. In this way learning is occurring through critical reflection by both mentor and mentee. The mentor starts to ask the important question 'why?'.

Asking the why questions allows the mentor to reflect, share practice and collaborate to improve the mentee's practice. Helping the mentee in a systematic way enables the mentee to develop processes by which they can interrogate their own practice through critical reflection and making explicit their tacit actions. Thinking systematically and analytically about what is taught and how it is taught requires commitment and understanding. Equally understanding and acknowledging ones own abilities, strengths and weaknesses within the teaching learning environments is a powerful form of professional learning. Through mentoring one can begin to identify and set ones own agenda for learning and development. Sharing practice is fundamental to professional learning.

## Part 5: professional development through mentoring

Mentoring can be thought of in a variety of ways. Earlier in the chapter I showed how mentoring can be seen as a means of educating an individual through the concept or role model. Later I suggest that mentoring is an excellent tool for professional learning both for the mentor and the mentee through systematic critical reflection. Mentoring can also have a crucial role in staff development, particularly when used in the context of induction. The mentor's role in this context is one of support normally offered by a more experienced member of staff, whether this is school, college or work place. Mentoring within induction should be seen as a positive mechanism for developing management, communication and organisational skills. The mentoring process should move through a series of stages whereby the mentor helps to induct the new member of staff or trainee over a period of time followed by the development of the individual and finally allowing the individual to move forward and taking on the role as friend.

Mentoring in this way is an active relationship built on negotiation and trust. It is not the mentor's role to dominate, judge and be overtly critical. Rather the mentor should develop a relationship built on constructive criticism, support and a relationship that allows for development. In short, mentoring is a process through which knowledge and understanding, skills and abilities, may be passed on to less experienced practitioners (Blandford, 2000).

## Part 6: teaching and learning and the mentor

This chapter has focused on the variety of roles a mentor may have and the differing context in which those roles maybe implemented. Increasingly today in a world where education and training is seen as a key mechanism for enhancing the quality of student learning, workforce skills and organisational change, mentoring has re-emerged as a fundamental role in the enhancement of learning. Mentoring is seen as a tool by which an individual may learn and understand the ethics, rules and skills of a given community, whether this be teaching, nursing, medicine of work-based skills. Mentoring is also seen as a powerful tool for professional development and learning for the mentor. It is seen as a means for encouraging systematic critical reflection. It is also a powerful tool to help the mentor articulate the skills and knowledge they may have which is frequently tactic. Making explicit what one does and thus allowing someone else to learn from that knowledge is a powerful tool to have, mentoring facilitates the learning of such tools.

# References

Anderson, E. and Shannon, A. (1995) Towards a conceptualisation of mentoring, in T. Kerry and A. Shelton Mayes, *Issues in Mentoring*. Milton Keynes: Open University Press

Blandford, S. (2000) *Managing Professional Development in Schools*. London: Routledge

Carmin, C. N. (1988) Issues on research on mentoring: definitional and metho-dological. *International Journal of Mentoring*, 2(2), pp. 9–13

Carmin, S. (1993) *The Return of the Mentor: Strategies for the Workplace Learning*. London: Falmer Press

Carruthers, J. (1993) The principles and practices of mentoring, in *The Return of the Mentor: Strategies for the Workplace Learning*. London: Falmer Press

Hillgate Group (1989) *Learning to Teach*. London: The Claridge Press

Jacobi, M. (1991) Mentoring and undergraduate academic success: a literature review. *Review of Educational Research*, 61(4), pp. 505–532

Levinson, D., Darrow, C., Klein, E., Levinson, M. and McKee, B. (1978) *Seasons of a Man's Life*. New York: Knopf

McIntyre, D. (1996) *Mentors in Schools: Developing the Profession of Teaching*. London: Fulton Press

Maynard, T. and Furlong, J. (1995) Learning to teach and models of mentoring, in T. Kerry and A. Shelton Mayes *Issues in Mentoring*. Milton Keynes: Open University Press

Merriam, S. (1983) Mentors and protegees: a critical review of the literature, *Adult Education Quarterly*, 33, pp. 161–173

Rothera, M., Hawkins, S. and Hendry, J. (1995) The role of subject mentor in further education, in T. Kerry and A. Shelton Mayes. *Issues in Mentoring*. Milton Keynes: Open University Press

Wrightsman, L. S. (1981) Research methodologies for assessing mentoring, presented at the Annual Conference of the American Psychological Association, Los Angeles (*ERIC Document Reproduction Service No. ED 209 339*)

# Chapter 13

# The learning community

## A strategic dimension of teaching and learning?

*Paul Tosey*

## Introduction

The term 'learning community' is in common usage and refers to a wide variety of educational practices and principles. This chapter aims to identify ideas and practices of 'learning community' in currency in formal education, and to consider in detail its application at the level of a programme group or cohort. The chapter argues for a strategic rather than tactical view of educational design, both of the learning community itself and of the relations between a programme and its institutional and social setting. Learning communities could, and perhaps should, be designed with as much intentionality as other aspects of the curriculum, in tune with Bass' (1999) view of teaching as an 'extended process that unfolds over time'.

I begin with a brief survey of literatures. I then discuss practice in a UK higher education context with reference to a particular model, that of the 'peer learning community' (Heron, 1974). Based on this I propose six main functional dimensions that may be applied to the design of any learning community within a formal educational programme.

The chapter goes on to consider two contrasting theoretical perspectives on the notion of learning community. The first is critical, and draws particular attention to the political dimension of a learning community. This perspective tempers especially the potential for the notion of community to invoke connotations of harmony and unity. The second perspective is informed by theories of complexity. This perspective portrays behaviour in a learning community as emergent and thus challenges notions of who is in control.

## The concept of the learning community

Any group of participants on a course or learning programme could be said to constitute a 'learning community'. Thus, 'The learning community is something of an umbrella term to describe learning situations where a group of people come together to meet specific and unique learning needs and to share resources and skills' (Burgoyne *et al.*, 1978, p. 29, cited in Reynolds, 1998, p. 6). The term itself therefore does not differentiate between designating a group of learners as a 'community' because of proximity alone, such that participants on a given course are regarded by default as a learning community and encouraged or assumed to support and share with each other; and designing and facilitating a learning community according to explicit principles as part of a learning and teaching strategy. As Dewey (1916) notes, 'the terms society, community, are… ambiguous'.

Reference to the notion of a 'learning community' is widespread in literature on education[1] and, for example, in the field of management. As Bitterman notes, the literature is 'vast, sometimes elusive, and hard to synthesize' (Marsick *et al.*, 2000, p. 21). It is a multi-faceted notion, embracing themes such as:

- communities of practice, and communities of inquiry;
- professional and societal learning communities;
- curricular learning communities;
- collaborative, co-operative, peer and group learning.

What these conceptions share is an emphasis on the relational nature of learning. This stands in contrast, sometimes' starkly, to assumptions embedded in formal education that learning is essentially individual. Many sources are also motivated by concerns about the increasingly fragmented and potentially alienating nature of higher education, influenced among others by Dewey (1916) and Freire (1996).

The concept of 'communities of practice' (Wenger, 1999) refers usually to groups defined by their interaction through common problems or workplaces. They are not formal educational groups created intentionally in order to learn – in Wenger's view, such communities emerge through collective learning:

> Over time, this collective learning results in practices that reflect both the pursuit of our enterprises and the attendant social relations. These practices are thus the property of a kind of community

created over time by the sustained pursuit of a shared enterprise. It makes sense, therefore to call these kinds of communities 'communities of practice'.

(Wenger, 1998, p. 45)

Senge *et al.* (1994) have emphasised the notion of community in relation to organisational learning. The concept of a 'community of inquiry' (Fisher and Torbert, 1995; Reason, 1998) is similar, and emphasises an action research orientation.

Related to this is the notion of the 'professional learning community' which emphasises the participation of stakeholders in (usually) school improvement processes. Thus, 'Professional learning community, as applied to schools, is a term used to refer to a school organization in which all stakeholders are involved in joint planning, action and assessment for student growth and school improvement' (Huffman and Jacobson, 2003, p. 240). Societal communities may also be framed as learning communities. Bitterman, for example, takes a sociocultural perspective and focuses on learning through 'communities formed by lifestyle choices' (Marsick *et al.*, 2000, p. 21).

In formal education, there is a significant movement in the United States that emphasises the creation of learning communities, often bridging across two or more programmes in 'commuter colleges', in order to 'humanize the scale of higher education and promote community' (Smith, 2001). There is a National Learning Communities Project, based at the Evergreen State College, Washington, whose website contains many resources.[2] Here,

the term 'learning community' refers to the purposeful restructuring of the curriculum by linking or clustering courses that enroll a common cohort of students. This represents an intentional structuring of the students time, credit, and learning experiences to build community, and foster more explicit connections among students, faculty, and disciplines.

(Smith, 2001)

Other sources in this vein include Gabelnick *et al.* (1990), Levine and Shapiro (2000), Malnarich (2005) and Smith *et al.* (2004).

There is also a growing literature on collaborative and co-operative learning (e.g. Cooper and Robinson, 1997), concerned principally with interactive methods of learning within a programme context. This includes emphasis on peer learning (Boud *et al.*, 2001) and group learning (Jaques, 2000). Marsick and Kasl call for 'a pedagogy of group learning', which they define as 'when all members perceive themselves as having contributed to a group outcome, and all members of the group can individually explain what the group as a system knows' (1997, p. 1). Other literature on learning communities in educational and developmental settings includes contributions from Pedler (1981), Fox (1994) and Critten (1996).

A final strand is from the human potential and personal growth movements, with ideas related to therapeutic community practice (e.g. Scott Peck's 'community building', Peck, 1993). This strand also incorporated an emancipatory agenda, emphasising the development of individual autonomy and authenticity. It has also influenced recent thinking about participative forms of research through collaborative and co-operative inquiry (Reason, 1988; Heron, 1996).

The related notion of the peer learning community (PLC) is also sourced in humanistic educational practice. Put forward originally by Heron (1974) this is perhaps the archetypal 'growth community' model for adult education. Key principles of the PLC model according to Heron are:

- The notion of an educated person (emphasising self-direction, self-monitoring and self-correction), in which the staff-student distinction is secondary to the fundamental parity between human beings.
- Participative evaluation of course objectives ('In its basic educational procedures it cultivates the acquisition of self-directing competence in the student', 1974, p. 2).
- Two fundamental principles of parity: Equality of consideration (i.e. whatever each person brings is equally worthy of consideration) and equality of opportunity (it is equally open to anyone to contribute to or intervene in the course process at any time).
- Education of the whole person (particularly education of the affect, and the notion of emotional competence – for example, Heron, 1992a; Postle, 1993).
- Political modes of power sharing (particularly a progression from hierarchical to co-operative to autonomous modes of facilitating educative processes within the learning community – Heron, 1992b).

According to this radical concept a learning community is a process, not an entity or 'product'. These principles underpin the MSc Change Agent Skills and Strategies (CASS) in the School of Management, University of Surrey,[3] which has sought to embed the notion of learning community in the architecture and life of a programme from its inception.

Operating to PLC principles within the formal structures of higher education, however, raises various tensions and dilemmas. We rely on a variety of non-standard features to support this mode of education, including a specific entry criterion (that participants have undergone substantial personal development prior to entry, and continue their personal development throughout); clear setting of the expectation that the programme will involve holistic, experiential, interpersonal learning; a closed, small (approx. 20) group, on a continuous programme; interaction with peers on workshops lasting four days, led by staff with expertise in group facilitation; and a first module that is designed for community building, as well as teaching specific models and methods of learning used throughout the programme.

## Six dimensions of peer community learning

Clearly the above features are designed for a specialised programme, and many of them would need to be modified for other educational contexts. Nevertheless, the principles behind this practice could be applied to learning communities more generally, with any particular programme choosing the degree of application according to the type of community that is envisaged.

The following set of dimensions (summarised in Table 13.1) is derived from reflection on experience with the MSc CASS (e.g. Tosey and Gregory, 1998). As a framework, this may be compared for example with the six core processes for 'creating and sustaining organizations as communities'[4] (cited in Senge *et al.*, 1994, pp. 512–517). I do not claim this to be a definitive model, and other factors (e.g. critical thinking, Brookfield, 1987) are crucial to the quality of learning. The intent here is to stimulate educators' thinking about their own domains of practice.

### Holistic education

This dimension concerns the philosophy of the programme towards the education of the whole person – mind, body and spirit. Of especial significance is the education of the affect, which on the MSc CASS we regard as essential for effective experiential learning so that, for example, each person shows their vulnerability and opens themselves to receive the group's support. Emotional competence is related to, but not identical to,

Table 13.1 Six dimensions of peer community learning

| Dimension | High emphasis | Low emphasis |
|---|---|---|
| Holistic education | Intrapersonal and interpersonal events are a potential source of learning. Community process may be integral to the programme's educational agenda | The psychological and emotional life of the community are more likely to be seen as separate from the educational agenda. Community process and dynamics are treated as incidental or peripheral |
| Community interaction | More interaction and communication (quantity and channels, especially face-to-face) means the community has more opportunity to progress through stages of group formation | Lower interaction (less quantity, fewer channels) means (e.g.) that community is less likely to 'form' as a group and move through developmental stages |
| Facilitation | Skilled facilitation supports learning from the community's dynamics | Absence of facilitation, or facilitation that does not attend to process or the affective life of the community, means the focus is on programme content more than community learning |
| Structural integration | Collective tasks, shared interests, and formal interdependence reinforce the emphasis on community learning | If tasks, rewards, etc. remain individual, structures may conflict with our fail to support a stated intention to create a learning community |
| Power sharing | The community is more likely to develop co-operative and autonomous modes of working, to complement a hierarchical mode | Participant autonomy may be limited to carrying out hierarchically-defined tasks |
| Boundary management | Community identity may be clear; interactions with the environment may be a source of community learning; and members may participate in managing the interfaces with e.g. the institutional setting | Community identity may be diffuse, perhaps transitory; and/or interactions with the environment are taken for granted, routinely managed by staff, and not used for community learning |

Goleman's (1996) concept of 'emotional intelligence', and refers to: 'A person (who is) able to manage their emotions awarely in terms of the basic skills of control, expression, catharsis and transmutation... In every day living, emotional competence means being able to spot the stimulation of old emotional pain and to interrupt its displacement into distorted behaviour' (Heron, 1992a, pp. 131–134).

Broadly I contend that *most* formal programmes in higher education pay lip service to dimensions of the person other than the cognitive; the enormously rich potential for learning that exists in the interactions and dynamics between people is largely lost. Experiential learning is common, of course, yet tends to emphasise activity (learning through doing) and cognitive reflection much more than the emotional dimension, which many staff regard as outside the remit of education. The argument here is that the potential of a learning community whose emotional life is largely excluded from the educational agenda is diminished. Admittedly, it is no simple matter to include this dimension. It may well introduce conflict with the culture and norms of HE, as well as requiring specialist staff skills and designs for learning.

### Community interaction

A group of participants becomes a community through interacting, especially through experiencing common events. There are many models of group development that help to map this process, including among others M. Scott Peck's practice of 'Community Building' (Peck, 1993) and Tuckman's stages of 'forming, storming, norming, performing and mourning' (Tuckman and Jensen, 1977).

For obvious reasons, a learning community that has little interaction, in either quantity for quality, may not move through even the forming stage. At the other extreme engaging in experiential learning together, participating in and being exposed to the group's dynamics, and attending explicitly to the group's psychosocial processes, creates far greater opportunity for the community to build and develop. For example, the MSc CASS attends early on (i.e. in the initial attendance block) to group 'ground rules', allowing concerns about (say) confidentiality to be discussed and addressed by participants. These 'rules' may be revisited any number of times during the programme.

Learning communities will vary according to their opportunities to meet together, and the legitimacy of attending to (say) group process. An issue this raises is of the extent to which community learning is influenced by the possibility of face-to-face interaction. Virtual learning communities, mediated primarily by electronic communication, can enhance interaction in useful ways; equally they raise concerns about student alienation. Sensing others' physical and energetic presence, and experiencing direct interaction in the present, represents significant potential for community learning in a group that has the opportunity to interact face-to-face.

## Facilitation[5]

The style and quality of facilitation will influence the extent to which the potential of community learning can be realised. Most approaches to teaching emphasise a hierarchical, controlling mode of facilitation. Skilled facilitation enables the resources individuals bring to be manifested through community interaction, and enables personal development to flourish within the community setting. In Heron's model, the facilitator is 'an educationalist, not a therapist', occupying a role that is relevant to 'experiential learning groups of all kinds...any group in which learning takes place through an active and aware involvement of the whole person – volitional, affective and cognitive – in the group process and its particular focus' (1977, pp. 1–2). The qualities and skills of facilitators are emphasised also by Bitterman (Marsick *et al.*, 2000, p.30). Skilled facilitation is not the exclusive domain of appointed facilitators (i.e. a staff team), as every participant influences the group's process. In this respect in particular, peer community learning can enhance learning of transferable skills such as working in groups and teams.

If the structure and dynamics of the learning community are not on the educational agenda of the programme, aspects of group process – conflicts, projections, transference and so on (see, for example, Benson, 2001) – 'go underground' or are dealt with incidentally rather than intentionally. This is not to say that the community cannot or will not be psychologically healthy, but that it becomes more reliant on chance. One possible consequence is that the sense of community develops informally among the student group, who come to support each others' 'survival' of the course.

## Structural integration

Structural aspects to course design can, and indeed need to, support the development of peer community learning. The potential of peer community learning is more likely to be realised if it is integral to the philosophy and the design of the course. This is related to Biggs' (2003) principle of 'constructive alignment', such that learning outcomes, activities and assessment are mutually reinforcing. Structures will also support community learning where they create interdependence (Thompson, 1967), which means that participants must rely on and work with each other in order to pass the course, rather than do so only if they choose. On the MSc CASS for example, in addition to building intentionally a community that has cultural norms of peer support, students are required to participate in learning sets and in self and peer assessment processes. This requirement is enshrined in course regulations, and is non-negotiable, therefore is a contractual feature that is a condition of joining.

### Power sharing

Heron's view (e.g. 1992b) was that ideally a hierarchical mode of facilitation should shift towards co-operation – where negotiation largely replaces direction – and then towards autonomy, where the community becomes more self-sufficient and relinquishes dependence on those with hierarchical status. In the early phases, trained staff facilitators help to keep the boundaries, model the culture of a learning community, and teach key processes for interaction. Heron also makes the point that the politics of facilitation are more complex than this; that what on the surface may appear to be a shift towards autonomy and peerhood may at another level be seen as a more subtle form of hierarchical control.

The possibility of moving away from a hierarchical mode is contentious in formal education, where programme design and issues relating to accreditation and quality assurance typically are controlled by the institution in which the programme exists. Possibilities for some power sharing exist through use of processes such as enquiry-based learning (Kahn and O'Rourke, 2004), in which learning is guided by questions designed by participants. However it is in this dimension that Heron would, I believe, see the greatest contradiction between the PLC model and a formal education setting.

### Boundary management

Miller (1993) identifies boundary management as a vital task in any system's functioning. In formal education a learning community exists within an institutional context that both gives it legitimacy and impinges strongly on the structures, scope and life of the community, as acknowledged by Fox (1994, p. 251).

The interface with formal university systems feels at times like a clash of cultures, at others as a comfortable or necessary structure – perhaps a 'defence against anxiety' in Menzies (1970) terminology. This in itself is an educative experience for programme staff who necessarily occupy a key 'boundary management' role. The more power is shared with the learning community, the more conflicts and tensions are likely to appear at that boundary, and the harder life may feel for staff caught between the community (who are in one sense customers) and the institution (which, for all its espousal of customer-orientation, may remain remarkably immune to customer influence on many matters). But the consequence of staff retaining this role – which in one sense is the easier option for staff – is that participants gauge very easily the extent to which their choice and influence are real.

In practical terms, our MSc community needs a private space in which to meet where at least furniture can easily be rearranged, and noise can be made without disturbing others. Institutions' financial constraints, standard room booking systems and norms about course design and resources, can all militate against having the necessary inputs. There is also a clear community boundary in that all participants join each community group (i.e. one annual intake for the course) at its formation, and thereafter it remains a closed group. This is antithetical to contemporary trends towards fully modularised courses and the principle that students can define their own learning path through a menu of offerings. This is not to suggest that rigid boundaries are appropriate. On the contrary, this could result in a self-sealing group. It is a question more of attending to boundaries and their management.

## A critical perspective

Alongside discussion of the principles and mechanics of a learning community, there is a need for critical reflection on the concept and practices. This is offered by, for example, Cervero and Wilson (1999), Humphries and Martin (2000) and Reynolds (2000).

Reynolds argues that 'community' can be a normative concept based on sentiment, and he explores the shadow side of community, such as its dependence on conformity and its diminution of the significance of power. He summarises work such as critiques by Benhabib (1992) and Smith (1988) of 'communitarianism', and Shulman's (1983) critique of community as 'pastoral idyll', among others. Humphries and Martin (2000) equally address the way that the notion of community 'posits fusion rather than separation as the social ideal', and identify Knowles *et al.*'s (1984) concept of *andragogy* as typifying a liberal humanist emphasis.

One angle of critique challenges the notion that 'community' is automatically a context in which people can be 'authentic', or truly themselves. Behaviour within a learning community is still socialised, driven by perceived or actual norms, rewards and sanctions. The pursuit of individual autonomy by no means places all participants on an equal footing. The notion of 'authenticity' itself is value laden, and claims for its essentiality must be open to question. People's ability and inclination to 'be authentic' (or perhaps to produce 'authenticity displays' congruent with a discourse of peer community) in a group setting varies. It may be that those who are more adept find their behaviour rewarded, and perhaps find themselves more highly valued and influential members of the community.

Another criticism of 'communitarianism' is its idealisation of consensus and harmony. Boot and Reynolds note the 'disquiet among critical educators and more politicised professionals that the emphasis on openness, trust and self-disclosure in some versions of group-based training serves to obscure realities of power, difference and the conflicts of interest which characterise the workplace' (1997, p. 90). Reynolds points out that consensus is often unrealistic, and risks discounting important differences that exist in any social context. He thus proposes the 'bright lights' of the city as an alternative to 'pastoral idyll' and its connotations of utopian harmony.

These critiques are important, and have both informed and influenced our practice. They raise a series of dilemmas and render peer community learning problematic through posing moral and political questions that are present in any learning community, and that are suitable for inquiry themselves. Even so it seems important not to overdo the deconstruction of the notion of a learning community, for example by implying that creating a supportive learning environment predicated on constructive group interaction is either not worthwhile or somehow excludes issues of diversity and power.

## Complex adaptive systems

A conceptual frame informing my current thinking about learning communities is offered by theories of complexity. These contemporary ideas, reflected in work in the field of education (e.g. Fullan, 1999; Cunningham, 2000; Tosey, 2002; Fenwick, 2003; Cooper *et al.*, 2004; Haggis, 2004), offer an innovative perspective on professional educational practice, radical in that it challenges strongly the idea that staff are in control.

Complexity Theory is a cluster of ways of thinking that have developed from branches of 'new science' concerned with the behaviour of natural systems (Waldrop, 1994), such as Chaos theory, Dissipative structure theory and Quantum physics. These ideas lead to a view of human systems – of which a learning community may be an example – as 'complex adaptive systems'. 'A complex adaptive system consists of a large number of agents, each of which behaves according to its own principles of local interaction' (Stacey *et al.*, 2000, p. 106).

'Adaptive' indicates that the system both influences and is influenced by its environment, but accepting that no complex system exists in isolation from other systems. There is no unified view of the nature of Complexity Theory, however. It is contested territory and there are epistemological questions about the validity of treating learning communities and other human organisations as complex adaptive systems.

Complex adaptive systems have a self-organising capacity. Left to themselves – but with various conditions present, such as agents with sufficient opportunities to interact – patterns emerge from the apparently chaotic actions of the agents. 'No individual agent, or group of agents, determines the patterns of behaviour that the system as a whole displays, or how these patterns evolve, and neither does anything outside the system' (Stacey *et al.*, 2000, p. 106).

This contrasts (I suggest) with a more common, Newtonian assumption about learning communities in higher education, which is that they are entropic; in other words, that in the absence of some imposed order they will become inert and dissipate. Staff then become privileged agents who are seen as responsible for supplying order, and may blame students if their efforts are unsuccessful.

The complexity view is that instead of supplying order, the role of staff (together with students) is to help create and support conditions under which that self-organising capacity can operate. If we act as if the student group is entropic, we will be inclined to supply more energy and structuring than the community may need, efforts that could stifle the capacity of the community itself.

This links to another feature of the complexity perspective, which is that the universe is essentially participatory. No-one stands outside the system, and there are no privileged observers. We move from being external to the system to acting within it, and unable to stand outside it. Stacey (2000, p. 407) emphasises that in organisations, no manager can stand outside the system and choose how it is to operate. This means we have influence without control, which requires a shift:

> When one moves away from thinking that one has to manage the whole system, one pays attention to one's own participation in one's own local situation in the living present. Perhaps this humbler kind of 'management' is what the 'knowledge society' requires.
>
> (Stacey, 2001, p. 235)

A system self-organises in response to difference and interventions. We cannot determine how the system will self-organise, we can only anticipate what might happen and attend to what happens in practice. In this respect a learning community is like an eco-system. It changes and evolves; we participate in it, and cannot stand outside it or control it. Every change we introduce, indeed every act of participation, introduces difference. Human intervention can be precarious, and runs the risk of doing more harm than good. Predictions of the effects of changes, if based on 'linear' thinking, are likely to be disappointed. Changes will have unintended consequences, as well (hopefully) as some intended consequences, but 'solutions' often create new problems.

Paradox is inherent[6] in complex adaptive systems. As educators, naturally we encourage students to learn. For many of us it is our vocation and it seems self-evident that we would not intentionally prevent or obstruct learning. Yet I suggest that educators perpetually *regulate* how, where and when students should learn, tacitly teaching students about contexts in which it is legitimate (according to staff) for them to inquire,[7] and those in which it is not. Therefore, we are as active in discouraging learning in some respects as we are in promoting it in others. Mirroring this, and simultaneous with their 'legitimated' inquiring for programme purposes, students also inquire tacitly into the 'rules' of how to behave in any learning community, as is suggested by the concept of the 'hidden curriculum' (Snyder, 1971).

This is one way in which a complexity perspective may take up some of the critical concerns raised by Reynolds and others. Whatever educators say or do in relation to a programme is both an act of education and an act of regulation – which is an exercise of power, therefore power is inherent in every interaction with students. Communication cannot *not* be relational and political.

To make these processes of regulation open to inquiry in a learning community means asking educators to be open to challenge and able to display vulnerability. Perhaps the first step is for staff to be aware of when they may be closing down inquiry simply because it makes them uncomfortable, or threatens their authority, or appears inconvenient.[8]

A learning community predicated on ideas of complexity would also seek to value and allow for *emergent* learning, arising in unexpected ways from local interactions. This contrasts with a trend in formal education to value, and to emphasise the achievement of, predictable outcomes. Prescribed outcomes, and the schemes of assessment that follow, may leave no space for, and can fail to recognise or reward, emergent and accidental learning.

'Reality' (i.e. what people take to be reality) is also regarded as emergent, in the sense that it is constructed through interaction and dialogue. Such constructions of reality are recursive; in other words, dialogue about assessment criteria is not simply a process of clarification, it can change the assessment criteria because a new understanding emerges.

To allow for emergence we need to encourage, among other things, connectivity. The principle of 'connectivity' is that a system's behaviour relies less on the nature of individual agents (including staff, students and others who impinge on the learning community) than on the quantity and quality of connections between them. I suggest there is much greater scope for generally for connectivity in formal education generally between staff and students, among students themselves, and outside formal programme boundaries.

Richard Seel (2005) offers the following list of conditions that enhance emergence, and which can therefore also guide the design and facilitation of a peer learning community:

- Connectivity – emergence is unlikely to occur in a fragmented world.
- Diversity – if there is not enough diversity in the system it will be hard for different patterns to emerge.
- Rate of information flow – either information overload or too little information flow can make emergence unlikely.
- Lack of inhibitors – for example inappropriate power differentials, too much anxiety or threats to identity can all inhibit emergence.
- Good constraints to action – effective boundaries can enhance the possibility of emergence.
- Positive Intention – a clear sense of purpose can influence the chances of emergence occurring.

- Quality of Interactions – research by Marcial Losada (Losada and Heaphy, 2004) suggests that emergence is more likely to occur if there are significantly more positive than negative interactions within a group or team.
- Watchful anticipation – while a clear sense of purpose can influence the chances of emergence occurring, a period of expectant waiting is often necessary to facilitate emergence.

## Summary

This chapter has acknowledged multiple notions of learning community, which emphasise the relational nature of learning and attempt to counter the potentially alienating nature of higher education. It has proposed six dimensions of design that can assist with reflection on the intended nature of a learning community, and has also considered two further theoretical perspectives, those of critical theory and complex adaptive systems, that offer educators different ways of thinking about the notion of a 'learning community' and attendant issues. Broadly I have argued for a strategic rather than tactical approach to the design of a learning community, thus inverting the tendency to see the relational dimension of learning as an optional enhancement and instead embedding it in the architecture and practice of any educational programme.

## Acknowledgement

I acknowledge the contribution of participants on the MSc Change Agent Skills and Strategies peer learning communities, and that of academic colleagues past and present, particularly Dr Josie Gregory who co-authored an earlier paper on this subject.

## Notes

1 There is also contemporary interest in virtual or online learning communities, a theme not covered in this chapter.
2 http://learningcommons.evergreen.edu/, accessed 15 July 2005. I am indebted to Young (2005) for this link.
3 The MSc CASS began in 1992. It is an advanced, experiential course enabling participants to inquire about, and to develop their skills as facilitators of, human processes of change, learning and development in organisational and community contexts. Participants are postgraduates experienced in their field, which may be training, management development, organisational consultancy or a similar area. The course makes significant use of experiential learning

and principles of action learning, for example, through module by module tasks that involve drawing up learning contracts. There is also extensive, formalised usage of self and peer assessment.

4 Capability, commitment, contribution, continuity, collaboration and conscience.

5 Cross reference to chapter on Facilitation.

6 See, for example, Russell and Whitehead's theory of logical types, from which Bateson's theory of levels of learning is developed (Bateson, 1972, pp. 250–279).

7 I recognise a need here to tease out differences between 'learn' and 'inquire'.

8 Argyris (1999) describes such practices as 'defensive routines'.


# References

Argyris, C. (1999) (2nd edn) *On Organizational Learning*, Oxford: Blackwell

Bass, R. (1999) 'The scholarship of teaching: what's the problem?', *Inventio: Creative Thinking About Learning and Teaching*, Department of Instructional Improvement and Instructional Technologies, George Mason University, February, Vol. 1, No. 1 (accessed online at http://www.doiiit.gmu.edu/Archives/feb98/randybass.htm, 28.6.2005)

Bateson, G. (1972) *Steps to an Ecology of Mind*, London: Paladin, Granada

Benhabib, S. (1992) *Situating the Self: Gender, Community and Postmodernism in Contemporary Ethics*, Cambridge: Polity Press

Benson, J. (2001) (2nd edn) *Working More Creatively with Groups*, London: Routledge

Biggs, J. B. (2003) (2nd edn) *Teaching for Quality Learning at University : What the Student Does*, Buckingham: SRHE and Open University Press

Boot, R. and Reynolds, M. (1997) 'Groups, groupwork and beyond', in Burgoyne, J. and Reynolds, M. (eds) (1997) *Management Learning: Integrating Perspectives in Theory and Practice*, London: Sage

Boud, D., Cohen, R. and Sampson, J. (2001) *Peer Learning in Higher Education*, London: Kogan Page

Brookfield, S. (1987) *Developing Critical Thinkers*, Milton Keynes: OU Press

Cervero, R. and Wilson, A. (1999) 'Beyond learner-centred practice: adult education, power and society', *Canadian Journal for the Study of Adult Education*, Vol. 13, No. 2, pp. 27–38

Cooper, H., Braye, S. and Geyer, R. (2004) 'Complexity and interprofessional education', *Learning in Health and Social Care*, Vol. 3, No. 4, pp. 179–189

Cooper, J. and Robinson, P. (1997) 'Small-Group Instruction: an annotated bibliography of science, mathematics, engineering and technology resources in higher education', Occasional Paper no. 6, National Institute for Science Education, University of Wisconsin-Madison

Critten, P. (1996) 'A learning community in the making: Middlesex University's new MA in personal and organizational development', *The Learning Organization*, Vol. 3, No. 5, pp. 14–17

Cunningham, R. (2000) 'Chaos, complexity and the study of education communities', paper presented at *Education for Social Democracies: changing forms and sites*, Institute of Education, University of London, 3–5 July 2000

Dewey, J. (1916) *Democracy and Education: An Introduction to the Philosophy of Education*, New York: Free Press (1966 edn) (accessed through *The Encyclopedia of Informal Education*, http://www.infed.org/archives/e-texts/e-dewey7.htm, 15 July 2005)

Fenwick, T. (2003) 'Reclaiming and re-embodying experiential learning through complexity science', *Studies in the Education of Adults*, Vol. 35, No. 2, Autumn, pp. 123–141

Fisher, D. and Torbert, W. R. (1995) *Personal and Organizational Transformation*, London: McGraw-Hill

Fox, S. (1994) 'Towards a learning community model in graduate management education', *Management Learning*, Vol. 25, No. 2, pp. 249–262

Freire, P. (1996) (revised edition, transl. Myra Bergman Ramos) *Pedagogy of the Oppressed*, London: Penguin

Fullan, M. (1999) *Change Forces: The Sequel*, London: Falmer Press

Gabelnick, F., MacGregor, J., Matthews, R. and Smith, B. L. (1990) *Learning Communities*, San Francisco, CA: Jossey Bass

Goleman, D. (1996) *Emotional Intelligence*, London: Bloomsbury

Haggis, T. (2004) 'Theories of dynamic systems and emergence: new possibilities for an epistemology of the "close up"?', paper presented at SCUTREA 34th Annual Conference, University of Sheffield, UK, 6–8 July 2004

Heron, J. (1974) *The Concept of a Peer Learning Community*, Human Potential Research Project, University of Surrey

Heron, J. (1977) *Dimensions of Facilitator Style*, Human Potential Research Project, University of Surrey

Heron, J. (1992a) *Feeling and Personhood: Psychology in Another Key*, London: Sage

Heron, J. (1992b) 'The politics of facilitation', in Mulligan, J. and Griffin, C. (eds) *Empowerment Through Experiential Learning: Exploration of Good Practice*, London: Kogan Page

Heron, J. (1996) *Co-operative Inquiry: Research into the Human Condition*, London: Sage

Huffman, J. B. and Jacobson, A. L. (2003) 'Perceptions of professional learning communities', *International Journal of Leadership in Education*, Vol. 6, No. 3, July–September, pp. 239–250

Humphries, B. and Martin, M. (2000) 'Unsettling the "learning community": from "dialogue" to "difference"?', *Community, Work and Family*, Vol. 3, No. 3, pp. 279–295

Jaques, D. (2000) (3rd edn) *Learning in Groups: A Handbook for Improving Group Work*, London: Kogan Page

Kahn, P. and O'Rourke, K. (2004) 'Guide to curriculum design: enquiry based learning' (accessed online at http://www.heacademy.ac.uk/resources.asp?process=full_record&section=generic&id=359)

Knowles, M. S. (1986) *Using Learning Contracts*, San Francisco, CA: Jossey-Bass

Knowles, M. S. and Associates (1984) *Andragogy in Action: Applying Modern Principles of Adult Learning*, San Francisco, CA: Jossey-Bass

Levine, J. H. and Shapiro, N. S. (2000) 'Curricular learning communities', *New Directions for Higher Education*, No. 109, Spring, pp. 13–22

Losada, M. and Heaphy, E. (2004) 'The role of positivity and connectivity in the performance of business teams: a nonlinear dynamics model', *American Behavioral Scientist*, Vol. 47, No. 6, pp. 740–765

Malnarich, G. (2005) 'Learning communities and curricular reform: "Academic apprenticeships" for developmental students', *New Directions for Community Colleges*, No. 129, Spring, pp. 51–62

Marsick, V. and Kasl, E. (1997) 'Factors that affect the epistemology of group learning: a research-based analysis', paper presented at the 1997 Adult Education Research Conference (accessed online at: http://www.edst.educ. ubc.ca/aerc/1997/97marsick.htm, 15 July 2005)

Marsick, V., Bitterman, J. and Van der Veen, R. (2000) 'From the learning organization to learning communities toward a learning society', ERIC Clearinghouse on Adult, Career, and Vocational Education, Information Series no. 382, Ohio State University

Menzies, I. (1970) *The Functioning of Social Systems as a Defence Against Anxiety*, London: Tavistock Institute of Human Relations

Miller, E. (1993) *From Dependency to Autonomy: Studies in Organisation and Change*, London: Free Association Books

Peck, M. Scott (1993) *A World Waiting to be Born*, London: Rider

Pedler, M. (1981) 'Developing the learning community', in Boydell, T. and Pedler, M. (eds) *Management Self-Development: Concepts and Practices*, Aldershot: Gower

Postle, D. (1993) 'Putting the heart back into learning', in Boud, D., Cohen, R. and Walker, D. (eds) (1993) *Using Experience for Learning*, Buckingham: The Society for Research into Higher Education and Open University Press

Reason, P. (ed.) (1988) *Human Inquiry In Action: Developments in New Paradigm Research*, London: Sage

Reason, P. (1998) 'Political, epistemological, ecological and spiritual dimensions of participation', *Studies in Culture, Organisation and Society*, Vol. 4, pp. 147–167

Reynolds, M. (1998) 'Bright lights and the pastoral idyll: social theories underlying management education methodologies', paper presented at conference on 'Emergent Fields in Management: Connecting Learning and Critique', University of Leeds, July

Reynolds, M. (2000) 'Bright lights and the pastoral idyll: ideas of community underlying management education methodologies', *Management Learning*, Vol. 31, No. 1, pp. 67–81

Seel, R. (2005) 'Creativity in organisations: an emergent perspective', http://www.new-paradigm.co.uk/creativity-emergent.htm

Senge, P. M., Roberts, C., Ross, R. B., Smith, B. J. and Kleiner, A. (1994) *The Fifth Discipline Fieldbook: Strategies and Tools for Building a Learning Organization*, London: Nicholas Brealey

Shulman, G. (1983) 'The pastoral idyll of democracy', *Democracy*, Vol. 3, pp. 43–54

Smith, B. H. (1988) *Contingencies of Value*, Cambridge, MA: Harvard University Press

Smith, B. L. (2001) 'The challenge of learning communities as a growing national movement', *Peer Review*, Association of American Colleges and Universities, Summer/Fall, Vol. 3, No. 4 / Vol. 4, No. 1 (accessed online at http://learningcommons.evergreen.edu/pdf/PeerReview2001.pdf, 15 July 2005)

Smith, B. L., MacGregor, J., Matthews, R. S. and Gabelnick, F. (2004) *Learning Communities: Reforming Undergraduate Education*, San Francisco, CA: Jossey-Bass

Snyder, Benson R. (1971) *The Hidden Curriculum*, New York: Knopf

Stacey, R. D. (2000) (3rd edn) *Strategic Management and Organisational Dynamics: The Challenge of Complexity*, London: Routledge

Stacey, R. D. (2001) *Complex Responsive Processes in Organizations*, London: Routledge

Stacey, R. D., Griffin, D. and Shaw, P. (2000) *Complexity and Management: Fad or Radical Challenge to Systems Thinking?* London: Routledge

Thompson, J. D. (1967) *Organisations in Action*, New York: McGraw-Hill

Torbert, W (1991) *The Power of Balance*, Newbury Park, CA: Sage

Tosey, P. (2002) 'Teaching on the edge of chaos: complexity theory, learning systems and enhancement', Learning and Teaching Support Network, Generic Centre http://www.ltsn.ac.uk/application.asp?section=generic&app=resources.asp&process=full_record&id=55

Tosey, P. and Gregory, J. (1998) 'The peer learning community in higher education: reflections on practice', *Innovations in Education and Training International*, Vol. 35, No. 1, pp. 74–81

Tuckman, B. W. and Jensen, M. A. C. (1977) 'Stages of small group development revisited', *Group and Organizational Studies*, Vol. 2, pp. 419–427

Waldrop, M. (1994) *Complexity: The Emerging Science at the Edge of Order and Chaos*, London: Penguin

Wenger, E. (1998) 'Communities of practice: learning as a social system', *Systems Thinker* (accessed online http://www.co-i-l.com/coil/knowledge-garden/cop/lss.shtml, 14 July 2005)

Wenger, E. (1999) *Communities of practice: Learning, Meaning, and Identity*, Cambridge: Cambridge University Press

Young, G. (2005) 'Learning communities: literature review – curriculum development', unpublished paper, Faculty of Health and Human Sciences, Thames Valley University

# Part III

# Chapter 14

# Assessment in post-compulsory education

*Linda Merricks*

## Introduction

Assessment is vital to any teaching and learning. Minimally, students and teachers need to know that a required standard has been reached for particular awards. More importantly, without adequate information about what has or has not been learnt, whether subject knowledge or skills, students cannot progress, teachers cannot assess their own teaching and institutions cannot have confidence in the awards they offer.

Assessment is also a moral activity. As Peter Knight (1999, p. 14) claimed,

> What we choose to assess and how shows quite starkly what we value...Assessment systems advantage some learners and disadvantage others...effective assessment depends upon having a view of what it is that we are trying to do in a programme and hence of what we ought to assess.

This is echoed by David Boud (1995, p. 35) who wrote, 'Assessment acts as a mechanism to control students that is far more pervasive and insidious than most staff would be prepared to acknowledge.' The ideological aspects of assessment are unavoidable. Therefore, they should be recognised by all teachers and consideration of the effects of assessment made an element in the design of curricula.

Assessment is not simple. As the government's Lifelong Learning policies push towards a Learning Society, students in post-compulsory education are now diverse, of different ages and very different backgrounds. They also have different purposes for learning. Some study for interest, not award, while skills and vocational learning is becoming more necessary in response to economic changes in the workplace.

To achieve the new targets for employment in the various regions more people, and different socio-economic and age groups will need to develop new skills or find new ways of using those they have. Modes of learning reflect this diversity of students and purpose. Full or part-time; face-to-face or distance learning; the use of books; the Web; television and discussion are amongst the myriad ways of learning available to students. Courses too can be now more complicated. They cater for the range of students, by offering different levels of award, different speed of progress and different kind of subjects, sometimes in new combinations. Combined, major/minor, interdisciplinary, work-based learning is merely a selection. There is also an array of institutions to provide this learning. From Sixth Form Colleges, adult education, continuing education, the WEA, FE Colleges, Universities, Trade Unions through to the University of the Third Age, there is an enormous choice. However, as a result of this multiplicity of provision and learners, assessing need and progress has become more complex.

Research and discussions during the last ten years have led to an emphasis on assessment as an essential part of teaching and learning. The Academic Audit Unit in 1991/1992 said very little about assessment in its reports of visits to universities and in a number of instances found nothing to report. Since then assessment has become more important as a measurement of the quality of provision in institutions. For example, the 2001 Quality Assurance Agency (QAA) Handbook contains a separate 'Code of Practice for the Assessment of Students', which will be one of the tools for Academic Review procedures. This is one of the three 'standard codes', together with 'Programme Approval, Monitoring and Review' and 'External Examining', which are used to measure academic standards.

This degree of change in perceptions of the importance and role of assessment is not yet found in the FE sector where regular inspections and the verification role of bodies like the City and Guilds or GCSE have, and will for the near future at least, demanded particular modes of assessment. These have tended to concentrate on the achievement of specific learning as set out in the curriculum. However, some changes in vocational education now affecting the sector have been developed in the relatively new and fast-growing Work-Based Learning programmes. Because of the lack of tradition, these programmes have started from almost from scratch and an important part of their progress has been a careful examination of the role and processes of assessment. They also work within an ethos of students' involvement in all aspects of their learning, and this naturally highlights assessment. Foundation degrees, offered mainly within the FE sector raise new questions. As programmes designed to bridge the vocational/academic gap, assessment must address both elements.

## Why assess?

Assessment takes place for a number of reasons, for a number of different audiences – students, tutors, mentors, employers and educational systems – the management bodies of teaching institutions, government bodies and funding councils. Increasingly assessment is also seen as a vital part of the quality assurance processes. It therefore has many different purposes, takes many different forms, has different levels of reliability and validity, takes place at different points in the learner's career and has findings communicated in different ways. These can be summarised as follows:

- students expect it and are motivated by it;
- to diagnose learning needs – especially important for mature students and adults, to select for next educational stage or work; to certificate learning;
- to provide feedback; help remedy mistakes; help with option choice and selection; help diagnose faults;
- to provide a performance indicator for students and enables final grading (e.g. degree classification);
- to ensure that the learning outcomes for different awards and programmes are met;
- to provide a performance indicator for staff;
- to provide a performance indicator for course and institution;
- we have always done it.

## Assessment is learning

Assessment is basic to learning: to students' learning; to academics learning about becoming better teachers and facilitators; to systems' learning about what they are Doing well and less well. However, as the QAA attempt shows, the difficulty lies in defining how this might be accomplished, unless there are some principles for measuring what has been achieved by all teacher sand learners, learning from the experience will be negligible.

The primary purpose of assessment is to ensure that the learning outcomes of any course or programme are achieved, and sometimes to measure the level of that achievement. To accomplish this deceptively simple aim, a number of stages are necessary.

- The learning outcomes, both in terms of subject knowledge and of skills and competences, must be clearly defined at the curriculum development stage.
- The methods of assessing ALL these should be established at this point and forms of assessment established and questions about whether self- or peer-assessment would be appropriate, or the need for formal examination should be asked and answered.
- The uses of the results of the assessment also need to be considered here. Formative assessment, designed to provide students with feedback on their work, can be used very differently from summative assessment, whose primary functions to measure achievement towards the award of grades.
- The contribution to learning also should be considered. Mere repetition of information from memory rarely encourages learning. More useful aims might be to encourage team-work, as well as developing specific skills in a subject.
- Finally, the students must be involved in the process. The teacher should EXPLAIN the assessment processes early in the course to ensure students understand what is required of them and then explain the aims of each assessment task. Many research projects have shown that his stage is rarely completed and that students are left to guess the intentions of any task, hoping that they are right. Criteria for marking and grading also should be clear and comprehensible. The mystery of B++ might amuse the teacher, but it can be totally obscure to the learner.

Assessment contributes to the learning process only when learners and teachers share an understanding of the purposes of the assessment and the criteria for marking and grading.

## Teaching through assessment

One way in which understanding the processes of assessment can be clarified is through consideration of the purposes of the task. A convenient way of doing this is by using the summative/formative/ipsative definitions.

Summative assessment, as its name suggests is primarily designed to provide a description of what has been achieved and includes end of course assessment. It often results in grading of this achievement, which will indicate to learners, teachers and outsiders, for example employers, the level of that achievement. Because of this, reliability of the process, including marking and communication of the results is an essential feature. It is clearly desirable that there is parity between First Class degrees awarded by different institutions and that this can be measured. To ensure the validity of the results, the marking should be criterion-referenced against pre-determined criteria. Comparison with other students' work is not necessary in this context, but in some forms of examination this is an essential part of the allocation of grades – the grades are norm-referenced, not criterion-referenced. Feedback to the learner beyond the grade awarded is not necessarily a part of this process. The actual use of summative assessment in this unmediated form is coming under question. Students accustomed to public examination systems do not expect feedback on their examination papers, but new learners, especially perhaps adults recognise that little learning can take place without comments on their practice. Teachers are now beginning to question the whole process, but time in a climate of rising student numbers makes any change that will increase workloads unlikely to be popular. Immediately, the importance of the process is that the process of assessment is transparent and clearly explained to all concerned. Students expecting a norm-referenced grade may be disappointed when another measurement is used.

The judgement of reliability depends on the purpose of the assessment. The purpose of formative assessment is to provide an estimate of achievement, which is principally designed to help in the learning process. It often takes the form of pieces of work in addition to those demanded by summative assessment, but can also be a part of continual assessment. As the primary purpose of formative assessment is to be a part of the learning process it does not necessarily measure achievement with the award of a grade, although 'informal' and unrecorded grades are often given to indicate the level of achievement. Thus, reliability is not an essential issue as the comparison is with earlier learning, not a grade that compares with other learners.

The essential part of the process is to identify strengths and weaknesses in the learner's work so that improvements can be made and gaps in knowledge or skills filled. In this case, feedback is essential and should identify the level of knowledge of the subject, the presentation of the work and the competences demonstrated in generic skills. The assessment of these areas may refer to both criteria-referenced and norm-referenced levels. The process here needs to be both valid and reliable, but as with all formative assessment, the process must reflect the learner's achievement and provide guidance for the future.

Ipsative assessment measures personal achievement and is designed to provide information for the individual learner so they can check their own achievement. It must be criterion-referenced but need not be assessed by any outsider. The benchmark of achievement is oneself. It can be especially useful in some distance learning programmes where the learners can keep a note of their understanding and knowledge on a regular basis.

An additional complication is that formative and summative assessments are not necessarily mutually exclusive. One assessment can have a dual purpose and often does in continual assessment. The distinctions between the two are, in any case, not always clear. This is less important than ensuring that the assessment during the whole course of study achieves its prime purpose which is to ensure that students achieve the outcome of the course. To this end, and to overcome some of these difficulties of explanation, as Sally Brown and Peter Knight (1995, p. 15) have pointed out, 'the notion of reliability in HE assessment is being displaced by the concept of quality assurance in assessment'.

## Who should assess?

Traditionally, teachers have assessed students. The teachers have set the assessment tasks, explained what is required and then marked the results. Assessments have usually been defined in curricula but, especially in HE, have tended towards standard forms of 'the essay' or the 'seminar presentation'. So long as the majority of students came from traditional backgrounds this was adequate and tended to work well. However, with the increasing numbers of non-traditional learners there is the need for change towards more varied and more explicit forms of assessment. There has also been a difficulty with standardisation and parity across courses and subjects. University lecturers have traditionally expected a degree of autonomy in their teaching and have relied on external examiners and examination boards for any regulation. This process has been changed within the HE sector by a number of QAA initiatives including the publication of subject benchmark statements during the last year which describe the learning outcomes for individual subjects. The impact of these benchmarks has yet to be felt, but the intention is some standardisation of learning outcomes.

The learners' role has been merely to complete the task and await a grade. With the new complex mix of learners, demands for more owner-ship of the process have been growing and this has coincided with the realisation that students can learn more, and differently, from peer- and self-assessment. It has also coincided with teachers finding they have less time for the marking of assessments, especially if formative assessment is developed as a coherent part of the curriculum.

Self-assessment and peer-assessment can lead to greater ownership of learning and to greater motivation by learners. It 'is fundamental to all aspects of learning. Learning is an active endeavour and thus it is only the learner who can learn and implement decisions about his or her own learning: all other forms of assessment are therefore subordinate to it.' When successfully implemented, it

- allows sharing of learning
- leads to autonomous learners
- leads to more competent learners
- promotes the reflective student who is likely to become a lifelong learner
- develops skills – team wok, group work leadership, problem solving.

Self- and peer-assessment can work with a number of different assessment methods. For example, a record of achievement or Personal Statement of Learning ask students to reflect on their learning through a course of study and to ask themselves to what extent they have achieved the learning outcomes of the course. They might also ask for an evaluation of the course itself and the teaching. Consideration of thee questions demands reflection on the course itself and the learning that has taken place.

Questions about future study can also require consideration of the generic learning outcomes in addition to the subject-based achievement. Similarly, portfolios of work assembled during the course comprising learning journals and other materials demand careful assessing of what is being learnt. When the portfolio comprises an ongoing part of the whole course it can also help to reveal shortcomings in learning, which can be rectified before any summative assessment. Self-assessment forms require rather different skills for their completion. They are most useful when used in conjunction with clear criteria and examples of good and bad pieces of work so that learners can examine their own, or their peer's practice and offer comments on the resulting assessment.

However, learners often find it difficult to grade their own work and can both under and over-estimate their achievement. In view of this, self-grading should be used with caution, especially with returners to learning whose confidence in their abilities and understanding of what is required may need development. There are other limitations to the use of self- and peer-assessment. Peer-assessment of group work can be very useful as a means of persuading the group to ask who actually contributed what to the project, but it can be spoilt be the personalities in the group. Friends can over-estimate each other's achievement while enemies can under-estimate. There may be caution about actually saying that one member did very little. Similar difficulties can arise with other forms of peer-assessment and versions of 'I will scratch you back if you scratch mine' can arise so that grades are inflated.

There is also resistance to the process. Outside agencies can distrust it, arguing that only trained teachers can adequately assess the achievement of learners, thus ignoring the learning that takes place as a part of the assessment. Perhaps more surprisingly, learners themselves can react against it, they also argue that they are not able to assess their achievement. These can be overcome only by demonstration and persuasion, and, as in all other kinds of assessment, making the process and its expected outcomes clear to all concerned. Confidence in self- and peer-assessment will normally grow once it is a usual apart of the assessment strategies.

Finally, it should be clear to everyone concerned that peer- or self-assessment can only be a part of the whole. They are not normally used for summative assessments and almost never for graded examinations. They play a part, alongside teacher-assessed work, in providing varied learning for self-confident reflective learners.

## Forms of assessment

There are almost as many forms of assessment as there are teachers and learners. A number have already been mentioned. They vary from traditional, unseen, timed examinations whose grade contributes directly to a final award to self-assessed learning journals, from seminar papers or book reviews to formal essays with full academic references. They can be written, oral or pictorial. With the use of IT their range will increase. What the forms have in common is that they should be designed as a coherent part of the curriculum. They should each be able to test specific learning outcomes, and all the learning outcomes of the course, subject specific and generic should be assessed. This full coverage may be ascertained by a curriculum map or less formally by some kind of checklist, but it is important that teachers and learners can demonstrate the relationship of assessment of all outcomes. Transparency of theses processes is becoming increasingly significant as the demands of equal opportunities legislation are met. Finally, the kind of outcome of the assessment, grades or developmental, needs consideration in the context of the whole programme of learning.

Where there are progression routes, as through a three-year degree programme, there might be learning outcomes from the whole programme, as in definitions of graduateness. There is a need for the learning associated with these outcomes to be assessed as well as those of the individual modules. Mapping outcomes becomes more sophisticated and complications as processes become more transparent. The development of student progression files places further demands on the mapping of outcomes.

There also might be demands from the awarding bodies for some kinds of assessment to measure the achievement of specific learning outcomes. As already described, HE institutions have specific outcomes associated with degrees. Further Education and Work-Based Learning programmes normally have clear vocational aims and objectives and lead to externally referenced awards. These might be NVQs with specific already agreed learning outcomes in the form of competences which need to be achieved and are set out in advance. The outcomes for Work-Based learning Programmes are usually negotiated with employers and learners at the outset. Like vocational awards, GCSE students need to demonstrate that they have completed a national curriculum, which must be marked against nationally agreed criteria, with norm-referenced grades awarded on basis of all students' achievement.

In contrast, HE tends to be largely autonomous with external examiners providing the external references. This form of peer review means that as a result assessment tends to be valid. Parity is achieved across an institution or subject, but it is not necessarily reliable across the sector. Subject benchmarks and the work of the QAA are attempts to address these issues without going so far as the FE/GCSE models.

Adult Continuing Education has traditionally been more flexible than any of these. However, the moves towards certification and accreditation since the changes in funding resulting from the 1992 Further and Higher Education Act mean that assessment here is coming under increasing scrutiny. The difficulty lies in retaining flexible processes designed to meet the needs of numbers of students with very different abilities and experiences while including summative assessments on which judgement of overall achievement can be made. In addition, these results must measure reliably against other those of other HE institutions.

All these processes put heavy and growing demands on staff who struggle to cover all aspects. As a result, in all areas, interest in computer-assisted assessment (CAA) is growing rapidly. As Sally Brown (1999, p. 1) has said, it is hoped that CAA can help by

- reducing the load on hard-pressed staff;
- providing students with detailed formative feedback on their learning much more efficiently than is usually possible with traditional assessment;
- bringing the assessment culture experienced by students closer to the learning environments with which they are familiar and confident.

Bull and McKenna (2004, p. 143) claim that it also can add to the authenticity of the assessment process. However, they warn that although attractive, CAA cannot be the sole form of assessment. It is particularly appropriate for formative assessment, it is perhaps more suitable to scientific and technical subjects than more discursive disciplines. In a newly developing and fast-growing form of assessment, these restrictions may be challenged.

Recent legislation means that all forms of assessment will be subject to additional scrutiny. The Disability Discrimination Act, 2005, insists that access to education should be available to all and adjustments should, wherever reasonable, be made to ensure this. A part of this requirement will be the provision of forms of assessment geared to the needs of particular students.

## What is assessed?

The simple answer to this question should be learning – of the student, the teacher and the institution and the essential question to be asked of the process should be whether or not the learning outcomes of the course of study have been successfully achieved. The outcomes of the course should be of two kinds. Conventionally, assessment has concentrated on one part of the first, which is knowledge of a subject or discipline. This can be assessed as just a question of memory and the learner can be asked to rehearse that learning. While formative assessments during a course may be used to test memory in this way it is now more usual to also assess understanding of the subject through some kind of explanation of process either in written form, in essay or examination or verbally in class presentation or discussion.

Generic competences and skills appropriate to the subject areas should also be assessed. As described above, this may be achieved through self-assessment, but the teacher as well as the student should record the achievement of an acceptable level. In some courses these skills are specifically assessed and the learning outcomes refer to them, for example, the ability to analyse and synthesise the results of some limited research. In others, the achievement of generic skills is assumed to be a part of the programme and there is an expectation that students who cannot adequately write an essay will fail. The latter procedure is tending to be phased out, as in many other instances, the changing student body demands more clarity and guidance.

As well as the learning of the students, the teaching of the course should also be assessed. If the majority of learners have not achieved the learning outcomes of the course then it is likely that there are problems with the teaching, either in the presentation of the materials or in the design of the course. In the most serious cases, some kind of institutional failure might be the cause. It is possible, but less likely to raise comment, that too high grades might lead to the same questions.

## Quality assurance and verification of assessment

This is increasingly important and a number of external agencies are involved at course and institutional levels. At present, HE institutions are relatively autonomous with their own award-giving powers. The FE sector tends to be more regulated by outside stakeholders and other external agencies, most notably OfSTED and the Adult Learning Inspectorate.

Increasing differences between learners and their learning needs leads to a need for regulation by both internal and external bodies. All quality assurance agencies recognise the importance of this, but all also recognise impossibility of standardisation across institutions and sectors. The various level descriptors and subject benchmarks show the beginnings of attempts to provide a level of standardisation, but although some progress has been made within the various sectors, there is little advancement across post-compulsory education as a whole. At present, there are different external agencies and methodologies within and across the various parts of the whole.

External verification of results takes place at course level primarily in Further Education. GCSE and GCE courses normally have appointed external examiners to mark examination scripts and to check samples of teacher-assessed work. For NVQ and GNVQ programmes external verifiers are appointed by the awarding body, RSA, Edexcel or City and Guilds, to confirm that assessment procedures are appropriate and that work is marked to national standards. The validating HE institution usually checks degrees taught in Further Education colleges.

Awards by Higher Education Institutions are more autonomous. They have in general been subject to external scrutiny only by external examiners. There are exceptions to this, primarily in vocationally based programmes where the professional body acts as an additional verifier of the course and the results. For example, the British Psychological Society verifies psychology degrees. However, the external examiner system is becoming more difficult. As workloads increase there is a growing reluctance to fulfil this role by academics in the sector. Simultaneously, there is the development of auditing by external agencies that develop tools by which HE assessments can be measured.

In addition to these procedures, there is increasing scrutiny from the quality assurance bodies although in HE this tends to concentrate on process not results of the process. The QAA for Higher Education is responsible for auditing the quality of all HE teaching. It has also been responsible for the production of subject Benchmarks. OfSTED, with the Adult Learning Inspectorate has increasing responsibility for much FE work and will be responsible for all non-higher education post-compulsory learning. In addition, the Further Education National Training Organisation has set professional standards in Education and Teaching.

The QAA code of practice for assessment sets out guidelines for all HE institutions. The attitude of the Agency is encapsulated in their *Precept 2* – 'The principles, procedures and processes of all assessment should be explicit, valid and reliable.' However, the effect of this publication may be disappointing. Despite a very positive introduction, the code itself emphasises procedures and measurement. The Introduction describes assessment as 'a generic term for a set of processes that measure the outcomes of students' learning, in terms of knowledge acquired, understanding developed, and skills gained'. Specifically, the many purposes of assessment are defined as –

- the means by which students are graded, passed or fail;
- it provides the basis for decisions on whether a students is ready to proceed;
- it enables students to obtain feedback on their learning and help them improve their performance;
- it enables staff to evaluate the effectiveness of their teaching.

The Code continues, 'Assessment plays a significant role in the learning experience of students', and goes on to describe the different forms of assessment as diagnostic, formative or summative. At this point though, the Agency quietly demonstrates the difficulties of measuring the complicated view of assessment it has set out. The Introduction concludes, 'The code of practice assumes that these understandings of the nature and purpose of assessment are broadly accepted and implemented by higher education institutions.' The precepts that follow this introduction then concentrate on the 'measurable' of assessment procedures and emphasise that assessment should demonstrate the achievement of learning outcomes. Even here, the Agency explains 'It is not the intention of the Agency to prescribe specific ways of implementing the precepts set out below'. An opportunity to examine the various possible methods of assessment and some kind of account of best practise in the sector seems to have been lost. The valuable work at a number of conferences, in books and the work of the Staff and Educational Development Association which have all contributed to changes in the view of assessment in HE seem to be judged too complicated to assess.

## Implications

The implications of the assessment methods, and the changes now taking place are that the results of assessment are designed more closely to emphasise the learning that can be achieved. This learning is set out more clearly, in terms of learning outcomes of any course and how those outcomes will be assessed. However, there is a need for staff development if full advantage is to be taken of the full possibilities of nee methods and there is a demand for increased staff time, at least in the development phase. If these can be meet, then assessment can become a truly useful part of learning and teaching, not just the bugbear of examinations.

## References

Boud, D. (1990) *Implementing Student Self-Assessment*, Higher Education Research and Development Association of Australasia, Sydney

Boud, D., Keogh, R. and Walker, D. (1985) *Reflection, Turning Experience into Learning*, London: Kogan Page

Brown, S. and Dove, P. (eds) (1991) *Self and Peer Assessment*, Staff and Educational Development Association

Brown, S. and Glasner, A. (1998) *Assessment Matters in Higher Education*, SRHE and Open University Press

Brown, S. and Knight, P. (1994) *Assessing Learners in Higher Education*, London: Kogan Page

Brown, S., Rust, C. and Gibbs, G. (1994) *Strategies for Diversifying Assessment*, Oxford: Rewley Press

Brown, S., Race, P. and Bull, J. (1999) *Computer-Assisted Assessment in Higher Education*, Staff and Educational Development Association

Bull, J. and McKenna, C. (2004) *Blueprint for Computer-Assisted Assessment*, Routledge, Falmer

*Code of practice for the assurance of academic quality and standards in higher education. Section 6: Assessment of Students*, The Quality Assurance Agency for Higher Education, May 2001

Knight, P. (ed.) (1995) *Assessment for Learning in Higher Education*, London: Kogan Page

Miller, A. H. (1998) *Student Assessment in Higher Education*, London: Kogan Page

*Standards for teaching and supporting learning*, Further Education National Training Organisation, January 1999

## Useful websites

www.niace.org.uk

www.qaa.ac.uk

www.tesfefocus.co.uk

www.lilfelonmglearning.co.uk

www.fefc.ac.uk

www.education.guardian.co.uk

www.seda.demon.co.uk

# Chapter 15

# Assessment of experiential learning in higher education

*Josie Gregory*

In this chapter I intend to illustrate some key educational processes involved in self- and peer-assessment and indicate some of the reasons why higher education has been slow to adopt this method of reflective learning for HE students. I consider the extent to which self- and peer-assessment, particularly of experiential learning can meet its developmental and emancipatory aims (Heron, 1974) within a formal academic structure. Thus the practice of self- and peer-assessment is compared to the philosophy of the education of adults (Knowles, 1990) and Torbert's (1991) concept of a 'liberating structure'. Self- and peer-assessment does possess the potential to operate as a liberating structure, and so to contribute to emancipatory education (Habermas, 1972). At the same time there are various pressures within a higher education setting that may militate against this, and which may lead to self- and peer-assessment being operated in impoverished forms. I want to argue that this represents a failure to apply knowledge about adult learning within higher education, and an example of educational institutions as non-learning organisations.

## Self- and peer-assessment educational theory and intentions

The literature on self- and peer-assessment within professional education stretches back more than 30 years (Kilty, 1978; Heron, 1979a; Bond, 1988), yet only attracted serious study and application to learning and academic grading since the late eighties (Boud 1989, 1995; Ford 1997). The form of self and peer group assessment discussed in this chapter was developed through experiential inquiry with groups of professionals in the medical, nursing and public service fields, before gradually extending to a formal Master's programme, where it is an integral part of the teaching and assessment processes. (The MSc in Change Agent Skills and Strategies.) As progressive liberal educators, seeking congruence between our philosophical values of individual liberation and empowerment within social and hierarchical systems, we use educational methodologies aimed at keeping the power of 'knowing thyself' (Baume and Baume, 1986, p. 65) with the individual.

Heron (1974) stated that an educated person is one who is self-directing, self-monitoring and self-correcting. This premise continues to be used to benchmark what should constitute 'being educated' in higher education. The link between Heron's definition and Fisher and Torbert's (1995, p. 7) 'liberating structures' is not difficult to see, for:

> A liberating structure is a type of organizing that is productive and at the same time educates its members towards self-correcting awareness. Engaging in a process of mutual self-correction requires ongoing effort among participants to recognize and correct errors and incongruities in the midst of action, an effort we find to be the primary requirement for continual quality improvement.

'Mutual self-correcting' in Fisher and Torbert's statement is the linchpin of self- and peer-assessment. The values of self-direction, that is, believing that human beings have choice, and with that, responsibility, that they are intentional, aim at goals, and are aware that they cause future events and seek meaning, value and creativity (AHPP, 1998, p. 15) are all reflected in the self- and peer-assessment process. Heron writes 'Using self- and peer-assessment combines three strands: (1) it is a form of professional development; (2) it is an advanced continuing educational procedure; and (3) it is an action research inquiry into professional practice' (Heron, 1994). These three strands are essential in professional development and offer an educational rationale for the inclusion of this form of self- and peer-assessment on the MSc course. Self-assessment is therefore a teaching and learning activity as well as an assessment practice for accreditation purposes, a point confirmed by Boud (1995). He documents very clearly the conflicting purposes of assessment in higher education. One purpose is 'to improve the quality of learning' through formative feedback from tutor and 'the other concerns the accreditation of knowledge or performance' (Boud, 1995, p. 37), that is, summative assessment. Boud goes on to say that formative assessment is intended to facilitate the learner, helping him or her to improve performance, while the latter is 'for the record', that is, it serves the academic institution and the external world. It certifies competence to certain standards and provides for easier selection in the workplace.

The theoretical rationale for self- and peer-assessment has been suggested already through the philosophy of self-directed adult learners (Knowles, 1990) and under the principles of the Peer Learning Community (Heron, 1974; Tosey and Gregory, 1998; Chapter 13 of this volume); and on the notion of the educated person. Self- and peer-assessment in principle are supported by a number of educational theorists. The modern philosophical base, which gave rise to humanistic educational thinking during the 1950s and 1960s, has its origin in progressive education (Dewey, 1916). This link between Dewey's educational philosophy, humanistic psychology and the education of adults is discussed in an earlier chapter of this volume.

Dewey's educational philosophy with the use of Kolb's (1984) and Heron's (1989) experiential learning cycles provides the basic for a reflective self-assessment cycle used as part of the self- and peer-group assessment processes. Rogers' injunction that: 'The only man who is educated is the man who has learnt to learn' (Rogers, 1983, p. 120) forms the mandate for developing learning to learn skills, the most important of which is, accurate self-assessment (Heron, 1974; Jarvis, 1995). This facilitation of learning has been the challenge of adult education for the past thirty years and philosophically has been the main change in professional educational thinking and direction over the same period (Jarvis, 1995).

Torbert (1991, p. 41) refers to a 'liberating structure' under the framework of a paradigm of 'just action'. This he states is an educational process. In summary, parts of these liberating structures include 'a cultivation of awareness that embraces the realms of the intuitive whole, the rational strategy, plan or rules, congruent action, and outcomes and that observes and corrects errors and incongruities in translations from one realm to another'. Torbert emphasises that this should be part of raising children, and if done successfully then adults would be able to work within these premises in organisational work and, we believe, in education for professional and organisational work.

Much of traditional education is deemed to re-enforce oppression. Inappropriate or oppressive pedagogy is considered to create imbalance in the psyche of the individual, causing unaware under-development of potentiality and distortion of self-identity and self-esteem. (Freire, 1972; Knowles, 1990; Heron, 1992; Boud, 1995; *inter alia*). On the other hand liberating structures seek to empower, and empower in a way that Knowles (1990, p. 57) described under the term 'the psychological adult', that is, when individuals arrive at a self-concept of taking responsibility for their own life, of being self-directed. Hence one particular intention in developing students' skills in self assessing is to facilitate their liberation from oppressive self perception to a more spontaneous, accurate and empowered view of their own knowledge and abilities with the main emphasis being on learning from experience. This theme is developed in both Habermas's (1974) critical social science and Mezirow's (1981, 1999) transformation theory, where the two most important tenets are critical dialogue and the need to examine social and cultural environments as well as the subjective when assessing what needs to change and how to make prudent decisions.

## Self- and peer-group assessment on the Master's programme

The introduction of the MSc in Change Agent Skills and Strategies in 1992 gave an ideal opportunity to review and adapt the model of self- and peer- group assessment for an award-bearing Masters programme. Previously the model had been used for a non-award baring Diploma course and other professional development short courses that had run for twelve years. The adaptation moved away from the ideals of the complete self-determined model to a more formally assessed and graded evaluation of learning outcomes.

The MSc provides a postexperience training for people such as management consultants, trainers and other professionals in the human resource field. The course group operates as a learning community (Tosey and Gregory, 1998 and Chapter 13 in this volume) and the assessment process creates peer learning through its two main educational methodologies: to operate as an experiential learning group and foster learner participation in educational decision-making. The course community works as a closed group over the two year programme and fits the definition of peers as; those who have shared knowledge and expertise in the subject matter, accessibility to the professional context and are accepted by each other as legitimate peers for the purpose of the educational process (adapted from Heron, 1974). This provided a rationale for the involvement of the peer group in the assessment of individual learning. For as Heron (1974, p. 1) stated: 'In all three stages, (of the educated person), as a self-directed, self-monitoring and self-correcting being, the opinions of his peers in the same domain of experience are an important source of influence'. On the MSc, There are eight modules, seven of which are taught as experiential workshops where the module is assessed by four main criteria:

1   the diagnosing of learning needs, with the development and implementation of a learning contract within prescribed contract criteria;
2   satisfactory self-assessment of the learning contract within the self- and peer-assessment format and submission of a portfolio summary in the form of reflections on learning and self accreditation of the module;
3   demonstration of advances in learning how to learn and change from modular activities;
4   the submission of a satisfactory theoretical assignment.

The first three criteria form part of the assessment for the experiential component of the programme and is the focus of this chapter. The theoretical assignment is also self, peer and tutor assessed using Masters' level learning descriptors and Masters' level marking criteria. Two Internal Examiners and one External Examiner assess the dissertation in the traditional way. The theoretical assessments will not be discussed further.

Self-assessment as a procedure has embedded within it many processes and skills that need to be teased out and developed in the student. These skills include the student's ability to self-assess their learning needs, followed by other skills such as; being able to set achievable learning goals or outcomes; being able to form a learning contract with peers' help to address the goals set; having the necessary resources and ability to make the changes or pursue the learning identified in the learning contract and finally being able to self assess their learning outcomes. Self-assessment in this case means being able to reflect on what one knows within the subject area of the module. It means knowing what one does not know but needs to know to meet academic learning criteria. The self-assessor needs to have the skills to determine the causes of success or failure, illuminating his/ her practice in the light of theory and to make correct and realistic judgements about achievements. The individual and the whole group are able to self audit in terms of academic and professional performance and standards to a rigorous degree with sufficient recourse to outside agencies, be that the programme tutor or professional auditors, to help them to decide for themselves whether they demonstrate sufficient knowledge or skills to succeed. According to Habermas (cited in Carr and Kemmis, 1986, p. 143):

> The structure of communication is free from constraint only when...all participants must have the same chance to initiate and

perpetuate discourse, to put forward, call into question, and give reasons for or against statements, explanations, interpretations and justifications.

Such democratic discourse is part of the inquiry process on the programme generally and in the development of learning contracts in particular and goes a long way towards facilitating its liberating and emancipatory aims.

Peer-group assessment requires the same skills and knowledge of the process as for self-assessment. 'Mutual self-correcting' implies that only peers who have gone through the same training in the necessary skills and are able to self assess to an equally good standard are eligible to peer assess others.

What makes self and peer group assessment liberating, in Knowles and Torbert's terms is in the shared knowledge and power of decision-making. This is incorporated in the assessment process as shown in italics below:

- self-directedness – *selection of personally and programme relevant learning goals, which is brought about through developing a learning contract (see example in Appendix A)*;
- recognition of the ability to develop self criticism and to make valid judgements about performance, *demonstrated through the use of self-assessment*;
- competence to give and receive feedback directly and honestly, *actioned through the peer learning community feedback systems and peer-assessments (Appendix B)*;
- willingness to engage with and understand group dynamics, *through interpersonal and group skills development in working in learning sets and the course group as a whole.*

## The learning contract

In our view as a course team, one of Knowles' (1986) greatest contribution to progressive adult education was in the formulation of learning contracts where many of the facets of self-directed learning come alive. Knowles observed in his studies of workers in part-time adult education, that providing a learning contract was a powerful strategy for engaging students in their own learning. Within the MSc, the use of learning contracts forms the first phase on which self-assessment and peer group assessment is built. Following Knowles model each learning contract has a description of individually identified learning needs and intended learning outcomes in relation to some aspect of intentional change. The outcomes may be personal, interpersonal or professional within the context of the module themes, and usually involves all three. The learning outcomes need to be developmental, usually based on experience of shortfalls or reduced competence in specific areas (Appendix A). The intended outcome could range from minimum competency to standards of excellence. The various parts of the learning contract are:

1   a description of the learning task;
2   learning objectives and criteria of good practice;
3   a list of resources and a plan of action;
4   evidence of accomplishment, a specification of what evidence will be used and how learning is to be validated.

Learning sets (Hughes in Pedler, 1983) are formed with four to five people per set who facilitate each other in creating the contracts in a peer helping relationship (Rogers, 1967). The importance of creating interdependence within the peer group is made very clear from the start of the process. They must explore each individual learning contract, looking for feasibility of the intended change, its scope and depth, significance for the individual and its relevance to the module objectives. This is followed with developing criteria for achievement, some minimum and others standards of excellence for the intended change. The module study guides offer guidelines on minimum criteria as well as a list of generic experiential criteria, which the learning set adapts to the particular themes of the module. Tutors act as resources to the learning sets while they learn the skills of creating realistic yet challenging learning contracts. The peer-group also learns the interpersonal skills necessary to facilitate each other and play Devil's Advocate to the contract to test its robustness before the individual learner engages with the contract task. In that process the peer-group is activating the first stages of the self and peer-group assessment procedure.

The development of the learning contract and the self- and peer-group assessment procedure are interpersonally intense experiential learning encounters (Heron, 1989), and is an example of the learning and teaching strategy described earlier. Much of the professional development and action research inquiry mentioned by Heron (1994) is contained in the forming and refining of the learning contract. The dialectical process of inquiry by the learning set about personally perceived developmental needs and progress can and often is a challenge and includes degrees of personal disclosure and feedback as described in the Johari Window (Hanson, 1973). The challenges involve honesty on the part of all concerned, being transparent, trusting and non-collusive. It requires that the group is facilitative and supportive as well as being emotionally competent (Postle, 1993) – all valuable attributes of personal and professional development (Claxton et al., 1996). In developing the learning contract, individuals are often confronted with self-reflective processes such as distortions in the person's self-formative processes which prevents a correct understanding of themselves and their actions (after Habermas, 1974). Such insights are brought to conscious awareness, to facilitate a change in personal constructs. Equally, there is a need to examine frames of references that are socially and culturally mediated, so that a valid diagnosis is made of what the subjective developmental needs are and what is socially constraining. Both may need attention. But to do the first without the second lends itself to the postmodern critique of individualism and psychologism, while to only attend to the latter negates the individual's ability to construct their own reality, subjectively, and to take some responsibility for creating the social and cultural milieu they reside in. Much of the experiential learning on the modules offer students experiences to engage them with their belief systems, their interpretive frames of references, and their actions, as students, peers in the learning community and as change agents in particular.

Following agreement with peers that the learning contract is ready for implementation, students work on the stated developmental task(s) outside the course contact time. Learners will also observe their own progress-in-action and reflect-on-action (Schon, 1991) using a (mandatory) personal journal to record progress and any significant aspect of their learning and intended change. A particular learning contract stays in operation from two to three months until the module is finished. In the final days of the module the self- and peer-group assessment procedure on the learning contract takes place.

## The self- and peer-assessment procedure

The self- and peer-assessment procedure itself has a prescribed format (See Appendix B). Following completion of the learning contract the learner prepares an evaluative summary on each aspect of the task(s) and a reflexive account on the mode of engagement with the task and progress made. This will include developments / change in self-awareness, attitudes, values, behaviour, thinking, emotions and spiritual levels if appropriate and learning to learn as well as the degrees of completion and achievement acquired. The learning set come together for a three-hour period during which each person takes time as self-assessor, when he or she evaluates his or her accomplishments, celebrates achievements and acknowledges any underachievement. The individual receives feedback on their self assessment. A crucial principle within the programme philosophy is that the power and ownership of the learning stays with the learner, therefore peers respond within the parameters set by the content delivered by the self-assessor, which they will all have been party to during the contract development. Peers will agree or disagree with the evaluation of learning against the criteria created in advance. They will state whether they accept the evidence to be as valid as promised. They will challenge under or over-assessment of the individual, and any deprecating remarks as well as any grandiosity in the delivery of the self-assessment. They will finish by celebrating with the self-assessor what he or she has achieved, which may not always be the successful completion of the contract, but the value of the learning in the process of engaging with the task.

There is no doubt from our experience that this whole process serves all the students in the learning set and that the learning contract is a tool or channel through which self and professional development does occur. It is a teaching and learning strategy and its effectiveness lies it's the development of prudent and sophisticated decision-making. Our student have usually to spend from five to twenty years in work situations assessing or auditing these businesses in the light of national, international, and sometimes government criteria. Hence the need for them to have diagnostic and assessment skills to a high level of competence. Yet the academic self- and peer-assessment processes experienced on this programme seem more personally challenging and equally more rewarding.

Being mindful to separate out the two aspects of assessment (improvement of learning and institutional requirements) the self- and peer-assessment of experiential learning is formative as well as summative, and is in the control of students as to whether they will pass self and peers in the learning set. The grading is a simple pass or fail grade. A fail grade, while seldom needed, is more like a referral with some requirement to complete parts of the learning contract if necessary.

In all the years that the programme has been running, the self- and peer-assessment process has for the most part been agreed with by peers with little unresolved conflict. There is often conflict in the sense of challenges by the group to the individual if the student does not seem to be stretching him or herself sufficiently. Equally the individual can challenge the group if the learning requirements seem unreasonable or the assessment criteria too demanding. Such conflicts are considered a vital energetic learning opportunity for all concerned as it ultimately challenges the whole learning set to work with achievable standards that they can all be confident to identify with. The level and intensity of dialogue within the learning sets around the development land implementation of each learning contract and the assessment together form an action inquiry cycle.

## Self- and peer-assessment – a liberating structure?

According to Broadfoot (1996, pp. 41–42), liberating assessment techniques are explicitly designed to promote rather than assess learning. In her review of assessment in mainstream education she states: 'although the battle to liberate the learner though assessment has been temporarily lost to schools, the war continues with aspirations of a paradigm shift away from testing to learning'.

Broadfoot also asserts that assessment drives learning, therefore the type of assessment will play a large part in determining the learning attitude and strategies that learners adopt. If we accept that assessment drives learning, and our aim is to promote learning then making assessment a teaching and learning strategy will allow these two aims come together. The learning contract provides the optimal strategy for this alliance and provides a liberating structure while still aiming for valid academic standards.

The literature on the application of modified forms of self- and peer-assessment highlight the varying degrees of commitment to the process as a completely liberating one. The most obvious modifications of the original model are that while the assessment of educational tasks (be they scientific experiments or practical) and processes, (such as team building or group involvement) are devolved to learners, the assessment and marking of theoretical work continues to be held by the 'professional' assessors (Stenhouse, 1975; Burnett and Cavaye, 1980; Earl, 1986; Brown and Dove (ed.) 1993; Conway *et al.*, 1993; Boud 1995). The percentage of grades allotted to self- and peer-assessment procedures also demonstrates a weakened commitment to the fundamental postulate of the educated person, as tutors hold on to an unequal allocation of grades thus maintaining an in-balance in decision-making (Boud, 1995). For example, Earl (1986) reported that in the BSc in Mathematical Science, 10% of the course marks were peer awarded for group communication skills as these were seen as an essential part of the group-based projects. However students were not allowed to self-award and were neither given nor expected to set exacting assessment criteria. There appears to be a lack of trust in students' ability to set exacting standards for themselves and their peers nor to accurately or honestly assess themselves, yet being able to do this for their peers.

Within a course for the training of adult educators known to the author, the course staff were content to allow self and peer award of 15% of the total course marks based on self- and peer-group assessment of student competence in creating a positive learning environment among themselves. However one of the Course Validation Bodies (Nursing in this case) reduced the proportion to 5% of the total marks, making the acquisition of such a grade irrelevant to passing or failing the course. Students' motivation to engage in the exacting task of criterion setting and the self- and peer-group assessment process was seriously challenged.

As a final example, in Fineman's report (1980) on peer teaching and peer-assessment as part of an undergraduate Business Administration course, a more self-determined strategy is described where students took complete charge of different parts of a module on Organisational Behaviour. Here the self-and peer-assessment was almost totally in the hands of the students. The tutor held the equivalent of one student vote and no more when dealing with content of subject, assessment criteria and the award of grades. This model fits the liberating structure as described by Heron (1994) and in Higher Education is closely aligned to Baume and Baume's (1986) self-determined self- and peer-assessment.

One of the key principles of a liberating structure is that of ownership of power and power sharing. On our Master's programme, while we remain mindful to work with the various combination of power sharing as part of our facilitation style (see Chapter 9), the module tutor holds hierarchical control of the module content to varying degrees depending on the module requirements. Part of this control is the setting of parameters for the learning contract within the context of the module themes. For example, the module on personal development prescribes that the learning contract must include an improvement of an interpersonal relationship, increased self-awareness and development of a (new) competence (Gregory, 2000). This degree of educational direction is intended to be an authoritative mode of facilitation, rather than autocratic (Heron, 1999), although purists of the self-determining, self-directed philosophy would dispute this. Indeed the prescription reveals the tutor's intention to comply with the modular aims and objectives, which they have hierarchically imposed as curriculum developers. The need here is for the curriculum designers to conform to the University's expectations to enable the course to be approved by the Validation Board before students ever join the programme. Yet, just such an argument (or excuse in Freire's terms) makes for the de-liberation of students when it comes to complete self-determining behaviour. As Freire (1972, p. 23) stated 'Every prescription represents the imposition of one man's choice upon another, transforming the consciousness of the man prescribed to into one that conforms to the prescriber's consciousness'. Freire goes on to say that such prescriptions create fear of freedom particularly if the consequence of not following the prescription is punitive, 'as freedom would require them (the prescribed to) to reject this image (of oppression) and replace it with autonomy and responsibility (p. 23). Freire's argument is that oppressed people learn to fear freedom because they have not learned to be autonomous and responsible. Our experience on the course would support this view, as students demonstrate discomfort and sometimes even disbelief when they realise that they really do have the power to self and peer assess and accredit each other on the programme.

This is experienced as a huge responsibility to group members, and not unlike Freire studies, they show a fear of working with this freedom and look to see what punitive measures might be taken if they get it wrong. One student stated:

> I was quite struck last week to hear that there was no peer review/ assessment for the dissertation and my immediate reactions was relief I suppose. In some ways I feel pressure with peer assessment and perhaps feel uncomfortable with it sometimes. That is my first reaction. That is about trust and confidence in the peer and its also about the assessment process itself being assessed, leaving it in somebody else's hands, that feels uncomfortable, risky and difficult.

Another student said:

> I think the fear has subsided over time. I am not nearly as terrified as I was at the start. For reasons, which were, I suppose, about fair hearing or handling of the responsibility. I think what has happened is, as the peer community works better, so does the peer assessment process. And it's something to do with giving people time and attention and getting an awareness of the work (to be assessed)....But I don't ever lose the terror of the assessment as such.

The programme tutors recognise such fears and allocate time during the workshops to discuss the assessment process and hear participants' fantasies and fears. The whole learning community is offered coaching until they feel confident with their knowledge and skills in criterion setting, the assessment process itself, managing the group dynamics in the learning set and managing emotionally and intellectually challenging situations as well. To tip the balance of power back to students in educational decision-making, we encourage students to develop personal learning criteria, particularly standards of excellence in one or more areas of the contract that the individual has a particular passion to develop. So again, if we take the example of the personal development module, while a relationship is to be improved, the learner is the only one who will decide which relationship to improve and state how he or she will navigate thought the complexities of that relationship.

The experiential learning assessment remains firmly in the hands of the learning sets who can award a module pass or fail grade to any one of the learning set members including themselves. The tutor's role is that of moderator of the process which they hold in co-operative mode (Heron, 1999) with the learning set. Therefore any collusion, scapegoating, 'dumping' of unfinished business or other biased or prejudicial behaviour will be flushed out as soon as identified and corrective, reparative action taken.

Part of the learning process for students is the need to do some un-learning about how people learn, and who is best placed to assess learning. Most learners have only experienced unilateral power – hierarchical and sometimes oppressive (Boud, 1995), where people give over responsibility and accountability to 'higher' or expert authority. Through the action inquiry process of self- and peer-reflection and assessment the skill of learning how to learn is developed and practised. Learning how to learn embraces Bateson's (1973) levels of learning as the inquiry deepens and broadens to take in change at different levels of being, and doing. It embraces Heron's (1989) four forms of knowledge, the experiential, imaginal, conceptual and practical as the learning contract is developed through these epistemological modes and assessed at a meta-level of analysis and critical reflection and evaluation. Learning how to learn is an emancipatory process. The educated person is one who has learned how to learn, they are self-organising, and can equilibrate their motivation, capacity to learn and transfer skills across contexts.

From the literature and in our experience it seems that critical compromises are often made for self- and peer-group assessment to be acceptable within the relevant institutional framework. We therefore argue that self- and peer-group assessment is a political structure, in that by its nature it will challenge institutionalised assumptions and practices. This political dimension is an inherent feature of liberating structures, an important theme, which needs further exploration. The aim will be to consider how such political pressures could be managed by academics wishing to introduce self- and peer-assessment.

The compromise within our programme is that the theoretical assessment is less liberating as a structure as the tutor's assessment and grade takes precedence over those of the student and peer assessor. This has created some disillusionment and at times disagreement among tutors and students. The programme regulations allows for serious disagreement to form the basis for a meeting between all assessors concerns, self, peer and tutors where each explains and justifies their reasons for the grades against the stated criteria. Here all voices are equal and the tutors' decision is open to scrutiny by students. However, the grade is seldom changed even after such a discussion. This transparency mitigates a little against the hierarchical power held by the tutors.

## Conclusion

There is a paradox that adult education remains, by and large, dominated by a hierarchical model of education. We know a very great deal about the learning preferences and needs of adults. Yet our education system has not only failed to implement these on any significant scale, but also the current trend is regressive in this respect.

Flexibility and accessibility do not, contrary to the popular view, enhance the 'adultness' of the learning experience. Primarily they facilitate the economics of education – enabling greater consumer access, and increasing the commercial opportunities of higher education institutions.

If the assessment strategy drives learning, then that strategy needs to mirror the values of the educated person in order to be a liberating structure (Torbert, 1991) The self and peer group assessment strategy for experiential learning we adopt aims to meet these criteria.

## Acknowledgement

This chapter has been developed from an internal Human Potential Research Group (HPRG) publication co-authored with Paul Tosey.

# Appendix A

## *Learning contract*

Learning contracts are based on the assumptions about how adults learn (Knowles, 1986).

The learning contract is developed out of an assessment exercise where the student compares own present competence against externalised personal standards or other competencies or standards (of professionals and peers).

A Competency diagnostic list needs to be complied and agreed by peers who will support the individual and assess achievement of the learning contract. Use of inventories or other personality styles/learning styles can be used; however the choice of level of standards is negotiated in the learning set. By competence we mean appropriate standards of knowledge, skills, attitudes and values.

Questions to ask yourself are:

How important is the competence to my personal and professional life?
What is the level to which I have developed this competency to date?
What is its level of priority in my life now?
What is the level to which I want to develop this competency?

Below you will find a sample layout of a learning contract. All sections need to be completed for each new piece of learning.

Sample of Learning Contract layout

*Name:*                                                  *Module:*

| Learning objectives | Resources and strategies | Targets date for completion | Evidence | Verification |
|---|---|---|---|---|
| No. 1 | | | | |
| No. 2 | | | | |

# Appendix B

## Self- and peer-assessment – formal assessment

| Stage | Purpose | Essential content | Options/examples | Suggestions |
|---|---|---|---|---|
| Disclosure of self assessment | Self-assessor gives assessment of performance in relation to the stated aims and criteria. The agenda throughout is what has been said or done, not what could be done in the future | • Have I (self-assessor) achieved the objectives in my contract to the standard agreed with my peers?<br>• What is my key evidence?<br>• What are the main strengths and weaknesses of what I have done? | • What else have I learnt? | • Begin by reminding peers of the learning contract. Then evaluate achievements, limitations and so on. Do not go into detail or 'story-telling' at the expense of a clear self-assessment |
| Clarification questions | Peers ask for clarification and further information. Self assessor responds to questions by giving the minimum information needed | • What else do I (peer) need to know in order to (a) know what feedback I will give and (b) whether I accept the / self-assessment? | • What else do I need/want to understand/know?<br>• For example: 'Please expand on... ?'; 'Tell me more about...'; 'What did you mean by?'; 'How did you...?' | |
| Negative feedback | Peers respond to self assessment with criticism, that is, bases on which they disagree with or challenge the self-assessment. Deliver in a way that remains supportive of the person (however challenging to their actions or self-assessment) | • Self-assessor does not respond to any feedback<br>• In what respects do I (peer) disagree with the self-assessment?<br>• Is there any incongruity between the self-assessor's claims and their evidence? | • Was the self-assessor congruent (e.g. did verbal and non-verbal messages match?)<br>• For example: 'I think/I don't think...'; 'I dislike/I like least...'<br>• For example: Rhetorical challenging questions; 'Do you | • It can be useful for the first peer responding to acknowledge the self-assessment (e.g. 'I'm delighted/ surprised to hear...')<br>• Ensure any challenges are challenges to the self-assessment (e.g. 'I challenge your claim that... on these grounds...'), |

| | | | | |
|---|---|---|---|---|
| | | really think ..?'; 'Did you notice the contradiction..?'; 'Are you aware that..?' | | NOT 'dares' to the person (e.g. 'I challenge you to....')<br>• Ground feedback in concrete data, examples |
| Positive feedback | Peers respond to self assessment with affirmation, that is, bases on which they agree with or support the self-assessment. Deliver in a way that remains rigorous to the procedure/educational aims of the process, and supportive of the person | • Self-assessor does not respond to any feedback<br>• In what respects do I (peer) agree with the self-assessment? | • Include appreciation, admiration, recognition etc.<br>• For example: 'I like...'; 'I value...'; 'I appreciate...'; 'I enjoyed...' | • Ground feedback in concrete data, examples |
| Self assessor responds | Self-assessor reflects on how they feel now, and how they experienced the self- and peer-assessment process – but NOT to respond to the content | • What am I (self-assessor) feeling now?<br>• How has the process impacted on me? | • For example: I felt very anxious when I heard your feedback.'; 'Now I feel ...' | • It is for the self-assessor to decide whether or not they accept any item of feedback; not commenting on the content does not mean that the self-assessor agrees with the feedback |
| Quality assurance | Group evaluates and 'quality assures' the self and peer assessment process, identifying modifications needed | • Have we kept to the principles and procedures?<br>• Has our process been degenerate?<br>• What do we need to improve next time around? | | • NB do not change principles<br>• Avoid tinkering with the structure of process; maintain same timing structure; sequence; etc. unless important to change it |

# References

AHPP (1998) Humanistic Values. *Self and Society – The European Journal of Humanistic Psychology*, Vol. 26, No. 3, July, pp. 3–60.

Bateson, G. (1973) *Steps to an Ecology of Mind*. London: Paladin.

Baume, D. and Baume, C. (1986) Learner, know thyself: self-assessment and self-determined assessment in education. *The New Era*, Vol. 67, No. 3.

Bond, M. (1988) *Self And Peer Assessment Manual For Nurse Tutors*. Unpublished. Guildford, The University Of Surrey, The Human Potential Research Project. Department Of Educational Studies.

Boud, D. (1989) The role of Self-Assessment, in student grading. *Assessment and Evaluation In Higher Education*, Vol. 14, No. 1, pp. 20–30.

Boud, D. (1995) *Enhancing Learning Through Self Assessment*. London: Kogan Page

Broadfoot, P. (1996) *Education, Assessment and Society*. Milton Keynes: Open University Press.

Brown, S. and Dove (ed.) (1993) Self And Peer Assessment. *Sced Paper 63* Birmingham: Society For Research Into Higher Education.

Burnett, W. and Cavaye, G. (1980) Peer assessment by fifth year students of Surgery. *Assessment In Higher Education*, Vol. 5, No. 3, pp. 273–287.

Carr, W. and Kemmis, S. (1986) *Becoming Critical: Education, Knowledge and Action Research*. London: The Farmer Press.

Claxton, G., Atkinson, T., Osborn, M. and Wallace, M. (eds) (1996) *Liberating The Learner: Lessons For Professional Development In Education*. London: Routledge.

Conway, R., Kember, D., Sivan, A. and Wu, M. (1993) Peer assessment of an individual's contribution to a group project. *Assessment and Evaluation in Higher Education*, Vol. 18, No. 1, pp. 45–56.

Dewey, J. (1916) *Education and Democracy*. New York: The Free Press.

Earl, S. E. (1986) Staff and peer assessment: measuring an individual's contribution to group performance. *Assessment and Evaluation in Higher Education*, Vol. 11, No. 1, pp. 60–69.

Fineman, S. (1980) Reflections on peer teaching and peer assessment: an undergraduate experience. *Assessment and Evaluation in Higher Education*, Vol. 6, No. 1, pp. 82–93.

Fisher, D. and Torbert, W. R. (1995) *Personal And Organizational Transformation*. London: McGraw-Hill.

Ford, A. (1997) Peer group assessment: its application to a vocational modular degree course. *Journal of Further and Higher Education*, Vol. 21, No. 3, October, pp. 285–296.

Freire, P. (1972) *Pedagogy of the Oppressed*. Harmondsworth: Penguin Books.

Gregory, J. (2000) *Understanding Personal Development. Study Guide-Module 2*. MSc in Change Agent Skills and Strategies. Guildford, School of Educational Studies, Human Potential Research Group. University of Surrey.

Habermas, J. (1972) *Knowledge and Human Interests*. Cambridge: Heinemann.

Hanson, P. (1973) The Johari Window: a model for soliciting and giving feedback, cited in *The Annual Handbook For Group Facilitators* (USA).

Heron, J. (1974) *The Concept of the Peer Leaning Community.* Guildford, University of Surrey, Department of Educational Studies. The Human Potential Research Project.

Heron, J. (1979) *Peer Review Audit.* University of London, British Postgraduate Medical Federation. University of Surrey. Human Potential Research Project.

Heron, J. (1989) *The Facilitators Handbook.* London: Kogan Page.

Heron, J. (1992) The politics of facilitation, in Mulligan, J. and Griffin, C. (eds), *Empowerment Through Experiential Learning: Exploration of Good Practice.* London: Kogan Page.

Heron, J. (1994) Self- and peer-assessment, in Boydell and Pedler (eds), *Management Self Development* (2nd edn) Chapter 8. London, McGraw-Hill.

Heron, J. (1999) *The Complete Facilitator's Handbook.* London: Kogan Page.

Hughes, M. (1983) The mixed set, in Pedler, M. (ed.) *Action Learning in Practice.* Chapter 6, Aldershot: Gower.

Jarvis, P. (1995) *Adult and Continuing Education* (2nd edn). London: Routledge.

Kilty, J. (1978) *Self and Peer Assessment and Peer Audit.* Guildford, University of Surrey, Department of Educational Studies. Human Potential Research Project.

Knowles, M. (1986) *Using Learning Contracts: Practical Approaches to Individual and Structured Learning.* San Francisco, CA: Jossey-Bass.

Knowles, M. (1990) *The Adult Learner: A Neglected Species* (4th edn). Houston: Gulf Publishing Company.

Kolb, D. (1984) *Experiential Learning: Experience as the Source of Learning and Development.* London: Prentice-Hall.

Mezirow, J. (1981) A critical theory of adult learning and education. *Adult Education*, Vol. 32, No. 1, pp. 3–27.

Mezirow, J. (1999) *Transformation Theory – Postmodern Issues. 1999 AERC Conference Proceedings.* http://www.edst.educ.ubc.ca/aerc/1999/99mezirow.htm

Postle, D. (1993) Putting the heart back into learning, in Boud, D., Cohen, R. and Walker, D. Chapter 2. *Using Experience for Learning.* Milton Keynes, SRHE and Open University Press.

Rogers, C. R. (1967) *On Becoming a Person.* London: Constable.

Rogers, C. R. (1983) *Freedom to Learn for the 80s.* Ohio: C. E. Merrill.

Schon, D. (1991) *The Reflective Practitioner: How Professionals Think in Action.* Aldershot: Ashgate.

Stenhouse, L. (1975) *An Introduction to Curriculum Development and Research.* Oxford: Heinemann.

Torbert, W. R. (1991) *The Power of Balance: Transforming Self, Society, and Scientific Inquiry.* Newbury Park: Sage.

Tosey, P. and Gregory, J. (1998) The peer learning community: reflections on practice. *Innovations in Education and Training International.* SEDA. Vol. 35, No. 1, pp. 74–81.

# Chapter 16

# Transforming learners through open and distance learning

*Peter Jarvis*

The year after I began my teaching career in Higher Education, the Open University (OU) was founded in the United Kingdom and for thirty years I was a part-time employee of the OU and, a decade or so after I started I was able to develop a Masters degree in Adult Education by distance learning at the University of Surrey, which was offered world wide. But in the past few years open and distance learning has changed dramatically and the opportunities for providing learners with the chance to learn appear fundamentally different. Now excellent books are being produced about these new approaches to teaching and learning, such as Laurillard (2002); Peters (2002); Jochem *et al.* (2004). While all these new approaches have rightly gained popularity, the traditional approaches to teaching and learning have remained and this is the main focus of this book. Nevertheless, it would be wrong for a book on teaching and learning not to include reference to these more recent approaches and so the purpose of this chapter is to do just this is a general way but it would take another book if we were to include all the changes that have occurred over the past thirty years. But what we have witnessed in this period has been a whole range of teaching methods that parallel the traditional approaches using a wide variety of media as the means of transmission of information or facilitation of learning.

All of the methods discussed in this book demand the presence of teacher and learners in the same place at the same time, but what modern technology has done has been to re-align space and time, so that one way of viewing open and distance learning is to recognise that the teachers and the learners need not be in the same place and learning need not occur at the same time as the teaching role is performed, not that it actually ever did. But this is not a new phenomenon since writing has always enabled this to happen; St Paul's letters, in the New Testament, might be regarded as an early distance education text where one person tried and succeeded to some extent in influencing early Christians in different churches in his absence through his writing. Like those letters, teaching through the media is a more timeless process because once the material is prepared and put out into the public domain it is open for anybody to access and for this reason the preparation of such material needs always to be of a very high quality since it is now not only the teacher's academic reputation that it at stake, it is the reputation of the institution which authorises and transmits it. No wonder that quality control procedures need to operate rigorously at institutional level.

When the OU was founded writing was still the main medium, although the use of radio and television was introduced from the outset, albeit in quite an unsophisticated manner. Much of this early material was didactic although there were some notable experiments with more Socratic and project approaches but it was towards the last years of the twentieth century when things began to change drastically as new media were introduced – although the fundamental teaching methods are still similar but the use of the media is rapidly becoming much more skilled. What was a rather traditional teacher-centred approach has not become much more student-centred through the sophisticated use of electronic media. Even so, one of the things about which we need to be aware is that we become so caught up with the slickness of the presentation that the actual aim of helping students to learn is relegated to second, or even to a lower, place. Therefore, some of the more general principles of teaching through the media remain the same as for the more traditional approaches. It is still necessary to understand how students learn and this is where we shall begin this chapter. Thereafter we will look at the way that different use of the media can facilitate learning.

## Part 1: students' learning

When we teach face-to-face we can situate the learners within the lecture theatre or class room but when we prepare distance learning materials it is impossible to think of the learners' situation but in both approaches it is even more difficult to know what the students are thinking, their academic histories, and so on. This is probably harder when we recognise the diversity of background from which learners using distance methods come. Peters (2002, p. 90) actually suggests that there are ten new learning spaces: instruction spaces; documentation spaces; information spaces; communication spaces; collaboration spaces; exploration spaces; multi-media spaces; hypertext spaces; simulation spaces; virtual reality spaces – each of which he discusses. Some of these we will refer to later when we discuss learning exercises. Consequently, it is impossible for us to assume a level of knowledge common to all of our students, especially in more open approaches to learning where there may be no prerequisite qualifications to starting a course of study. What then can we assume about the students? Clearly we can assume a level of motivation, perhaps even an eagerness to study. We can possibly assume that they will be working alone, although with many forms of e-learning there are numerous opportunities for interaction and even with more traditional distance learning methods we might have facilitated learning groups which meet regularly or even telephone networks – so that we can perhaps build into our courses opportunities for student interaction.

But what we do need is to try to start the students learning each session from a common starting point, or question, even if they do develop their ideas independently. The common question is actually quite significant because we all tend to take our world for granted and do not ask questions about it. Schutz and Luckmann for instance, write:

> I trust that the world as it has been known by me up until now will continue further and that consequently the stock of knowledge obtained from my fellow-men and formed from my own experiences will continue to preserve its fundamental validity… From this assumption follows the further one: that I can repeat my past successful acts. So long as the structure of the world can be taken as constant, as long as my previous experience is valid.
>
> (1974, p. 7)

In other words, we prefer not to question but to live 'instinctively', in harmony with our environment. Moreover, society is premised on the fact that we accept what we are told and that we do not question it and the last thing that we want as teachers is to have students approaching our lessons with the attitude of 'been there have done that'. This does not stimulate learning. There is a sense in which learning begins when we do not take our world for granted but when we question it. In my own research into human learning (Jarvis, 1987, 2006) I regard learning as beginning when we do not know, or that we do not know what to do, how to do it, etc.; it is what I call disjuncture. It is the point when my biography (memory of all my past learning) and my understanding of my present experience are not in harmony. This is disjuncture – it is a teachable moment. We have to create that disjuncture, that teachable moment, in our students. It is, therefore, important to stimulate our students, get them to start to question or be so excited by our introduction that they want to ask questions about it. Fundamental to all teaching is the maxim: if you do not strike oil in the first minute – stop boring! It is the disjuncture that occasions an experience and it is the experience from which we learn; it is the experience of not knowing that generates the learning process. There is a sense in which this disjuncture is rather like a lesser form of the type of experience that subjects have in a *Candid Camera* scene when they are confronted with a totally unexpected and even unimaginable situation – they just cannot take it for granted.

But experience is a problematic concept about which many books have been written (Oakeshott, 1933; Crane, 1992) but on which we cannot spend too long in this chapter. Even so there are two types of experience that we can create for our learners and these are primary and secondary experiences.

- *Primary experience.* This is the form of experience that we all have when we experience at first hand – we are actually confronted with a situation and we have to do something about it.
- *Secondary experience.* This is also sometimes called mediated experience. It is somebody else describing their experience to us and we are experiencing vicariously. Significantly, all theory, all didactic teaching and all distance teaching is secondary experience.

But we can use both in generating learning – by providing the learners with the opportunity of having primary or secondary experiences, or both. This can be done in a very wide variety of ways, such as:

- getting our learners to do something;
- confronting them with a scene, a scenario, a theoretical perspective;
- producing an argument/theory;
- giving them a picture to look at and criticise.

The disjuncture has to be sufficient to stimulate but not so far removed from their daily experiences that they automatically turn off because they feel that it is beyond them. Then we have to remember that we all learn through all of our senses all the time and even though we are either using distance material like the printed word or video/film clips our learners are not only learning through the words they read, the sounds they hear or the pictures they see – it is the whole person and all five senses involved in the learning. We should prepare this opening stimulus so that we can use the learning from all five senses.

And so we might ask, what precisely is learning? I now regard human learning as *the combination of processes whereby the whole person – body (genetic, physical and biological) and mind (knowledge, skills, attitudes, values, emotions, beliefs and senses – experiences a social situation, the perceived content of which is then transformed cognitively, emotively or practically (or through any combination) and integrated into the person's individual biography resulting in a changed (or more experienced) person.*

Figure 16.1 depicts simply the learning process from the point of view of the learner and it is useful to take them together as we try to understand learning. The first one is how we transform our sensations into solutions that we try out in practice and is we find over a period of time that they work we can internalise them; then we are enabled to take our life-world for granted again – provided that the life-world has not changed in the meantime!

But we can look at this from a different perspective in which we again start from the learners' perspective and see that the disjuncture leads to an experience, a short episode, about which they do something – they think, act and feel and as a result of their learning they become changed persons. Now this process is much more complex than this, as I have tried to show elsewhere (Jarvis, 2006), but the significant thing for us is that we are using media to take our learner through this complex process and in the remainder of this chapter I want to try to illustrate some of the ways in which we can do this (Figure 16.2).

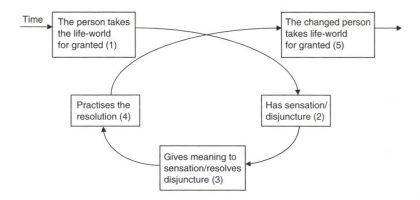

*Figure 16.1* The transformation of sensations in learning.

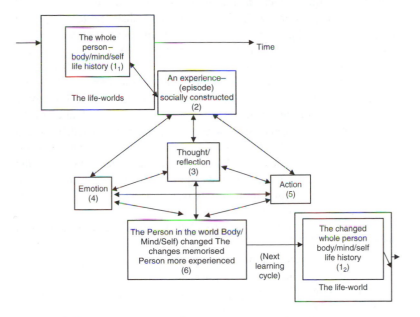

*Figure 16.2* The transformation of the person through learning.

In Figure 16.2 we can see that having had the experience the learners think/reflect, have feelings about it and may do something about it. But there are a variety of emotions and they interact with our thoughts in very different ways. There are numerous ways of thinking (Gilhooly, 1996) – not merely non-reflective and reflective – such as

- memorising and interpreting
- creative and critical thought
- directed and undirected
- problem-solving and decision-making
- deductive and inductive reasoning.

We need to be aware of these and utilise them in the learning exercises that we devise. In addition, we can do something as well – a project, an exercise, a piece of reading, and so on. These responses to the experience are the processes through which we learn and through learning we become changed or more experienced persons. The area of emotions is one that we have not used a great deal in teaching and learning but recent research (see Jarvis, 2006, for a summary of some of it) is beginning to show that emotions affect learning in many ways and eventually we will have to learn to work with the emotions in distance teaching and learning, but here I have made minimal and only basic references to the emotions. It is, therefore, our task to provide the initial experiences that start the learning process and then to provide/suggest activities in the three domains of thought, emotion and action through which our learners learn and become changed persons. These learning sequences may be part sessions or whole sessions, depending on the intention of the learning and preparing each session is a skilled process – one that is often developed in course development teams in distance learning organisations. This, in itself, changes the whole nature of teaching since the teachers used to design their courses and now distance learning is often prepared by groups working in collaboration. Merriënboer *et al.* (2004) have suggested that there are four components in the design of e-learning: the learning tasks provided for the learners; additional supportive information; just-in-time information – prepared and given to the students at the relevant time in the course in small packages; part task practice – exercises in order to integrate the outcomes of the learning into everyday practice. Most of what follows, however, will tend to focus on the design of the learning task itself.

## Part 2: the initial experience(s)

In the first instance most of us like to be able to contextualise our learning so that it is wise to begin a session by spelling out the aims of the teaching and learning session, even by specifying our aims and objectives – it will be recalled that earlier (Chapter 4) we suggested that behavioural objectives should not be used in teaching despite their popularity. We may also want to situate these aims within the whole course/module or programme so that at the start learners know precisely where this piece of learning fits into the whole. We need not do this latter element by merely telling the learners because we might want to combine that with questions and answers (see Chapter 7), or some other exercise that helps students recall and locate for themselves. However, it may be that we move from this to the initial experience.

If we recognise that students learn best if their curiosity is excited by something – if they themselves are asking questions about it, and so on. Consequently, we will do well to plan this carefully but, depending on the media in which we are working, we need to help students break away from their taken-for-granted and question. Our stimulus could be scene, a story, a critical analysis of a theory – and so on. It could also deliberately set out to use the emotions to get to feel a sense of affiliation, outrage, injustice, and so on – depending on the aims of the session. However, the object is to strike oil before we stop boring!

This is the springboard for part or whole of the session and we then need to guide our learners in the methods of learning – through thought, emotions and actions. It is here that we often run into problems about not being democratic in our teaching because we determine the methods of learning, even if our content is open-ended, and so it might be that we look at alternative ways of learning and alternative resources, rather than just specifying one way forward, and in this we can utilise thought, action and emotion. At the same time, this might be an ideal because we all function within the constraints of time.

## Part 3: facilitating the learning process

Clearly the process will depend to a great extent upon the medium within which we are working and the extent to which we are committed to providing sufficient material to achieve the objectives/pass the course. Some distance learning courses, for instance, make the claim that learners can pass the course on the material they are given in the course itself, not expecting the learners to go elsewhere. While this is a perfectly understandable intention if we are using distance learning print materials in certain situations or countries, but it is unwise to give learners the impression that they do not need to go beyond what we provide in the course. I can well remember in the early days of the British OU being confronted by some students at a summer school and being told by them that their tutor had told them that they did not need to learn anything more than what was in the course because there was enough there for them to get a good pass. I explained to them that there might be sufficient material in the module for them to pass the course, but the OU never claimed to provide all the knowledge about a topic nor did it say students could get a distinction just by learning information with which they were provided. Higher education is about more that memorising – but so too is learning, as we have indicated above and our aim is to help students learn.

Having had a stimulus with which to start, we transform our experiences through thought, emotions and actions and we can devise our teaching and learning materials and exercises in a wide variety of ways in order to incorporate them. Nevertheless, all learning starts with experiences and so in helping the students to keep on learning, it is up to us to keep on presenting our material in a learnable manner. Since this is a general introduction to teaching in open and distance education we will illustrate how we can utilise these human responses in relation to the different media. Laurillard (2002) suggests that there are five media forms: narrative, interactive, communicative, adaptive and productive and I will use these here to illustrate some of my points.

## Narrative

Basically this is teacher-centred teaching and learning material, such as a lecture printed or presented on video/compact disc/ DVD. In the same way, we can utilise documentaries, interviews with experts, panel discussion and so on. In many of these forms, the learners will have to teaching material so that they can play back or re-read what they are being taught. Nevertheless there are times when we use television or radio and not all learners will be able to record the material for future use and so, in these cases, students should be told to take notes at the time when they see/hear the material. In many instances, however, the material will be in a re-usable form and this can be utilised in future activities.

In each case the material is presented to the learners, but having presented the teaching material, we need not expect the learning to follow the same format. Consequently, teachers might want to prepare all types of learning exercises following the presentation, using a wide variety of teaching and learning methods. If we want students to think about the material we might undertake question and answer type exercises or we might focus on some element(s) of the presentation and raise questions about it – Socratic style. Here, we might focus on the legitimacy of an argument, the validity of the evidence, the logical progression of the ideas etc. In all cases, we can set exercises that enable the material to be considered at a deeper level. But we might want students to consider their emotional response to some teaching material, especially if it involves beliefs and values as well. We might ask students to keep a learning diary in which they record their emotional responses to the material, which they can subsequently be asked to analyse and discuss in groups, on-line networks or even in one-to-one discussions through all types of media. In addition, we might ask the learners to act upon what they have been taught – the action might merely be to discuss it with others, but it might be to observe what we see in our daily lives and check the validity of what we have been taught, and so on.

We are aware that many of these exercises that we set in some distance learning material is skipped by the students because they think just getting the material and trying to remember it for themselves is sufficient. We might have to explain to students that there are better ways of learning and that what we present might not actually be the whole answer to the question.

### Interactive

Interactive media mean that learners are able to interact with the media being used; traditionally, this has referred to the idea that the learners could control the speed of presentation, pause when they wanted to consider what has been presented, etc. However, there are now many other forms of interactive media. One is the preparation of programs using the Socratic method, whereby students are set exercises which require them to give their answers on the computer and the program does not progress until an acceptable answer is given. This is also a form of mastery learning.

Clearly in this approach there are fewer opportunities for building emotions into the learning process and the interaction itself forms part of the activity; indeed, each interaction might be regarded as a learning experience and, in a sense, the students go through the learning cycle again.

### Communicative

These are approaches that facilitate discussion between peers or between students and teachers. Teachers can, naturally, ask for feedback, questions and so on and have 'office hours' when they will respond to questions that have been sent them and even communicate their answers to all the enrolled students, but also there are programmes that enable students to communicate with each other, rather like the discussion group in face-to-face teaching. Such discussion should always be encouraged and students do have to learn that learning from other students is not a form of cheating, but a form of learning through mutual support. Students can discuss their emotional responses as well through these means, although many might be loathe to express their emotions and so this should not be expected.

In the same way that discussion groups tend to be informal learning, it is possible to create a formal conference, either audio by telephone or visual through other electronic forms. In these situations, which are sometimes quite expensive and so it is wise to know the cost before planning them. In addition, there tends to be much less informality in conferences of this form and so there needs to be a set agenda. Consequently, the preparation of such activities needs to be carefully undertaken. Such conferences need not just be on the teaching material but can usefully come after students have undertaken a small project or similar activity and then they will have opportunities to discuss their findings, the problems of conducting the work or even how they want to present their findings for assessment and so on.

It is significant that it is now possible to examine by this means, and I have taken part in a upgrading Viva from MPhil to PhD through video conferencing.[1] Naturally, all the normal examination procedures had to be taken care of and, in this instance, there was a representative of the awarding institution at the Viva but in the country with the candidate, although the examiner was in United Kingdom in the host institution with the chair of the examining committee. The actual viva itself was not too different from one that was face-to- face, but when the final PhD Viva was conducted we did it face-to-face in the host institution. Nevertheless, it is possible for such examinations to be conducted through this format, provided that all the examination procedures are carefully worked out beforehand.

### Adaptive

In the normal face-to-face educational activities, teachers tend to be adaptive to students' needs and modify their programmes and presentations accordingly. But this is much harder with open and distance education. Clearly the use of simulations and games allows this to happen and in these instances, students can also be asked to keep a record of their own emotional responses so that they can analyse themselves and their activities in these situations. Clearly, this is quite important when the topics under consideration are social or ethical in some way or another.

### Productive

A great deal of teaching and learning results in students undertaking mini-projects either individually or in groups. These can be built into open and distance learning and the outcomes of the activity can be presented face-to-face or through media networking. The use of Powerpoint presentations is useful here when copies of the slides are made available to all the students in the network. As in all group work, it is sometimes useful to record one's emotional response.

## Concluding discussion

This is only a very brief introduction to teaching and learning at a distance because, as I pointed out earlier, such a topic requires a book of its own. However, once we move into different media there is a potential problem, which is to forget all the basic theories about teaching and assume that every new development in e-learning is entirely new. This is not the case, most of the techniques we use are based on the ones that we have utilised in face-to-face teaching; it is just that the media are different. Distance leaning teachers still need a basic training in teaching and learning, even though they have to adapt their understandings to different media in which they should be experts.

Clearly in this globalised world, educational institutions are being forced to use the media for open learning as well as distance learning. There are great advantages of using such material – because it allows people to access learning opportunities who would not have been able to do so do for physical, social, economic and a variety of other reasons. The global network allows for the dissemination of more information and the sharing of many new ideas more widely. At the same time, there are potential dangers that through centralising teaching to some extent we expand the competitive aspects of the global market and gradually generate more mega-educational institutions at the expense of some of the smaller centres of excellence.

## Note

1 In some countries, such as United Kingdom, many research students are registered for MPhil/PhD and then undergo an upgrading interview during their studentship – some students, whose work does not look as if it will achieve PhD standard are encouraged to continue with the MPhil rather than the PhD after such an interview.

## References

Crane, T. (ed.) (1992) *The Contents of Experience* Cambridge: Cambridge University Press

Gilhooly, K. (1996) *Thinking: Directive, Undirected and Creative* (3rd edition) Amsterdam: Academic Press

Jarvis, P. (1987) *Adult Learning in the Social Context* London: Croom Helm

Jarvis, P. (2006) *Towards a Comprehensive Theory of Human Learning* London: Routledge

Jochems, W., van Merriënboer, J. and Koper, R. (eds) (2004) *Integrated E-learning* London: Routledge, Falmer

Laurillard, D. (2002) *Rethinking University Teaching* London: Routledge, Falmer

Oakeshott, M. (1933) *Experience and its Modes* Cambridge: Cambridge University Press

Peters, O. (2002) *Distance Education in Transition* Oldenburg: BIS, University of Oldenburg

Schutz, A. and Luckmann, T. (1974) *The Structures of the Lifeworld* London: Heinemann

van Merriënboer, J., Bastiaens, T. and Hoogveld, A. (2004) Instructional Design for Integrated E-learning in Jochems *et al.* (eds) pp. 13–23

# Chapter 17

# The professionalisation of teaching

*Peter Jarvis*

The traditional image of the practice of teaching as 'chalk and talk' has long been destroyed in contemporary society, although it is still widely practised. If distance education has done nothing else, it has demonstrated to a wider public new ways of teaching and learning. This book has also shown that even the old ways are undergoing tremendous change and, in a sense, rediscovering some of the techniques used in adult education for many years. The changing nature of teaching reflects the changing nature of society itself. For instance, there is a sense in which distance education began with letter writing but now, through the wonders of technology, the internet provides instant communication to masses of people world-wide. In face-to-face teaching there used to be wandering scholars, individual students travelled to the seats of learning, and now the generation of the 'knowledge factory' with hundreds of students all assembled in one place to receive the pearls of wisdom that would drop from the lips of one scholar. Now they do not need to travel. But even more so, as the learners are often older and more experienced, they play a greater role in the teaching and learning process. Teaching has not dropped the old in the face of the new, it has merely incorporated the new into the old and adapted to all the changes that are occurring. There are now a multitude of ways by which teaching is performed. It will continue to change in the future and we will briefly examine a few of the ways that teaching is changing and might continue to do so. We will do this in five sections:

- the continuing division of labour;
- the changing nature of what is taught;
- the changing nature of the learners;
- training the teachers;
- the professionalisation of teaching.

## Part 1: the continuing division of labour in teaching

Society has seen many forms of division of labour since Durkheim (1893–1933 edition) first wrote his classic study on the subject. Teaching has also seen a division of labour for traditionally a single teacher taught a course. However, in recent years a variety of different approaches to team teaching have occurred, and this is for a variety of reasons, including:

- the recognition that a great deal of teaching is about practice, which is not divided by academic disciplines, and practical knowledge is integrated. Hence it needs different subject specialists to combine to produce a practical course, including practice-based teachers;
- the fact that academic courses are being modularised – in a sense this is a Taylor-type means of production, with specialists concentrating on their own specialisms in the production of a course;
- the growing emphasis on modularisation, since it is also a useful approach to marketing since small pieces of a course can be marketed for lower cost, and so on;
- the need to update material very rapidly in a world where knowledge is changing very fast indeed;
- the growing complexity of knowledge production, especially in such approaches as distance education – where there are not only subject experts but process and production experts;
- the increasing need for practice-based teachers, such as coaches and mentors. This has led to training in mentorship and an increasing use of senior colleagues helping new teaching staff in a wide variety of ways;
- with the introduction of a wide variety of distance education universities and e-learning generally, there has been an increase in the diverse functions of the teaching and learning team with the ones who prepare the teaching material being but one part of an enlarged team.

In common with many production processes, teaching has become a team activity – groups rather than individuals prepare the teaching material, but in many cases the teaching material is determined by the level of technology being employed. Once this process begins, it is possible to envisage its expansion so that the production is not only by members of one institution of teaching and learning. Programmes are being prepared by teams spanning different educational institutions, and even from different countries, each using the expertise of members of these departments and universities. Now students might not know who their teachers actually are since one has prepared and another has delivered the learning material, and so on. The traditional teacher–student relationship is partially disappearing and with it the interpersonal ethic (Jarvis, 1997). Now students are clients purchasing a quality product.

However, this impersonality has given rise to other roles in teaching: the personal tutor, the academic counsellor and the advisor. If one wanted to be cynical and pursue the metaphor to its logical conclusion – this is becoming customer services. A major significance of the personal tutor role is that students still have a sense of continuity throughout a whole programme and there is still somebody who knows them. Nevertheless, the economics of teaching are such that fewer personal tutors perform the a counselling and guidance role which is becoming a specialist occupation in its own right. This role is less personal than that of the personal tutor since counsellors are not so closely associated with individual students and advise more students from a variety of different disciplines. American universities have for a long while now employed academic advisors.

However, in contrast to this division of labour in teaching, another approach is also possible: one well-known academic – a guru – can put together a single course for an academic institution and it can be marketed throughout the world, thereby putting at risk the jobs of many not quite so well-known subject specialists. If global capitalism continues to invade education, this will begin to occur. Already some commercial companies are employing well-known academics to produce lecture series that they can transmit over the internet. 'Star models' of teaching have already been considered and not rejected by educational institutions and consortia. Indeed, we can expect to see teaching develop in the same way as other manufacturing industries, as Otto Peters (1984) has already shown for distance education.

Traditionally in universities, academic specialisation was related to subjects being researched and taught by the same scholar but, as we pointed out in the opening chapter, there is a growing division between research, which is discovery – and teaching, which is the production and marketing of knowledge about these new discoveries. However, many of the discoveries are now no longer made in the traditional seats of learning, so that the material taught does not necessarily contain any that has been discovered by the teacher, or in fact by any teacher since, as Lyotard (1984) showed, knowledge is now often produced commercially, is of commercial worth and used in a knowledge economy.

## Part 2: the changing nature of what is taught

Teaching used to be concerned with disseminating knowledge, which was regarded as the truth. Truth, however, is a difficult phenomenon to envisage when knowledge changes daily and what was up-to-date one day becomes obsolete the next. Knowledge, in many scientific and technological areas does change almost daily, which means that the 'shelf-life' of some courses is very short indeed. Consequently, if teaching material is to be regularly updated, it can only be produced in small pieces, which allow for the substitution of new knowledge in a course between each time it is taught. Teachers, therefore, become more removed from the source of the knowledge as they seek to incorporate findings from diverse sources into their courses.

Knowledge is not necessarily truth. It is personal and subjective, as constructivism has shown us. Indeed, there may be competing interpretations of a single phenomenon and now teaching may assume a role of offering interpretations and evaluations of these competing perspectives (Bauman, 1987). This means that students have to be taught to understand that teachers no longer teach the truth and that they, the learners, have to be critically aware of what is occurring. Indeed, learners do have to be taught to learn in a critical and analytical manner (Barry and Rudinow, 1990). Consequently, the status of teaching is changing since it no longer legislates on what is true. Indeed, despite its high reputation in the past, Dearing (1997) could suggest that university teaching needed to professionalise and later in this chapter we will point to some of the developments in response to this that are taking place in the United Kingdom.

It is now widely recognised that a great deal of what is taken-for-granted knowledge is actually discourse (Foucault, 1972) and that the more powerful to propagators of the discourse, the more likely it will be taken as true. Curriculum specialists have always recognised this in as much as they have written about the hidden curriculum. Hence, the interpretative nature of teaching must also assume a critical function helping students to deconstruct the interpretations and the taken-for-granted and reach decisions for themselves. But this creates its own problems with many teachers of adults since, if they work within a commercial enterprise, they may be required to assist employees acquire a company culture and learn company knowledge (Meister, 1998). However, we are becoming increasing aware that the discourses of corporate capitalism relate far more to company interest than to truth, as Monbriot (2000) has clearly demonstrated. Teachers in such organisations may be refrained from teaching 'truth' and be required to teach company policy. The ethical nature of teaching is thus reinforced in the knowledge economy, especially as students are of all ages and all walks of life and bring varying levels of experience with them to the teaching and learning situation.

## Part 3: the changing nature of the learners

Adult educators have always endeavoured to recognise the differences between and the experiences of the students. In continental Europe, andragogics has always been separated from pedagogics, although in the United States Knowles (1980) used the term andragogy in a different way from continental Europe. For him, it was about responding to the experiences of older learners and the new teaching and learning techniques this demanded. Knowles' formulation has subsequently shown to be flawed in a number of ways (Hartree, 1983, *inter alia*) but the substance of what he expressed – the different approaches to teaching that experienced learners require – is standing the test of time. But then this was not a new discovery when he popularised the term 'andragogy'. Increasingly, education is becoming a lifelong process and so Knowles' argument, which was specifically about adult education, remains significant, as various chapters in this book have illustrated, but now it is built much more on theories of experiential learning. Once this comes to fore, it will should be increasingly recognised that teaching is both a humanistic and an ethical enterprise (Freire, 1998).

Learners do come to education with a great deal of knowledge and expertise. They should not be treated as empty containers to be filled, what Freire (1972) called banking education. Education should now both seek to use the learners' expertise and build on their knowledge which can be done through a variety of teaching techniques which include a mutual sharing of expertise amongst the learners (and the teachers) – hence the development of peer learning communities, and so on. At the same time, there is new knowledge and there are new interpretations to learn which calls for a skilled use of the different styles and methods of teaching. Lifelong education not only makes this demand, it is also a basis for generating new teaching and learning methods. Consequently, all the methods in face-to-face teaching are not exhausted by those contained in this book. There are others and there will be even more new approaches in the future. Clearly this calls for some form of teacher preparation, as Dearing (1997) has suggested, and while the approach in that Report was a little narrow its effects in the United Kingdom have been very wide.

## Part 4: the preparation of teachers

Until about the 1960s school teachers were the only teachers who were expected to receive formal training before they could enter the teaching profession: those in all forms of post-compulsory education did not need to be trained. However, in the latter part of the twentieth-century a concern for professional preparation among teachers of adults emerged. In the United Kingdom, Elsdon (1975, 1984) was amongst the foremost agitators for the introduction of such training. The Haycocks Committee (Haycocks – ACSTT, 1975, 1978, 1980) reported between 1975 and 1980, recommending that there should be a phased part-time training programme for adult and further education teaching. Significantly, the Committee also recommended training in management skills – something that is also occurring in higher education, as universities and colleges are becoming increasingly run as corporations. Early in the 1980s the Department of Adult Education at the University of Surrey introduced a Postgraduate Certificate in the Education of Adults, which was immediately seized upon by nursing as a qualification for nurse educators. In addition, we had a very few students from other branches of higher education and educational institutions found it very difficult to receive placements from such students. At that time nursing was the only occupation, apart from school teaching, that insisted on the professional preparation before teaching.

At the same time, the professional preparation was an issue for educators of adults throughout Europe as Jarvis and Chadwick (1991) showed. As the years have passed many courses in this professional preparation have emerged but now the field of practice has also developed into a field of practice and study: there are a multitude of post-graduate qualifications, masters degrees and a considerable amount of doctoral research on the topic. Much of this is actually occurring in institutions of higher education.

Dearing (1997) asked the same of post-compulsory education – this is not surprising considering the complexity of the teaching and learning process. Some might marvel at the lateness of this demand, while others might wonder why it has occurred at all. Nevertheless, its recommendations have been widely responded to in the United Kingdom. Surprisingly, universities were slow to utilise the expertise that their departments of adult and continuing education had acquired, probably because these department always occupied a marginal position in the academic hierarchy of universities. At the same time there is a growing emphasis on the professional preparation of teachers in higher education, leading to more accredited courses emerging including higher degrees and the amount of doctoral research will no doubt grow. Paradoxically this further separates teaching from research since the teachers are expected to become increasingly aware of this process, while the content may almost certainly be the research topic of others, although there is a real place for practitioner researchers here (Jarvis, 1999). Education is a process and its emphasis is on the knowledge of the process; this is a form of practical knowledge. Indeed, this is another indication of the division of labour in academia and the generation of new specialisms. Now the specialism is the process of teaching and performativity, as Lyotard (1984) argued, is a major basis for the legitimation of knowledge in this post-modern world. Consequently, it may be claimed, that this emphasis on the teaching process is a sign of the times, or a product of the learning society and the university teacher becomes separated from the university researcher.

Other professional groups have agonised over the extent to which professional preparation and continuing education should be compulsory. In the early days of professionalisation, the licence to practice was only granted after professional preparation and then the debate shifted to whether practitioners should be allowed to continue to practise without continuing education. Houle (1980) records some of this debate in the professions in the United States, but it reflects a similar debate in the United Kingdom. Dearing also suggested that continuing education might be introduced for educators in higher education. Naturally, this emphasis on teaching in higher and further education is to be welcomed, but the extent to which it separates teaching from research is to be questioned. Research institutes are already separated from teaching and this will no doubt continue and so the debate about teaching and research universities might well be resurrected.

## Part 5: the professionalisation of teaching

The Dearing Report called for the professionalisation of teachers in higher education and the higher education institutions were not as slow to respond to these suggestions as they had been in earlier times. I recall sending a memorandum on the need to reward good teaching in the university to a vice-chancellor in the 1980s, after I had attended a dinner at the University of Maryland to commemorate two academic staff to whom the university was awarding teaching fellowships because of their recognised expertise in teaching, suggesting that we should try something similar in the United Kingdom – but the vice-chancellor concerned did not even bother to respond. Now, however, that university has introduced a number of schemes to recognise good teaching and also to train teachers in higher education. However, the amount of innovation that has occurred in the past decade demands a book in itself and so a brief summary of some of these innovations is recorded here. Perhaps the most significant element has been the national focus on skills – reflecting the practical knowledge emphasis discussed previously – which has been reflected in the renaming of the national government ministry as the Department for Education and Skills. Now many of the activities for teaching come under the ambit of Lifelong Learning UK (LLUK), a part of the ministry, which is seeking to enhance 'the professional development of all those working in the field of lifelong learning' (www.lluk.org). The driving force behind many of these changes is not just the desire to improve teaching and learning for its own same, but rather the expressed need to improve the standards of the work-force so that the United Kingdom can be as competitive in the world market as any of its partners or rivals. This has led to a re-emphasis on skills in the transmission of knowledge, and so on.

For many years the London Institute of the City and Guilds validated one of the few nationally accredited courses in the training of teachers in adult and further education (City and Guilds 730) – it is now possible to get that training in many different institutions in the United Kingdom and it is coupled with the wider national qualifications framework and university qualifications, such as Certificates and Postgraduate Certificates. Since 2003, however, initial teacher training courses can also be offered by private institutions provided that they can meet the necessary standards for qualifications and their courses, like those of traditional educational institutions, are subject to regular monitoring and endorsement. Significantly, the University of Surrey which started the first Postgraduate Certificate in the Education of Adults no longer has a Department of Educational Studies and so this award is no longer offered there, although there is now a government funded Centre of Excellence in Teaching and Learning. Even so, there is a move to ensure that all new entrants to teaching in further and higher education should have initial qualifications and although they are not yet compulsory in all post-compulsory sectors of education there is a growing emphasis in this direction. In addition, there is an increasing concern for in-service training for already employed staff and institutions are being funded to establish Centres for Excellence in Professional Training and Education (CELT).

However, this concern for teacher preparation in further education has grown with the introduction of the FENTO (Further Education National

Training Organisation) scheme. FENTO is not only concerned with the training of teachers, it is also involved with the skills gaps of those who are in professional practice. In 2001 (FENTO, 2001, p. 2) suggested that among the skills gaps 35% of the further education sector work-force needed training in teaching the disaffected, 35% needed to examine performance management; 34% needed to learn how to support on-line learners, 21% lacked generic management skills, 20% needed general pedagogic training and 20% needed to know more about research. Such statistics indicate how concerned national agencies have been in introducing continued training for teachers in a wide variety of the skills that are necessary in the wider world of teaching. Clearly as approaches to teaching continue to change, so it will be increasingly necessary for teachers to specialise in one or more of these areas and to keep abreast with the innovations that are occurring within their sector(s). In this sense, we are seeing another form of division of labour in teaching, with an increasing number of positions for specialists in certain aspects of teaching. This process of segmentation is common in the growth and development of other professions. Additionally, it is not only going to be continuing learning of the necessary skills to perform a teaching and learning role, there is a growing emphasis being placed on research into skills performance and more evaluation of institution's teaching performance – with government research projects such as the teaching and learning projects that have occurred in the United Kingdom where emphasis has been both on discovering the amount of professional preparation available to new teachers in higher education and also seeking to discover their further training needs and career development opportunities.

In addition to these developments in higher education, the Quality Assurance Agency was established in 1997 by higher education institutions in the United Kingdom to be an independent body responsible for quality assurance in higher education. This is undertaken by visits to different institutions and departments by teams of professionals (many employed on a consultancy basis whilst being full-time employees of other educational institutions) who check on the quality of provision of that department or institution. Such visits involve scrutinising all the student records to ensure that they are being adequately catered for by the institution, by meeting past and current students to discuss their own experiences of the institution, in discussion with staff and by attending classes and watching teaching. The Agency then issues a report and an evaluation which eventually becomes a public document.

In a sense many of the developments have endeavoured to professionalise teaching in higher education and, perhaps, the formation of the

Higher Education Academy in 2004 illustrates this most clearly. Its focus is threefold: to support educational institutions to improve the quality of the students' learning experience; to support both subject and staff development; to provide an independent and authoritative voice on policies that influence the students' learning experience (www.heacademy.ac.uk). It has both a professional resister and accredits institutions' programmes of training. It also administers a Fund for Teaching and Learning and has a National Teaching Fellowship Scheme. After a slow start, we can see considerable impetus for change and development at the institutional level in recent years which will no doubt result in considerable developments in the preparations of teachers and the practice of teaching in the near future. This will be reflected in the way that higher education is funded in the next round as the Higher Education Funding Council for England is undertaking a consultation on the teaching funding method (www.hefce.ac.uk).

Finally in this brief overview of recent developments in teaching, at a European level, a consultation is being undertaken under the auspices of the German Institute for Education seeking to look at competence profiles for adult educational professionals. This is concerned with the professionalisation debate and with the extent to which various countries have produced competence profiles. This consultation began in 2005 and will continue for the next year or two. Consequently, we can see that what is occurring in the United Kingdom might be reflected in different ways in other countries in Europe and more widely as universities introduce their own centres for teaching and learning. The role of the university teacher might well be sub-dividing and more specialist roles beginning to appear and teaching in further and higher education itself appears to becoming a separate profession.

## Conclusion

This book has endeavoured to examine both theory and practice of teaching and it implicitly recognises that practice might well lead theory in teaching innovation. Naturally teaching techniques and debates about the efficiency, the philosophy and the moral issues in teaching will continue. While our emphasis has been on post-compulsory education, many of the points raised are relevant to compulsory education as well. The practice of teaching has changed and has become more complex, and so teachers do need to be trained for the complexities of their occupation, especially in a society in which education has become a marketable commodity and educational institutions more concerned about both the cost and quality of the process of teaching which, after all, might be seen as a major component in the production process of the educational product.

## References

Barry, V. and Rudinow, J. (1990) *Invitation to Critical Thinking* Forth Worth: Holt, Rinehart and Winston (2nd Edition)

Bauman, Z. (1987) *Legislators to Interpreters* Cambridge: Polity

Dearing, R. (Chair) (1997) *Higher Education in the Learning Society* London: Department for Education and Employment

Durkheim, E. (1933) *The Division of Labour in Society* New York: The Free Press

Eldson, K. (1975) *Training for Adult Education* Nottingham: Department of Adult Education, University of Nottingham in association with the National Institute of Adult Education

Eldson, K. (1984) *The Training of Trainers* Huntingdon Publishers in association with Department of Adult Education, University of Nottingham

Foucault, M. (1972) *Archaeology of Knowledge* London: Routledge

Freire, P. (1972) *Pedagogy of the Oppressed* Harmondsworth: Penguin

Freire, P. (1998) *Pedagogy of Freedom* Lanham: Rowman and Littlefield

Further Education National Training Organisation (FENTO) (2001) *Further Education Sector Workforce Development Plan – Consultation* (April) London: Fento

Hartree, A. (1984) Malcolm Knowles' Theory of Andragogy: A Critique *International Journal of Lifelong Education* Vol. 3, No. 3, pp. 203–210

Haycocks, J. (Chair) (1975) *The Training of Teachers for Further Education* London: Advisory Council for the Supply and Training of Teachers

Haycocks, J. (Chair) (1978) *The Training of Adult Education and Part-Time Further Education Teachers* London: Advisory Council for the Supply and Training of Teachers

Haycocks, J. (Chair) (1980) *Training Teachers in Education Management in Further and Adult Education* London: Advisory Council for the Supply and Training of Teachers

Higher Education Academy (2005 – downloaded 6th November) *About Us* http://www.heacademy.ac.uk

Higher Education Funding Council (2005 – downloaded 28th October) *Review of the Teaching Funding Method* http://www.hefce.ac.uk

Houle, C. O. (1980) *Continuing Learning in the Professions* San Francisco, CA: Jossey-Bass

Jarvis, P. (1997) *Ethics and the Education of Adults in Late Modern Society* Leicester: National Institute for Adult Continuing Education

Jarvis, P. (1999) *The Practitioner Researcher* San Francisco, CA: Jossey-Bass

Jarvis, P. and Chadwick, A. (eds) (1991) *Training Adult Educators in Western Europe* London: Routledge

Knowles, M. (1980) *The Modern Practice of Adult Education* Chicago, IL: Academic Press (2nd edition)

Lyotard, J.-F. (1984) *The Postmodern Condition* Manchester: University of Manchester Press

Meister, J. (1998) *Corporate Universities* New York: McGraw-Hill (Revised and Updated Edition)

Monbriot, G. (2000) *Captive State: The Corporate Takeover of Britain* London: MacMillan

Peters, O. (1984) Distance teaching and industrial production: a comparative interpretation in outline in Sewart, D., Keegan, D. and Holmberg, G. *Distance Education – International Perspectives* London: Routledge

# Index